ADAPTATION AND EDUCATION IN JAPAN

The Praeger Special Studies
Series in Comparative Education

General Editor: Philip G. Altbach

ACADEMIC POWER: Patterns of Authority in Seven National Systems of Higher Education
John H. Van de Graaff
Burton R. Clark
Dorotea Furth
Dietrich Goldschmidt
Donald F. Wheeler

ADAPTATION AND EDUCATION IN JAPAN
Nobuo K. Shimahara

CHANGES IN THE JAPANESE UNIVERSITY:
A Comparative Perspective
edited by
William K. Cummings
Ikuo Amano
Kazuyuki Kitamura

COMPARATIVE PERSPECTIVES ON THE ACADEMIC PROFESSION
edited by
Philip G. Altbach

FUNDING HIGHER EDUCATION: A Six-Nation Analysis
edited by
Lyman A. Glenny

US AND UK EDUCATIONAL POLICY: A Decade of Reform
Edgar Litt
Michael Parkinson

Published in cooperation with the
Center for Comparative Education,
State University of New York, Buffalo

ADAPTATION AND EDUCATION IN JAPAN

Nobuo K. Shimahara

PRAEGER

PRAEGER SPECIAL STUDIES • PRAEGER SCIENTIFIC

Library of Congress Cataloging in Publication Data

Shimahara, Nobuo.
    Adaptation and education in Japan.

    (Praeger special studies series in comparative
education)
    Bibliography: p.
    Includes index.
    1. Education--Japan--History. 2. Social
institutions--Japan. 3. Educational sociology--Japan.
4. Social adaptability. 5. Group relations training.
I. Title.
LA1311.8.S525   370'.952   79-9929
ISBN 0-03-049206-8

PRAEGER PUBLISHERS,
PRAEGER SPECIAL STUDIES
383 Madison Avenue, New York, N.Y. 10017, U.S.A.

Published in the United States of America in 1979
by Praeger Publishers,
A Division of Holt, Rinehart and Winston, CBS, Inc.

9   038   987654321

© 1979 by Nobuo K. Shimahara

Dedicated to My Mother with Affection

ACKNOWLEDGMENTS

This book is based on research that began two and a half years ago and ran for one full year during 1976/77. It was an extremely productive and eventful year for me as well as for my family, who had stayed with me in Japan for the entire period of the research. Nagoya was chosen as the central research location for one important reason: Nagoya University invited me as a visiting researcher in order to launch my study.

Owing to my promise to maintain the anonymity of my informants and the schools I studied, I must refrain from acknowledging their names here. They contributed enormously to my research; needless to say, it would have been impossible to carry it out without their generosity and cooperation. I will be pleased if this book contributes to improving their educational practices.

I wish to express my deepest appreciation to Professor Takeo Taura, who was dean of the Faculty of Education at Nagoya University during the period of my research, for making my study possible with his generous and continuous support and guidance, and to his family for their kindness. I am indebted to the following individuals for their indispensable advice: Professors Ikuo Amano, Hidenori Fujita, Mamoru Horiuchi, Toshio Kuze, Kyoji Eto, Toshio Ogawa, and Morikazu Ushiogi, all of Nagoya University, and Toshihiko Konno at Tokai University. The kind advice of Professor Ardath Burks at Rutgers has also been greatly appreciated. I wish to thank Professor Philip Altbach, editor of the Praeger Comparative Education Series, for his invaluable editorial suggestions. My colleagues and doctoral students at Rutgers took the special trouble of reading the manuscript at my request. I am especially indebted to Eleanor Horne, Dolores Lesnick, John Mamone, Marguerite Schlag, and Adam Scrupski. I am grateful to Rutgers University for granting me an academic study leave for my research and to Nagoya University for sponsoring it. In preparation for this volume, I was aided by funds provided by the Research Council of Rutgers University. I also wish to express my gratitude to Yolan Arlett, my doctoral candidate and friend, for serving as the custodian of our house while we stayed in Japan.

Above all, I am most thankful to my wife, Yasuko, who has given me unswerving encouragement and assistance from the outset of my project to the completion of this book. My lovely children, Erika and Mark, have been very helpful and understanding. Finally, I would like to extend my thanks to Hideji Sumikama and his family for offering generous support to me and my family.

New Brunswick, N.J.
October 1978

CONTENTS

LIST OF TABLES AND FIGURES

ADAPTATION AND EDUCATION IN JAPAN

1
INTRODUCTION

To state the central thesis of this study succinctly, schooling is a function of the social, economic, and political institutions of society, and schools are not agents of social reform. The manner in which education responds to the needs of these institutions is guided by the culture, which provides the orientational framework for people to adapt to the economic, political, social, and ecological pressures created by both internal (intrasocietal) and external (intersocietal) forces. Economic and political institutions are created and developed to promote the adaptation of society to its environment. The pattern of adaptation, however, is determined significantly by culture.

Hence, different societies exhibit different patterns of adaptation to, for example, pressures for modernization and industrialization. They do not follow a linear pattern of social change, nor are their patterns of adaptation exclusively determined by universal economic imperatives. Each society exhibits a specific evolution.

This volume attempts to provide an anthropological and sociological interpretation of Japanese society and schooling. Thanks to the development of social anthropology in Japan, though still limited in many respects, this interpretation rests upon an analysis of much literature that has not been presented thus far in the voluminous studies of Japanese schooling, either in Japanese or English.

As the title of the volume suggests, adaptation is the broad frame within which education in Japan will be examined. Adaptation is a continual process through which the organizations of society are modified to meet social and physical requirements; it is a dynamic strategy for solving problems of human existence. Central to the Japanese pattern of adaptation is the emphasis that Japanese society has placed upon group orientation throughout its modernization and the development of its adaptive efficiency. Hence, we give special attention to the nature of the Japanese group and its orientation.

1

In order to understand Japanese society and its modernization, one must give attention to the interaction between the cultural orientations and structural conditions of society. By cultural orientations, we mean a system of value orientations that gives "order and direction to the ever-flowing stream of human acts and thoughts as these relate to the solution of 'common human' problems."[1] They involve cognitive, affective, and directive processes in people's strategies to solve problems. Cultural orientations are a specific pattern of value orientations unique to a particular society and are generationally transmitted through the process of enculturation. They are tenacious, persistent, superorganic principles that resist pressures for change brought about by the institutional transformation of society.

Structural conditions, on the other hand, consist of those institutional arrangements of human life that are constantly subjected to change; for example, economic, political, and social systems undergo transformation resulting from pressures for adaptive efficiency, such as modernization. Institutional or organizational arrangements are amenable to modification, unlike cultural orientations, and such organizational amenability represents a societal competence to upgrade adaptability.

During its modernization, which spans the past century or so, Japan has undergone immense structural and organizational changes in the educational, political, economic, and social spheres. Organizational transformation in Japan occurred because of the intra- and intersocietal conditions that necessitated Japan's adaptation to a new political and cultural environment. Japan has been remarkably successful in its modernization. From a Marxist perspective, which would tend to overemphasize the effect of structural conditions upon people's cognitive patterns and ideologies, one might assume that such drastic structural changes will lead to equally radical changes in Japanese cultural orientations. Although it is not intended here to refute Marxism as a tenable economic and social theory, however, such an assumption is untenable relative to Japanese society. The fact is that Japanese cultural orientations have changed relatively little despite Japan's modernization.

This modernization, therefore, consists of the differentiation and adaptive upgrading of institutions and the absence of significant changes in Japanese cultural orientations. While modernization in general creates change and instability in the pattern of structural conditions, Japanese cultural orientations have served as a stabilizing and conserving force in the process of Japanese modernization. Consequently, drastic transformation in the structure of social organizations in Japan has not been accompanied by the simultaneous transformation in the content of organizations characterized by a particular pattern and intensity of social relations and interaction, which are guided by Japanese cultural orientations. Western observers explained that the lack of isomorphism between structure and content was anachronistic and predicted that it would be merely a transitional phase in Japanese modernization. Their prediction has proved fallacious, however, for the lack of isomorphism still exists even now that Japan has become one of the most advanced industrialized societies in the world. Thus, modern Japanese social change has been characterized by an interaction between changing structural conditions and stabilizing cultural orientations; Chapter 2 examines the process of Japanese modernization, of which the development of education is an integral part, and Japanese cultural orientations.

[As Japanese modernization began in the last half of the nineteenth century—following the dormant period of Tokugawa feudalism that had lasted for nearly three centuries—it introduced educational reforms; modeled after French, U.S., and German practices, they represented comprehensive and revolutionary changes. Such changes had been foreseen and even urged by Meiji leaders, who were deeply concerned with the unification and modernization of Japanese society, on the one hand, and its ability to cope with the external political and civilizational pressures of the West, which were impinging upon Japan, on the other. Those leaders saw education as an instrument that would assist the new nation-state to meet its imperatives. The provenance of schooling in Japan, for both the masses and the elite, as related to state imperatives can be traced back to that period.]

Lacking any viable antecedent models in Japan for the type of education that could fulfill the political and economic functions they identified, the Meiji leaders urgently looked to the West for educational models to emulate, in hopes of fostering technological, economic, and political development. Thus, their zeal for, and devotion to, educational reforms led to the introduction of new institutional patterns of schooling into Japan. The reforms involved importing fundamental educational orientations from the West that were entirely alien to the Japanese. As the Japanese were not willing to accept alien orientations, attempts to implement the reforms were doomed to failure.

Subsequently, Japanese cultural orientations were blended with Western educational systems to make a new system of schooling acceptable to the Japanese. In short, institutional changes in education were made on the basis of Western models, whereas the success of educational reforms required Japanese cultural orientations as the framework in which such reforms could take place. It is relevant to note that the educational reforms after World War II followed the same path.

The postwar reform, initiated by the United States Education Mission in 1946, was as comprehensive and revolutionary as the

Meiji reforms. Based upon the U.S. conception of democratic education, it emphasized progressivism, decentralized control of education, and the development of individuality. For five years the Japanese attempted to learn how to implement this reform, but by 1952 they realized the essential incompatibility of the U.S. educational orientation with Japanese cultural orientations. Japanese independence, coupled with the Korean War, which had a significant impact upon the Japanese economy and politics, served as a turning point in the development of postwar Japanese education and led to the "Japanization" of the U.S. educational system as it was transplanted in Japanese soil. That is, major structural features of the system have remained unchanged to the present time, but its underlying orientation gave way in the 1950s to an orientation compatible with Japanese culture. (The evolution of schooling outlined here will be the theme of Chapter 3.)

Socialization and schooling for the college entrance examinations receive extensive attention in Chapters 4 and 5, where they are discussed in particular reference to the Japanese pattern of adaptation. The college entrance examinations may properly be viewed as a "cultural focus," to borrow a term from Melville Herskovits. According to him, "Cultural focus designates the tendency of every culture to exhibit greater complexity, greater variation in the institutions of some of its aspects than in others. So striking is this tendency to develop certain phases of life, while others remain in the background, so to speak, that in the shorthand of the disciplines that study human societies these focal aspects are often used to characterize whole cultures."[2] As a conceptual tool, cultural focus enables the anthropologist to appreciate and understand culture by paying attention to those areas where its greater complexity and variations occur. We can apply the same methodology used by Herskovits to study contemporary Japanese education. The entrance examinations are an institutionalized practice that exhibits greater complexity and causes greater concern than other critical aspects of Japanese education. By exploring schooling and socialization for the entrance examinations as the foreground of Japanese education, we may better understand its background.

Although the reader may be acquainted with the pressure created by entrance examinations, the intense pressure of the Japanese college entrance examinations is a unique social phenomenon. The Japanese, including students, teachers, and parents, view their examinations as an institutional practice sui generis imposed of necessity upon adolescents. Such a view is understandable since, having experienced it year after year in the same manner, they do not know how to alleviate or change it; nor apparently does anyone know how to control it. It is not only adolescents who feel intense pressure but also their parents, particularly mothers intensively involved for years in their children's preparation, and their teachers. If one asks teachers or students to identify sources of their deepest concern relative to education, the answers would invariably include the entrance examinations. The mass media constantly focus upon them, and the highly developed, examination-centered educational industries depend on them for their very existence. By the same token, private tutoring and preparatory schools have grown rapidly all over Japan. Numerous bookstores in Japan, regardless of localities, cater to secondary-school students to satisfy their needs for information about the examinations. Given such intense examination pressures, it is not surprising that secondary education is organized to respond to them. We will explore this aspect of secondary education and socialization to meet such pressures. Detailed accounts of what is happening in Japanese education will be deliberately offered so that the reader may avoid journalistic, perfunctory impressions of schooling in Japan.

The reader may ask why the entrance examinations play such an unusually critical role in Japanese life. Simply, they are a rite of passage and the most vital culturally imposed obstacle that must be overcome to secure membership in the "right" groups: colleges and work organizations, where Japanese seek not only lifetime employment but also their personal and social anchorage. Japanese group orientation requires such a rite of passage for permanent membership in these organizations. The reader must become acquainted first with Japanese group orientation (explored in Chapter 2) as the basis of the Japanese pattern of adaptation in order to understand fully the relationship between the entrance examinations and group orientation. The entrance examinations are functional to Japanese adaptation and the group-oriented character of Japanese society.

It is suggested that the prolonged socialization and schooling for these examinations contribute to adolescents' development of particular patterns of motivational and cognitive orientations functional to the perpetuation of the existing political and economic systems. Further, it appears that one of the functions of the entrance examinations is to maintain the current structure of social stratification.

The thesis that schooling is a function of the social, economic, and political institutions of society is variably discussed in Chapters 3, 4, and 5. We will return to it again in Chapter 6, which examines how the economic forces of Japanese society have contributed to shaping educational policies in the postwar era. As Japan regained its prewar level of economic strength around the middle of the 1950s, its major focus shifted from economic recovery to expansion. Its major concern in the 1960s was twofold: the doubling of personal income within a decade and expansion into the international market and competition with advanced industrial nations. In short, adaptation to the international sphere of economic competition had become a critical policy consideration for private industries as well as for the government. Again, the schools were called upon to advance Japanese adaptation to the emerging phase of economic expansion by supplying private industries with the required human resources.

Chapter 7 presents a cultural and social perspective of Japanese education, with reference to the thesis of this study. We will look most carefully at the remarkable isomorphism, or compatibility, among the Japanese cognitive orientation, the pattern of "degree-ocracy," and the sociological functions of schooling. This chapter will provide a theoretical integration of our earlier exploration.

Finally, let me state what must be avoided for a proper understanding of Japanese education. Unfortunately, there has been a pervasive tendency, in Japan as well as in the United States, to look at education as an institutionalized activity in itself. Hence, the social and cultural context in which education takes place is more often than not disregarded by teachers, researchers, college educators, and school administrators. Let us note here two modes of orientation toward schooling, from among others, that they entertain.

The first mode makes a myopic, pseudoscientific assumption that educational activities can be isolated from their total environment for the purpose of understanding their nature and problems, as if they were extrasomatic, natural phenomena that could be simulated and replicated in a laboratory. Those who espouse this mode of orientation separate variables underlying educational activities from their context in the name of science and treat them as if their analyses alone were sufficient to comprehend these activities and their problems. Therefore, such researchers and scholars are extremely reluctant to interpret these variables in relation to the holistic context from which they have been extracted. In other words, complex relations of cultural and social phenomena created by men and women are grossly ignored. This mode of orientation leads, unfortunately, not only to a view of education as a contained entity but also to an attempt to solve its problems within its own institutional boundaries. It is a small wonder that countless studies of education, conducted every year in Japan, the United States, and elsewhere, are often academic exercises that contribute little to understanding and improvement.

The second mode of orientation is the naive ideology that education, in the formal sense, has regenerative and re-creative power. Therefore, whether or not education can contribute to the personal growth of the child and to social change is thought to be a function of the educational system and teaching. Proponents devote a great deal of attention to studying and improving teacher effectiveness and the general efficiency of the system. While this is commendable, the fallacy of such an effort lies in its fundamental assumption regarding schooling.

These modes of orientation toward education are rejected in favor of a holistic cultural and sociological approach. Such a perspective is preferred here since it allows the study of the educational process in terms of the larger cultural, political, economic, and social context.

The literature and other data used in preparing this book were largely gathered in Japan during 1976/77, when the author was a visiting researcher at Nagoya University conducting research on schooling and the college entrance examinations. The research involved an ethnographic study of schools as well as an extensive survey of the literature related to the Japanese patterns of adaptation, employment practices, economic policies, and the college entrance examinations.

NOTES

1. Florence R. Kluckhohn and Fred L. Strodtbeck, Variations in Value Orientations (Evanston, Ill.: Row, Peterson, 1961), p. 4.

2. Melville J. Herskovits, Cultural Anthropology (New York: Alfred Knopf, 1955), p. 484.

2

GROUP-ORIENTED SOCIETY:
THE JAPANESE PATTERN
OF ADAPTATION

The purpose of this work is to explore education in the holistic context of Japanese society. Such study requires an analysis of Japanese society and its development, and this chapter is designed to provide the cultural, social, and historical background for the ensuing discussion. The focus here will be upon identifying central orientations of Japanese culture that have guided the evolution of behavioral patterns and attitudes of the Japanese and have nourished their sense of personal and social identity. These cultural orientations have guided the Japanese in their attempts to cope with social, educational, economic, and political problems; adaptation is the term used here to describe such a social phenomenon. Japanese education is a function of Japanese adaptation, and its orientation is a reflection of the Japanese pattern of adaptation.

ADAPTATION

In order to survive and prosper, human beings not only must adapt to a habitat that imposes particular physical conditions upon them, but they also must actively attempt to utilize it. Energy is the source of human life, process, and organization, just as it is the source of the movement of inanimate objects, and constitutes the physical universe of which the human environment is a part. In this sense human life is understood as a mode of adaptation involving a process of capturing and utilizing free energy to put it to work in the service of people. Thus, human society, as the self-expression of human beings and their activities, is the process that constitutes the most vital basis for their biological perpetuation as well as the perpetuation and extension of their social lives.

Human society is an organization and a process of energy transformation; its foundation is a system of activities employed to harness free energy. In this sense, every society is an organization of activities intended to produce need-serving goods and services. What this means is that these human activities are organized to harness and transform free energy to meet the needs of people as they are culturally and biologically defined. Human society captures energy from nature and transforms it into people, so to speak, and into their social and political systems. The level of cultural development, seen from both qualitative and quantitative aspects, therefore, is determined by the extent to which the energy system of society is advanced. The question of how to harness energy is a problem that various societies have had to solve in one form or another.

I am discussing cultural adaptation as the process by which a population alters its relation with its environment in order to maintain its organization of social relations and to promote the effectiveness of order, regularity, and predictability in patterns of activities involving cooperation and competition. Social institutions, including schools, are developed as an integral part of a society's adaptation, and they are functionally designed, in part, to serve political, economic, and social needs deriving from internal and external sources of societal pressures. All societies result from adaptation, and all exhibit diverse patterns of response to cultural and environmental imperatives and problems.

Adaptation constitutes a basis of cultural evolution. Evolution is a dual process or phenomenon.[1] The first aspect is what may be termed specific evolution, which means that a specific culture improves its chances for survival through specific strategies. Specific evolution consists in a particular system's progress in capturing energy efficiently and adapting to an environment. It demonstrates, therefore, the phylogenesis of a given cultural system. The second aspect is general evolution. This is a directional, stage-by-stage process of cultural progress, a development of cultural forms measured by universal and absolute criteria without reference to the adaptive specializations of individual cultures. It is assumed that culture, in the generic sense of the term, evolves from lower to higher levels of energy capture, integration, and all-around adaptability. Specific evolution, however, is assumed to be a ramifying, specifying process of culture, that is, adaptive modifications of particular cultures. It is the notion of specific evolution that is particularly relevant to the present discussion of Japanese society.

The Japanese cultural orientation that was dominant in the eighteenth and nineteenth centuries has remained relatively unaltered, although Japan has become a modern, complex society that has undergone extensive structural changes since the Meiji Restoration (1868). In other words, the structural changes brought about by industrialism in the past century have not significantly modified vital aspects of the traditional cultural orientation that provide a rationale for social relations. These aspects of the orientation underlie the dominant pattern of Japanese adaptation to rapid social transformation since the inception of Japanese modernization.

As industrialism proceeds, it requires a particular pattern of orientation to guide the social action of individual members in social organizations. It is generally suggested that the more industrialism advances, the more articulated this pattern of orientation becomes. The notion of <u>pattern variables</u> has been introduced by Talcott Parsons in order to determine the value orientation of social action.[2] It is hypothesized that, as societies are modernized and industrialized, orientations undergo a change in emphasis from particularism, ascription, diffuseness, and group orientation toward universalism, achievement, specificity, and individualism.[3] While this hypothesis is generally applicable to Western societies with a high degree of industrialization, it cannot be employed to understand Japanese society fully despite the fact that it is one of the world's most industrialized nations. Japanese society continues to place a significant degree of stress upon the mixture of universal, achievement, and specificity orientations with particular, ascriptive, and diffused orientations as applied to human relations in social organizations. The seeming paradox exhibited by Japanese society makes it unique among highly modernized societies and constitutes a specific evolution.

JAPANESE MODERNIZATION

A major index of modernization is social mobilization—the process in which traditional economic, political, social, educational, and psychological commitments are replaced by new patterns of practice and socialization in major spheres of institutional activities. A structural characteristic of social mobilization is differentiation in the institutional system, such as the development of specialized and diversified types of social organization, of free resources channeled into these organizations, and of national and multinational group identifications. The process of differentiation leads to fundamental structural changes in the economic, political, educational, and social spheres. In the economic sphere proper, such changes are characterized by the growing specialization of economic activities and occupational roles and by the growth of the scope and complexity of the major markets for goods, labor, and money. Relative to the political sphere, there is the development of centralization of the polity and the differentiation of the political structure in terms of specific political roles and institutions. Concomitantly, the educational sphere exhibits a process of adaptive upgrading resulting from differentiation in its system and the centralization of control whereby policies developed at the national level are universally imposed upon local school systems. The processes of urbanization, secularization, and mass education characterize the social dimension in modernization. Social mobilization also results in a greater measure of educational and political participation on the part of the masses and in the development of a communications network. [4]

Japan has undergone a great deal of social mobilization in the past century; although the nation has become a modern society, however, it has preserved to a great extent the traditional mode of social relations in its present-day social organizations. In other words, Japan exhibits characteristics of modernization in a great many respects, yet it also reveals varied elements of modernization and tradition.

A look at the contemporary aspects of Japan's modernization reveals, primarily, that contemporary Japan is a highly industrialized society. The nation's total output of goods and services has approached $1 trillion (about half the total output of the United States), the third largest, after the United States and the Soviet Union, of the world's gross national products. Japan became the "economic miracle" of the postwar world. Its industry initially emphasized labor-intensive light goods in the 1950s, then moved on to capital-intensive heavy goods and chemicals in the 1960s, and on to technically sophisticated products in the 1970s. It is moving further toward the knowledge-intensive industries that require highly advanced technical skills, which Japan is capable of supplying abundantly. Japan has gained access to and inundated world markets with its goods: textiles, cameras, electronic equipment, ships, tankers, steel, chemical fertilizers, automobiles, and many others. Japanese exports and imports each account for about 10 percent of its GNP. Meanwhile, Japanese per capita income has risen constantly: $458 in 1960; $1,050 in 1967; $1,887 in 1970; $4,400 in 1975; and over $5,000 in 1976.

Relative to education, Japan enjoys the highest literacy in the world: 9,993 children out of 10,000 attend middle school, and nine adolescents out of ten complete high school. No longer exclusive, higher education is becoming a part of mass education.

When Japan was defeated in 1945, it was totally devastated in terms of its physical, social, and moral fabrics. Its economic recovery was inevitably very slow for a half decade, but gained unexpected acceleration in the first half of the 1950s—partly because of the Korean War, which stimulated Japanese industries. Subsequently, by the mid-1950s, the Japanese economy had regained the per capita production level of the prewar period. By the late 1950s, it was moving ahead rapidly, and it received additional stimulation in the early 1960s when the Ikeda cabinet launched a strong economy-centered policy to double personal income within ten years. For more than a decade, the economy averaged annual growth rates around 10 percent in real terms. Japanese began to feel its prosperous effect upon their consumption patterns. They acquired stereos, cameras, washing machines, air conditioners, television sets, and even private cars—unprecedented consumerism they had never dreamed of.

Japanese education had suffered from no less chaos for a half decade immediately after the defeat. It began to regain its stability in the early 1950s, reflecting economic recovery and political stabilization. In the 1960s it became a powerful instrument of Japanese economic expansion into the world market by supplying human resources for industry.

The transformation of the Japanese economy in the postwar period has had a great impact upon the demographic mobility of individuals. The general pattern of mobility indicates, on the one hand, a progressive shrinkage of the agricultural population and a gradual increase in manufacturing and construction employment and a growing prominence of tertiary industries, on the other. At the time of the Meiji Restoration, more than 80 percent of those gainfully employed were engaged in agriculture, and a little over 10 percent worked in commerce and secondary industries.

By 1930, Japan had been transformed into an urban society, and the agrarian population had dwindled to less than 50 percent. In 1940, the agrarian population declined to nearly 40 percent, while the population in the secondary industries increased to more than 25 percent. Wartime destruction of industries and evacuation from urban centers contributed to the waxing of the agrarian population, as seen in Table 1. Since 1955, when the economy turned from restoration to growth, however, the population has been steadily shifting from primary to secondary and tertiary industries. Of the 17.8 percent in agriculture, as shown in the 1970 census, only seven out of ten persons were engaged in full-time farming; the remainder worked in both agriculture and secondary and tertiary industries. Within 15 years, between 1955 and 1970, the proportion of the population in primary industries had dropped from 41 to 19 percent—an unprecedented phenomenon anywhere in the world. Consequently, rural communities in Japan are now populated by relatively old people because the young have found more lucrative employment in urban centers. These statistics demonstrate that Japan's urbanization, its industrialization, and particularly its recent expansion of tertiary industries have taken place with unusual speed.

Schooling responded to urbanization and the increasing prominence of secondary and tertiary industries, which required a greater degree of education as a condition for mobility. For example, prior to 1945 only 15 percent of adolescents advanced to the middle schools;

TABLE 1

Employed Population by Sector
(percent)

Sector	1940	1950	1955	1960	1965	1970
Primary industries	44.0	48.3	41.0	32.6	24.7	19.3
Agriculture	41.4	45.2	37.9	30.0	22.8	17.8
Forestry	0.9	1.2	1.3	1.0	0.6	0.4
Fishing	1.7	1.9	1.8	1.6	1.3	1.1
Secondary industries	26.1	22.0	23.5	29.2	32.3	33.9
Mining	1.8	1.7	1.4	1.2	0.7	0.4
Construction	3.0	4.8	4.5	6.1	7.1	7.7
Manufacturing	21.3	16.0	17.6	21.9	24.5	25.8
Tertiary industries	29.2	29.6	35.5	38.2	43.0	46.7
Trade	12.7	11.0	13.9	15.9	17.8	19.2
Finance, insurance	0.9	1.0	1.6	1.8	2.4	2.7
Transportation, communication	4.3	4.5	4.6	5.1	6.1	6.2
Electric power, gas, water	0.4	0.6	0.6	0.5	0.6	0.5
Service industries	9.0	9.2	11.3	11.9	13.0	14.7
Public service	1.9	3.3	3.5	3.0	3.1	3.4
Not classifiable	0.7	0.1	0.0	0.0	0.0	0.1

Source: Tadashi Fukutake, Japanese Society Today (Tokyo: Tokyo University Press, 1974), p. 23.

in 1955, however, 51.5 percent attended high school, and by 1970 that figure had increased to 82.1 percent. The numbers of eligible youth attending college doubled between 1955 and 1970.

In the wake of a postwar baby boom, Japan was highly successful in controlling its birthrate during the 1950s and 1960s, with an annual population growth of 1 percent. This stabilization of the population has contributed to the growth of the national economy, as well as to the economic status of each family. Typically, the Japanese family limits the number of children to only two.

In politics, the Japanese government accepted a constitutional reform drafted by General Douglas MacArthur's staff in 1946 and the new constitution went into effect in 1947. Ironically, although it was drafted by U.S. citizens, it was not based upon the U.S. political system, but upon the British parliamentary government, probably due to Japanese familiarity with the British model, which had been partly in operation in the 1920s in Japan.

Under the new constitution the national Diet, composed of the upper and lower houses, assumes ultimate political power to which all competing units of power are clearly subordinated. The members of the Diet are elected and the cabinet, appointed by the prime minister who is himself elected by the lower house, is directly accountable to the Diet. The status of the emperor is unambiguously that of the national symbol; powerless, as in the past, in the political sense, his significance for the Japanese is as a symbol of national unity. The constitution includes a very wide range of popular rights, and prohibits Japan's rearmament—perhaps the most ideal document in the entire world if it is fully enforced. Despite Article 9 of the constitution, which prohibits rearmament, Japan established the Self-Defense Forces in 1954. This rearmament is the subject of frequent parliamentary debates and occasional court rulings regarding its constitutionality. Nevertheless, it continues to exist in the absence of national consensus on its constitutional status.

Meanwhile, education is allegedly neutral relative to politics. Yet, in Japan's attempt to stabilize its political order, educational policies have been forged, both overtly and covertly, so as to reinforce the dominant ideology of the state through education. Major changes in curriculum, laws governing educational administration, and the introduction of moral education, for example, reflect clearly the emphasis the state places on a particular pattern of political socialization promoting its political ideology.

Turning to the historical background, we must evaluate Japan's postwar industrialization and political system partly in the light of the revolutionary social changes begun in 1868, when the Meiji reform began to modernize Japan as a unified nation-state. Japanese modernization was stimulated by the threatening forces of the West, but it was neither an accident nor purely a reflex. It had been carefully planned by national leaders and set in motion during the Meiji era (1868-1912), a most critical and turbulent transitional period that transformed a static, feudalistic society into a modern industrial state.

Prior to the Meiji Restoration, Japan consisted of a number of autonomous domains that formed the feudal system of the Tokugawa era (1603-1868). The Tokugawa shogun, or military governor, divided the country among his own domains and those of his vassals. His vassals were of three kinds: immediate relatives, hereditary vassals—who had served the Tokugawa shogun prior to the establishment of his government—and outer vassals. Although these feudal lords maintained theoretically autonomous domains defended and administered by their samurai retainers, they were ascriptively tied to, and controlled by, the shogun. They were required to spend alternate years in residence to serve the shogun at Edo, now Tokyo, seat of the Tokugawa government. Moreover, their families were kept in Edo as permanent hostages—a method devised to prevent possible revolts by local lords against Tokugawa. The Tokugawa administration eventually grew into a large bureaucratic system staffed by the hereditary lords and immediate retainers. This feudal system brought about lasting peace and stability and permitted the development of a rich cultural heritage, homogeneity, and social identity. It also contributed to the urbanization of Edo and other major castle towns where the economy had flourished.

As discussed in Chapter 3, Tokugawa education evolved to serve the feudal system of Japan. Domain schools for the samurai, the ruling class, were run by each domain to inculcate the Confucian ethic, which was the ideological mainstay of Tokugawa feudalism, and to cultivate letters for samurai bureaucrats; private common schools were developed for commoners. There was no central control of education, reflecting the social structure of feudalism.

The Tokugawa era lasted until 1868, but its preindustrial economy and its archaic structure of autonomous domains were not powerful enough to respond effectively to the external military threats posed by industrialized Western nations who enjoyed a technological advantage over Japan. In 1853 the U.S. Navy, under the command of Commodore Matthew Perry, finally forced Japan to admit U.S. ships to Japanese ports. The treaty, signed in the following year, gave the United States a limited access to Japan. Unable to mobilize whatever potential powers it had to resist foreign pressures, and also intimidated by the big, steam-powered ships and cannons of Western nations, the Tokugawa government was forced to succumb to unfair diplomatic and trade treaties, such as those that limited Japan's tariffs and provided U.S. citizens the extraterritorial privilege of trial by their own judges under their own laws. With these events, the collapse of Tokugawa feudalism was clearly inevitable. Meanwhile, following internal revolts against the central government, a coalition of several domains took control of the imperial court in Kyoto in 1868 and declared the resumption of direct imperial rule. Thus, the Meiji Restoration began, ending 265 years of Tokugawa rule.

Incessantly confronted with external imperialist pressures, Meiji leaders perceived industrialization and political centralization as focal elements of the formation of an independent and unified state capable of coping with such Western pressures. Hence, while selected Japanese, most of whom were exsamurai, were sent to Europe and the United States to study advanced technology and political systems, foreign engineers were invited to Japan to build industries and transportation and communication systems.

Among criteria for modernization, structural differentiation is critical because it leads to basic changes in the economic, political, and social spheres. The processes of political centralization and industrialization, undertaken in the Meiji era, contributed both to differentiation in these particular institutional spheres and to the mobility of the population.

In order to achieve a centralized political structure, Meiji reformers replaced the feudal domains with prefectures under the direct control of the central government. The feudal lords were required to return their land registers to the emperor, and they received, in return, appointments as governors of the new prefectures, whose lesser officials had also been appointed by the central government.

At the same time, the samurai, the bureaucratic and military retainers of those lords, lost their hereditary status as a privileged class—a radical change—and in 1873 universal conscription went into effect for the purpose of national defense. Thus, within the first ten years of the Meiji Restoration, the samurai lost most of their privileges. Though many exsamurai still occupied high governmental and bureaucratic positions by virtue of their previous training for such roles, the criterion for gaining access to positions of prestige in the government was rapidly shifting from ascription, such as heredity, to education and achievement. Comprehensive educational reforms (see Chapter 3) were under way in the 1870s and 1880s, and university education for the training of bureaucrats began in the late 1870s. Such education was expanding rapidly by the time universal schooling for six years became the norm in 1907.

The functions of the central government, modeled after those of the West, were differentiated into ministries with specific divisions of responsibilities. Tax reform, which substituted a monetary tax for the feudal system based on agricultural yield, was another measure to stabilize national revenues. A modern banking system was instituted in order to reform the economy. In another effort to industrialize the nation speedily, the government took a direct initiative in building certain industries important to mining, weapons production, transportation and communications networks, and other fields. These industries were later transferred to the private sector, however, when the government plunged into a deep fiscal crisis in the early 1880s.

Another significant aspect of modernization was the establishment of the Meiji constitution in 1889, based on the nineteenth-century German model. The constitution gave the emperor supreme authority to rule the country, but, in actuality, his power was largely nominal; he functioned only to validate decisions made by the cabinet of the central government. The constitution required the creation of a bicameral national assembly composed of an upper house, equivalent to the British House of Lords, and a house of representatives. The members of the upper house were appointed, and representatives were elected by those male citizens who had paid the required tax. While the assembly served as a legislative branch of the government, the cabinet constituted the executive branch under which were ministries. An efficient civil service system was created in those ministries, which served as a foundation of the contemporary civil service.

The educational counterpart of the Meiji constitution was the Imperial Rescript on Education, again partly based on the German educational model of the times. It had served as the ideological fulcrum of the centralized, imperial system of schooling for nearly two-thirds of a century.

Japan warred with China in 1894/95 and with Russia in 1904/05, emerging victorious. As a consequence of these campaigns, military and industrial developments were advanced, and Japan assumed the stance of an imperial nation, emulating the colonialism of the West.

Shortly after the turn of the century, Japanese began to enjoy enhanced political freedoms. Individual rights and political ideologies—Marxism, universal suffrage, and other related issues—were frequently debated, emphasizing the intellectual growth and political sophistication of the times. In fact, universal suffrage for men, without tax qualifications, became a full reality in 1925. The period between 1910 and 1930 was characterized by the growth of Japanese democracy. Nevertheless, soon after the development of its fragile democracy, Japan reversed its course and turned to militarism and the Pacific war.

GROUP ORIENTATION: A
CHARACTERISTIC OF JAPANESE SOCIETY

In the general process of modernization, the level of integration of a society changes from the local and concrete to the national,
generalized, and abstract; we have seen such a transformation in the
modernization of Japan. The boundary of society relying upon local
integration, on the one hand, is relatively loose, and subsocieties
(or subcultures) within the loose boundary are based upon ascriptive
and particularistic social relations, such as kinship-based relations,
which exhibit a high degree of autonomy. The boundary of society
relying upon national integration, on the other hand, becomes firm,
with the result that the local group boundaries tend to disappear.
The major conditions determining the level of integration are the
degree to which industrialism and political centralization are developed.

With reference to the general evolutionary process of modernization, the group orientation of Japanese society indicates that a
unique specific evolution has occurred. Politically centralized and
industrialized societies tend to exert pressure upon subsocieties,
formed on the basis of local cohesion, ethnicity, religion, race, and
nationality, to conform to national expectations.[5] They attempt to
subvert subsocieties so as to achieve a conformity of individual cognitive and motivational patterns, as well as a uniformity of institutional norms and values: a vital condition for political stability and
national integration. Subsocieties are subjected to conditions of dependence upon the national system and are required to respond to national imperatives of the social, political, economic, and educational
institutions. Hence, it is the national political and economic framework that shapes the conditions of continuity or discontinuity for subsocieties.

The centralization and standardization of schooling begin to
emerge in such a framework. Educational reforms developed during
the Meiji period, for example, represent a converging force of Japanese society by which locally controlled school systems were integrated into a national system so as to respond to the state's needs.

Individuals in advanced industrial societies are expected to participate directly or indirectly in national and multinational institutions,
as well as in national social structures in general without the mediation
of ascriptive or particularistic (for example, kinship and ethnic)
groups. Individuals are also expected to be mobile psychologically,
socially, and geographically. In other words, individuals are seen
as mobile participants of society, and their social status is a consequence of the extent to which they gain access to social resources
and institutions. The stratification of societies is a system regulat-

ing the access of individuals rather than groups to social resources; thus, the individual is a unit of social mobility.

Japanese society is highly homogeneous. At the time of the Meiji Restoration, there was no minority group other than a very small collection of Ainu in Hokkaido. Hence, during the period of the Meiji reforms, it was relatively easy to integrate the feudal domains and to achieve the conformity of Japanese cognitive and motivational orientations, particularly to instill national purposes into their minds.

Generalizations made about industrial societies here are by and large applicable to Japanese society, but, as mentioned earlier, Japan demonstrates a significant degree of difference from industrialized Western societies. In Japanese society the group is the basis of individual life, whereas it is the individual in the West who constitutes such a basis of life. The individual is not generally expected to be a socially and psychologically mobile participant in Japanese society, but rather a stable member of a group (see Figure 1).

In his classic work, Clan, Caste, and Club,[6] Francis Hsu speaks of two types of society. The first type is a society of centripetal orientation, where social relations are guided by centripetal forces contributing to the convergence of individuals within a group such as a clan. Mutual reliance is the central orientation of individual social behavior and in terms of which activities, constituting centripetal forces, are organized. Individuals seek harmony with each other and mutual reliance and, thus, individual desires are subordinated to the needs of the group. Subordination of the person to a situation takes precedence over the need of the individual to protect his or her individuality. The prototype of this type of society is traditional China, where clans were extensively developed.

The second of Hsu's societies is one in which centrifugality is the central principle underlying individual behavior. Individuals diverge, rather than converge, in their pursuit of individual freedom; self-reliance is the central orientation of behavior. The individual is viewed ideally as immutable and not subject to competing forces in a given situation. The society of the United States is a typical example. Even when middle-class Americans are seen as other-directed,[7] the underlying orientation of other-directed behavior is deeply rooted in their desires to express themselves vis-à-vis their peers. Other direction and individual submersion in the group are quite different. Other direction is a pattern adapted to an advanced state of industrial development—in the United States, for example, in which the nexus of social relations is highly complex and is influenced by centrifugal needs.[8]

The characterizations of these two societies are oversimplified but sufficient for the present discussion. The relevance of the comparison of the two societal types is to suggest that such a comparison

FIGURE 1

Modernization of Social Orientations

Subsocial boundary, firm;
social boundary, loose

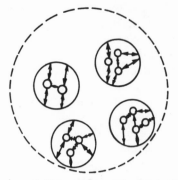

Ascriptive and particularistic
social groups: kinship-based
structure

Subsocial boundary, loose;
social boundary, firm

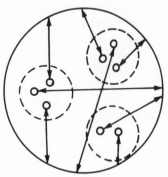

Universalistic social relations:
subcultural boundaries tend to
disappear

Underlying forces of movement: industrialism and political
integration

Modern Japanese subsocial boundary, firm;
social boundary, firm

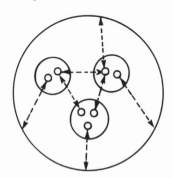

Source: Constructed by the author.

also applies to Japanese, vis-à-vis U.S., society. Japanese society is centripetal and situation-centered, as was traditional China. Contemporary Japanese social relations, however, are centered on nonkinship groups, whereas the traditional Chinese orientation was on the kinship system.

THE JAPANESE CONCEPT OF GROUP

The aspect of Japanese culture to which we give special attention here is the pattern of Japanese behavior for which the group functions as its framework. As argued cogently by Chie Nakane and others, the group is most fundamental to all vital aspects of Japanese social, economic, political, and educational behavior. It constitutes the pervasive basis of contemporary social relations and mediates the relationship between individuals and their larger society; thus, it is vital, not only in a functional sense but also as a general framework that defines an individual's personal identity and social participation.[9]

The Japanese concept of group is central to understanding the evolution of education and, particularly, the orientation of contemporary schooling in Japan toward entrance examinations. Yet little attention has been given to this concept and its sociological roles relative to education in available literature and research.

The concept of group refers to the social organization. The Japanese group emphasizes the "frame," in Nakane's term, which constitutes its boundary and the common identification by which its members are bound and seek social and personal anchorage. Anthropological and sociological studies to date identify the archetype of the contemporary Japanese group in terms of ie, the traditional household developed during the Tokugawa era, and dōzoku, an sion of the ie that evolved from the middle of the Tokugawa era through the Meiji. Dōzoku came into existence as an entity of households based upon both the genealogical and economic relations among them, and it functioned as one of the corporate groups in the village community. Contemporary social organizations in Japan still exhibit distinct characteristics of ie and dōzoku, although they are structurally more complex and differentiated. Four aspects characterize the group in contemporary Japanese society. These characteristics are overgeneralized below for heuristic purposes and are not inclusive.

The first is a strong orientation toward homogeneity—a stress on the conformity of motivational orientation. Once individuals with different attributes become members of a group, the group exerts lasting pressure on them to conform to its orientation, that is, to its frame. Various means for assimilating new members into a group (a corporation, for example), are employed: lifelong employment, frequent intermingling of superiors and subordinates in cafeterias, parties, group trips, sports events, and company-financed housing for employees in the same geographical area. Through these practices and other means, employees gradually internalize the orientation of their company and are expected to demonstrate a sense of identification with it as belonging to a distinct group. A paramount individual need is not only to belong to a group but also to become a permanent member, so as to establish lasting identity with it. Japanese are not so much concerned with the realization of self or individuality as with group identity and the establishment of one's sense of belonging. Japanese clearly perceive education as a process of socialization guided by a concern with one's placement in a group; rather than being individualists, they are strongly inclined to submerge their identity in some large group and are often obsessed by a sense of duty. Japanese obsession with duty and group identity is fostered by the cultural expectation that the group takes precedence over the individual. It is internalized through processes of primary and secondary socialization in one's life; for example, even elementary schoolchildren exhibit a strong need for belonging, and their behavior is commonly group-oriented. Children's relationships with peers usually are established not on a one-to-one basis but, rather, on a group basis. If one is excluded or fears exclusion from the group, it threatens the sense of personal identity and causes a feeling of alienation. Fear of exclusion, in turn, tends to intensify motivational and behavioral conformity on the part of children, as it does on the part of adults working in a company.

The second characteristic is inclusiveness. Once individuals become employees of a private firm or a governmental bureau, they are equally protected by their organizations, regardless of their positions, and the means referred to above to assimilate the new members are also used to extend inclusiveness to them. Thus, employees of large organizations are rarely dismissed, although everyone may recognize that certain employees are incompetent; even at a time when serious recession reduces corporate profits, corporations are expected to keep their employees unless they go bankrupt. The public image of large companies is often determined by the extent to which they can offer such protection to permanent employees as members of their groups. A national university will lay off a lecturer who does not have a tenured status only after it finds him or her employment elsewhere. This practice is regarded as a moral obligation for an academic institution. Overt individual competition among the members of a group is reduced significantly by offering rewards according to the longevity of service, not so much according to individual achievement. Although this pattern of controlling competition among individuals is changing to allow for the expression of individual achievement, the underlying cultural orientation is still dominant. Individuals are likely to be motivated to depend on each other to seek security in the inclusive group. This makes Japanese less self-confident and more concerned with maintaining the good opinion of others.

The third characteristic is verticality of social relations, a central structural principle of Japanese social organizations. The social relations of a group are hierarchically structured, based on a scheme of the dyadic relations between superior and subordinate that lacks horizontal collegial relations. The accumulation of such dyadic relations makes up a chain of vertical relations in the entire structure of a group. The individual awareness of hierarchy is a more vital functional requirement for the Japanese group than for other cultural groups in Asian and Euro-American societies. The Japanese group cannot properly function without individuals being highly sensitive to hierarchical social relations. Individuals are always keenly aware of their positions vis-à-vis others; without such awareness they would be publicly embarrassed, looked down upon, and regarded as having transgressed the cultural code.*

---

*An episode I experienced during my research in 1976/77 may elucidate the importance of sensitivity to hierarchy. I was invited to a meeting of a study group of prefectural high school teachers from more than a dozen high schools in the Nagoya area to comment on presentations made by selected teachers. Headed by a high school principal, this group consists of about 30 teachers and meets four times every year so that members know each other and their ranks. The meeting began with a congratulatory speech by the prefectural director of formal education; this was followed by another short ceremonial address by a senior principal, under whom the chairman of the study group had worked previously as a head teacher; then the chairman addressed the group. They were seated together in the row facing the members, and my seat was next to theirs. I was then introduced to the group. These ceremonial speeches took almost a third of the entire session. Six presentations occurred in succession without a break or interaction between.

Since this meeting was the last of the academic year, a dinner party was planned for after the session. When we moved to the banquet hall, everybody took a seat nearly automatically, as if the seating arrangements had been made in advance. The chairman of the group was not with me at that moment, and, being new to the group and not knowing where to sit, I decided to take a seat at the end of a side row next to a teacher. When the chairman came, he immediately recognized me, and asked that I sit next to him in the front row with

The fourth characteristic is a strong tendency toward exclusiveness vis-à-vis other groups. This is a function of the first three characteristics that contributes to the relative lack of interinstitutional mobility on the part of individuals. This tendency has resulted in the evolution of Japanese social stratification by institutions rather than by individuals.[10] What this means is that various organizations are rated according to a national scale of prestige, and the individual who belongs to a particular organization derives social status from the institution's prestige. The social status of an employee in a private corporation or a government bureau is normally rated in this frame of reference.

Japanese schools also reflect this fourth orientation, particularly at the college level. Like corporate employees, university graduates are evaluated and their prestige is determined in terms of the institutions from which they graduated. Prestigious academic institutions claim their exclusiveness vis-à-vis other institutions. While this is true to varying degrees in other societies, it is emphasized much more in Japan.

As pointed out by Nakane,[11] Japanese perception of social relations involves two separate worlds: _uchi_ (one's own group), and _yoso_ (the world outside one's own group). This notion of two worlds is frequently referred to by Japanese, young and old, to discriminate consciously between one's family and others, one's village and others, one's college and others, one's political party and others, one's company and others. The _uchi_ world is often perceived as intimate, supportive, and protective, whereas the _yoso_ world is comparatively alien, unkind, and hostile. Hence, the norms that operate within the _uchi_ are different from those applied to the other world. Japanese tend to develop feelings of superiority or inferiority toward _yoso_ groups, and they are restrained and unfriendly when confronted with such groups or individuals of the _yoso_ world.

Apparently, the Japanese group is dominated by centripetal social relations that foster relationships of dependence. It is relevant here to refer to Takeo Doi's theory of the psychology of _amae_ peculiar

---

the director of formal education, his former superior, and other head teachers present at the banquet. The chairman and the director again made brief speeches before the toast. For 20 minutes or so, everyone stayed in their seats, but as the sake and beer began to affect them they began to move around informally.

As seen in this episode, one dominant principle regulating the whole process is the order of hierarchy accepted consciously and unconsciously by all members of the group. If one were to ignore it one would be not only embarrassed but also ostracized by the group.

to Japanese. [12] Amae implies dependence, desire for dependence, or the seeking of another's indulgence (what might be called "passive object love"). It is intensely bred in the pattern of Japanese social relations, stressing inclusiveness and motivational homogeneity. Doi's theory of the psychology of amae is built upon Freud's theory of libido, as specifically related to an instinctive desire to be united with the mother. According to Doi, therefore, amae itself is universal, but the fact that Japanese seek amae to a far greater extent than members of other societies, he contends, makes the Japanese psychology of amae distinct.

In this connection, Doi offers a fascinating observation on the distinction between identity formation in a Western frame of reference, of which Erik Erikson has written, and the Japanese personality process. [13] Identity formation, according to Erikson, begins with the first meeting between mother and baby and develops into a process of active interaction between individual and environment—a process that creates tension and challenge—a series of experiences that must be overcome and assimilated by an individual as an independent person; on the other hand, a Japanese tends to lack a dialectical self-process undergoing tension and assimilation—since a Japanese individual is born into a group where individuals are not separable as independent persons—and grows in the group's environment. One is also inclined to dissipate in a search for harmonious dependence and certainty. The identity process involves interaction between opposites and assumes a dialectical occurrence of polarization and synthesis of experience, whereas the development of amae personality involves the minimization, if not elimination, of opposites and inclusive embracement by a large whole.

Erikson refers to a letter of William James in order to explain what identity means:

> A man's character is discernible in the mental or moral attitude in which, when it came upon him, he felt himself most deeply and intensely active and alive. At such moments there is a voice inside which speaks and says: "This is the real me!"

Such an experience always includes

> an element of active tension, of holding my own, as it were, and trusting outward things to perform their part so as to make it a full harmony, but without any guaranty that they will. Make it a guaranty . . . and the attitude immediately becomes to my consciousness stagnant and stingless. Take away the guaranty, and I feel (provided

I am _verberhaupt_ in vigorous condition) a sort of deep
enthusiastic bliss, of bitter willingness to do and suffer
anything . . . and which, although it is a mere mood or
emotion to which I can give no form in words, authenti-
cates itself to me as the deepest principle of all active
and theoretic determination which I possess.[14]

A sense of identity, thus, involves an active tension, and
creates a challenge without guarantee. The conceptualization of
self-process by Erikson presents an interesting contrast to that of
Japanese personality development by Doi. Such a contrast reflects
differences in patterns of social relations in Euro-American and
Japanese societies. It similarly reflects differences in patterns of
individual dependence on academic institutions as one's basis for
claiming exclusiveness. By the same token, while schooling at the
elementary and secondary levels in Japan is highly oriented toward
achievement, the goal is not the growth of one's identity involving
active tension and challenge, but one's orientation toward dependence.
This goal requires a high degree of conformity to the group in which
one is nurtured, reliance upon authority (teachers in this case), and
a demonstration of resilience to meet external expectations. In return, one is treated as an inclusive member of a group.
    In group-centered Japanese society, _ninjo_ and _giri_ are central
day-to-day concerns of which exact correlates do not exist in Western societies. Respectively, _ninjo_ and _giri_ literally mean "human
feelings" and "a bond of moral obligation." The former is normally
referred to as spontaneously occurring between close individuals,
whereas the latter is thought to develop often in secondary group relations, as in the relationship between employees. Doi interprets
ninjo to mean one's sensitivity to another's overt and covert need for
amae, or dependence, and _giri_ to refer to a social relation cemented
upon _amae_ in which individuals are bound to be dependent upon each
other.[15] If one is insensitive to _giri_ and _ninjo_, he or she will be
seen as ignorant, inhumane, and unworthy. They play a significant
role in one's life in a group, emphasizing inclusiveness, and in the
formation as well as the perpetuation of vertical relations in it.
    This is only a schematic description of orientations underlying
typical, but not all, Japanese social organizations. There are variations of groups and their orientations to which the present analysis
cannot be applied. It presents central orientations of Japanese groups
and society, however, crucial to understanding Japanese behavior.

CULTURAL ARCHETYPES OF CONTEMPORARY GROUPS

    In the development of Japanese modernization, the Japanese
have effectively employed primordial patterns of social relations and

cultural orientations so that they could adapt to the new environment
and pressures generated in the political, economic, and social
spheres. This also constitutes a Japanese adaptation to the contemporary, complex industrial environment. It is possible to identify
three cultural archetypes that have had the most significant impact
upon the evolution of contemporary Japanese groups.

Ie

The primary archetype of the Japanese group is ie,[16] the traditional household appearing during the Tokugawa era. In sociological literature, the term ie is often employed as equivalent to the
term family. Equating these two terms is technically fallacious,
however, for while family involves primarily kinship and affinity ie
consists of a unit of coresidents under the shelter of the same house,
defined by the criterion of local residence. The latter normally centered around an elementary family and sometimes included other
relatives and nonrelatives as coresidents. Represented and organized by its head, who was always male, it functioned under his leadership.

Once established, ie persisted through generational changes
and maintained its identity, regardless of particular residents, as a
basic social unit in a rural community. Here the stress on the
group's frame should be noticed; there was a strong sense of closeness
or oneness among the members of ie who participated in a common
economy, regardless of their kin relationships. One perceived a
greater degree of proximity toward unrelated coresidents in the
same ie than toward close kin living outside it. This reveals an orientation of inclusiveness toward all members of the same frame,
while it reflects an orientation of exclusiveness toward other individuals. Ie provided a frame in which conformity of motivational orientation toward a common entity evolved among its domestic members.

Ie continued through the generations by the succession of headship, and the line of succession from the father to his son was the
axis of the ie structure. The father who assumed the headship held
exclusive authority to manage his ie and to choose his successor.
The latter might be one of his sons or his adopted son, but, as uni-
geniture was practiced in Japan, the rule stipulated the successor
must be a "son" and that only one son be chosen for it. The ie structure represented a clearly defined structure of status differentiation
in which the father-son axis constituted a hierarchy of power.[17]
While the son was subordinate to the father until his retirement from
the headship, he held, as successor, a position to which his brothers
were subordinate. The traditional ideal of the father was that he was

authoritarian. The recognition of status difference among the household members was central to the function of ie. Hence, one was constantly sensitized and subordinated to the vertical relations within it.

The notion of ie as a perpetuating institution was legally defined in the Meiji Civil Code, promulgated in 1898. According to the code, ie was an a priori entity to which individuals belonged. The ie head had power to which the other members were absolutely subordinated. For example, he had the authority to grant approval for marriage to his family members and for adoption of a child; to decide the residence of family members; to remove family members from the family registration (koseki) when they were disloyal to him and to reinstate them; to approve establishment of a branch house; to officiate at the ceremonies for ancestral worship; to decide the inclusion of an outsider as a member of the household.

Dōzoku

As an extension of the ie institution, dōzoku evolved from the middle of the Tokugawa era through the Meiji era. It was a group of ie, consisting of the main (honke) and branch (bunke) households. By 1750, while the rural population was increasing, new arable land had become so scarce in the village communities that it was necessary to apportion land owned by relatively wealthy households (honke) among their poorer branch households (bunke). Subsequently, the institution of dōzoku contributed to the stabilization of village communities, on the one hand, and to the absence of land monopolization by landlords, on the other.

Dōzoku came into existence as an entity of households based on both genealogical and economic relations, and functioned as one of the corporate groups in the village community. A bunke was established when the head of honke built it on his house-site land and apportioned part of his cultivated land, if not to his son, to a member of his ie who was about to become independent upon marriage. But bunke's economic dependence upon honke did not necessarily mean the former's ownership of land; it could be any type of economic assistance offered by honke that enabled it to carry on its economic life. The genealogical relations between them were not constituted strictly in terms of descent but in terms of household. In fact, bunke could be established not only by a son-in-law married to a daughter of the honke head but also by a servant who had worked for honke for a long period of years. Hence, dōzoku was not organized according to patrilineal lineage. Over a period of time, it could expand to a group of a half dozen ie and last as long as three generations. During the Tokugawa and Meiji eras, it had been a vital functional unit of close-knit social relations in the farming village.

Distinct features of dōzoku reflected, by and large, those of the ie institution. Like ie, dōzoku was a group defined in terms of common residence. Households identified with the same dōzoku were located in the same vicinity to promote close relations between honke and bunke. Like ie, it was an economic corporate group in which the dyadic relations between honke and each of its bunke were defined. They were characterized by the latter's economic and political subordination to the former, which resulted in a hierarchy of status. In the framework of dōzoku, relations other than the dyadic relations, such as collateral relations between two bunke, were not functionally important. The hierarchy of status subordinating bunke to honke was a structural principle of dōzoku that promoted its cohesiveness.[18]

Dōzoku, like ie again, stressed inclusiveness by permitting the spouses of the dōzoku members to be fully included. Meanwhile, those who left dōzoku because of marriage or adoption were excluded from it. This points to the emphasis upon the institutional frame of dōzoku, in which any member of a household identified with a dōzoku was automatically a member. Thus, dōzoku required tracing genealogical relations for the head of each household representing the institution of ie, rather than particular individuals.

Cohesion and the conformity of motivational orientation were crucial to maintain the role of dōzoku in the perpetuation of ie. While dōzoku accrued from the economic and genealogical relations, a variety of unifying rituals were conducted under the leadership of the head of honke. Weddings and funeral ceremonies for members of his dōzoku, for example, involved all dōzoku members and were carried out under his direction. Also, only he had the authority to officiate at the ceremony of the dōzoku shrine. The rituals that commemorated the dōzoku ancestors were said to be a "collective expression of dōzoku unity." Further, in order to stress the unity of dōzoku, its members usually had the same design for their ie insignia.

Iemoto

The urban equivalent of dōzoku was iemoto, which fulfilled similar functions. Merchant dōzoku existed, but dōzoku was dominant in agricultural villages and was extensively adopted by farmers to cope with economic and ecological problems. Iemoto evolved in urban settings, where urban Japanese had different problems and occupational commitments from those of the farmers. Its membership was not determined by criteria of residence and geographical proximity; potential iemoto constituents were geographically unlimited and not strictly bound by such ascriptive factors as place of birth and kinship. Iemoto permitted a greater degree of individual volition in determining membership. In other words, individuals gained membership by their own choice.

Characteristics of iemoto social relations, however, reflected to a great extent those of dōzoku. Once one joined iemoto, he or she was subject to organizational constraints—similar to those of dōzoku and ie—but was also under its protection. Hence, while iemoto and dōzoku were different in origin, they exhibited similar orientations that stressed institutional continuity, motivational conformity, inclusiveness, hierarchy, and exclusiveness vis-à-vis other groups, distinguishing the uchi (one's own world) from the yoso (outside world).

The traditional patterns of ie and dōzoku no longer exist. Ie has undergone a great deal of modification, particularly since the revision of the civil code by the occupation authorities in the postwar period; dōzoku was already in decline toward the end of the Meiji era, and broke up entirely in the early twentieth century. Variations of the original iemoto, however, exist at present. Since it was an urban corporate group, it exhibited a greater degree of continuity in the urbanized Japanese society.

In Iemoto: The Heart of Japan, Francis Hsu contends that iemoto is an archetype of the present Japanese social structure.[19] His analysis of iemoto, partly based upon Takeyoshi Kawashima's work,[20] sheds fascinating light on Japanese social relations.

Iemoto was a group whose principle of solidarity was based on what Hsu calls "kin-tract"[21]—a fixed hierarchy of social relations in which individuals gain membership on a voluntary basis for specific activities based on a given ideology and a code of behavior. It encompassed a variety of groups including schools of flower arrangement, the tea ceremony, judo, sumo, painting, calligraphy, dancing, kabuki, no drama, archery, singing, clothes designing, koto playing, gardening, cooking, the art of manners, and others.

Several distinct features of iemoto deserve discussion here: first, its basis in the master-disciple relationship. The master demanded complete loyalty from his disciples, who were expected to learn by observing and imitating him carefully. Self-understanding based on empathy was stressed as a technique for learning. The disciple was absolutely prohibited from modifying the master's teachings. Once accredited, he received a name, as a prospective master, from his master, and incurred permanent indebtedness (on) to him. In turn, the master was expected to protect his disciple and help him promote his work. Giri and ninjo entered their relationship. In Doi's term, "dependent relationships" developed between them.

Second, iemoto was based on a stratified structure of interlocking hierarchy. It consisted of the highest master and apprentices as

FIGURE 2

Order of Hierarchy in Iemoto

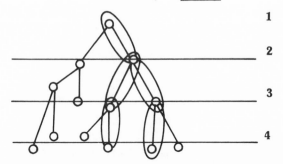

Source: From T. Kawashima, Familial Institution as Ideology (Tokyo: Iwanami, 1957), p. 338.

shown in Figure 2. Hierarchy was central to the maintenance of ie-moto, as it was to dōzoku. Third, iemoto functioned on the principle of territoriality, which defined the sphere of the master's influence and the needs for mutual protection within the entire organization of iemoto. Fourth, the highest masters, who were called iemoto, assumed supreme authority over the disciples in the schools. They had the right to control and preserve the styles, ideologies, and standards of excellence of their iemoto organizations and to receive part of the disciples' incomes as fees for accreditation, as well as to expel disciples. Fifth, iemoto was based on a fictitious ie system, which exhibited pseudokinship relations between master and disciple, and other characteristics of ie discussed earlier.

The orientations underlying the three traditional institutions have been extensively incorporated, with varying degrees of modification, into contemporary Japanese social relations. Those orientations have served to provide adaptive solutions to the emerging problems that Japan confronted in its evolving phases of modernization since the Meiji Restoration, and this underlies the unique Japanese pattern of modernization. Modernization in Japan has been superficially Western in a variety of respects, but its substantive features of modernization are uniquely Japanese.

THE GROUP IN CONTEMPORARY JAPAN

One cannot fully understand Japanese behavior only in terms of the group, since it is motivated and conditioned by a number of other factors. Yet, the Japanese concept of the group deserves further attention, for it is so central to Japanese behavior and motivation that, lacking sufficient knowledge of it, one may fail to appreciate its ramifications in contemporary Japan.

The Group and Contemporary Institutional Practices

An article in the Japan Times (1976) reported a survey conducted by a European tourist organization about Japanese tourists. It described Japanese as polite, respectable, and well mannered; but, it went on, Europeans felt that Japanese are awkward, unnecessarily restrained, insecure, and do not enjoy individual freedom because they are always in a group, wherever they go and whatever they do: sightseeing, shopping, going to theaters or restaurants. The Europeans suggested that Japanese should be more relaxed and enjoy individual freedom while touring in Europe. Obviously, this is an expression of a European ethnocentrism; the fact is that Japanese tourists feel more secure, relaxed, and content when they are in a group than when they tour alone following their own curiosities. The mode of Japanese tourist behavior abroad is little different from the one exhibited in their own country. Japanese children of all ages and grades frequently participate in group tours to parks, historic places, and distant cities for a few days. Similarly, farmers and men and women in private corporations often charter buses to conduct group trips that last several days as well for picnics nearby.

Lifelong employment, invariably adopted by relatively large private corporations and government institutions (bureaus of central, prefectural, and municipal governments), is a unique Japanese practice that reinforces major ideological characteristics of the Japanese group. While the extensive institutionalization of this practice started around the second decade of this century, its archetype evolved during the Meiji era. Several factors contributed to the practice of lifelong employment. Two influential ideologies, perfected during the preindustrial Tokugawa era, carried over into a modernizing Japan. One is a familism based on the concept of ie, which formerly governed the traditional pattern of commercial and agricultural management in Tokugawa Japan. The other was the Confucian ethic emphasizing paternalism blended with managerial familism. Both notions were adopted as practical for management in modernizing industries. Finally, when the labor market was relatively fluid and unstable toward the end of the nineteenth century as a result of increasing industrialization, management began to develop a system by which workers could be employed for life so as to provide for the stability of the labor force.[22]

After World War I, this practice was further institutionalized so that large companies could recruit and train boys fresh from school, such youths being more amenable to being molded to meet a company's needs. They were given not only technical training but moral and character training as well, for Japanese companies, as they still do, regarded the latter as essential as the former. The fact that the character of both company and employee has been an important concern is clearly seen in today's company mottoes. The motto of Hitachi Corporation, one of the giants, is "Let harmony be the highest ideal." "If the ideal is the same for all, we become a unified entity living in spiritual harmony and striving on a supreme moral path" is the motto for Mitsubishi Electric Company, another large company.

Let us look at some unique aspects of lifelong employment as currently practiced in private firms. Firms recruit new employees directly from schools, not from the labor market, and emphasize particular personal qualities—"vitality," "adaptability," "conformability," and "native intelligence"—which are considered necessary for becoming permanent employees. Individuals are not usually recruited for particular positions, nor do they often apply for them. Rather, they are recruited as additional unspecified labor with the expectation that they will be needed for certain positions in the near future for which firms offer intensive training. Employment lasts for one's entire career. Both employers and employees assume that there will be no layoffs nor changes of employment to other employers. One's salary and promotion are decided by the number of years of employment, and initial salary is a function of the level of one's education.

Firms offer employees a variety of benefits: bonuses twice a year, equivalent to normal salaries for three to five months; company housing; welfare schemes for families (for death, marriage, child care, education, and the like); low-interest loans; recreational facilities; and so on. Through these programs, therefore, not only the employees but their families, too, are involved in their companies in one way or another. In turn, the companies require permanent loyalty from their employees, that is, lifetime commitment to them. In short, lifelong employment provides the employees with security (inclusiveness) as long as they conform to the framework of their firms (conformity of motivational orientation and permanent involvement in particular hierarchical social relations).

Incidentally, it is this pattern of employment practices that is in large measure responsible for the current infernal entrance examination pressures, which have molded contemporary patterns of adolescent socialization. Its implication for schooling is mentioned only in passing here, since it is discussed extensively in Chapters 4 and 5.

It is difficult to determine the proportion of firms practicing lifelong employment or an equivalent form of employment. But, in general, large and stable corporations are invariably committed to this employment practice. In 1970, the percentage of people working for firms employing more than 500 persons was only 26 percent, while 22.4 percent of the total number of workers were in the firms with less than 500 employees; of the total labor force 11.1 percent had jobs in firms with less than 100 employees, and 40.5 percent in smaller firms having less than 50 employees. Probably it is the first and second categories of firms that can provide relatively stable employment with a lifetime commitment. In recent years lifetime employment has not been the rule for a small portion of individuals involved in large companies for they seek horizontal mobility among other firms, but this is not yet a significant trend. Whether or not Japanese can get jobs in big private firms and government bureaus, their dominant ideal is still to secure lifetime employment in such organizations particularly because most Japanese are anxious security seekers.

As related to personnel policies of business organizations, another distinct feature of Japanese management is what is called ringisei, or a system of decision making by consensus. Although an administrative technique, it exhibits a basic characteristic of administrative behavior, organization, and management. As Brzezinski points out, "The Japanese decision-making process is a study in prudence, circumspection, and collective responsibility."[23]

When a company confronts a problem, it is first studied by lower-level managers and their staffs. Subsequently, a ringisho, a document outlining the problem and its possible solution, is prepared and circulated among different echelons of management for their reactions and approval. Eventually, it reaches the desk of the chief executive for final approval, but by the time approval is finally rendered, a ringisho is discussed and modified to reflect the views of all levels of management, so that it may represent a consensus of an organization. Lower-level managers take every collective precaution, minimizing conflict and disagreement among themselves, to ensure that the ringisho does not meet disapproval by the chief executive. In this entire process of decision making, they spend such an enormous amount of time patiently learning each other's opinions and feelings that their consensus usually represents a final decision that will merely be formalized by the top executive who, in turn, feels obliged to approve a consensus collectively reached by the group. Obviously, the major concern is to maintain group harmony. As seen here, ringi always starts at a low level of an organization and attempts to achieve a consensual decision—a highly democratic process. Once the decision is made, no specific individual is singled out as responsible for it because it is always a group decision.

The underlying assumptions of the ringi system constitute a framework that guides decision-making processes in schools, including colleges and universities. Efforts are always made to arrive at consensus if possible. Faculty meetings often continue for hours while the participants search for unanimity at both the overt and covert levels. In these efforts the role of a principal or dean is frequently reduced to that of a coordinator, rather than that of the decision maker, of a group.

Another vital facet of group orientation in Japanese society is batsu, which may be termed clique or faction, although, unfortunately, these English words do not convey the full meaning of batsu, a unique Japanese phenomenon. It may be viewed as an extension of iemoto—a kin tract fulfilling the functional requirements of a group. It is a territorial group, formed on the basis of particularistic personal ties and defending its exclusive interest vis-à-vis other groups. It involves the relationship of patronage and dependence, the model for which can be found in ie, where oyabun (paternal parent) and kobun (child) constituted ascriptive, hierarchical relations. Hence, once it is formed, it tends to become a familistic group with emphasis on vertical social relations and internal solidarity.[24] The members of batsu are protected on an ascriptive basis. In the development of Japanese modernization, batsu has played a highly significant role, and it has subsequently been incorporated into contemporary social organizations.

Probably the first important batsu was hanbatsu or "domain batsu," which functioned in the political field. After the Meiji Restoration, political leaders, particularly from Satsuma (in southernmost Kyushu) and Choshu (in southernmost Honshu), dominated political power at the national level until the close of the second decade of this century. These feudal domains played the key role in overthrowing the Tokugawa shogun and in bringing about the Meiji Restoration. Leaders in those domains had close personal ties with each other, which served as a basis for common goals, mutual protection, and exclusion of others.

Related to the politically significant hanbatsu is the Japanese term habatsu, political faction, the role of which cannot be ignored in the development of political parties, particularly the ruling conservative party in the postwar era. The Liberal Democratic party, a dominant, postwar party, is a conglomerate of several major factions. The election of the prime minister and the formation of the cabinet are always contingent upon negotiations between the factions and a demonstration of the power of an influential faction of which the premier is head. Similarly, national policies reflect more often than not the dynamics of conflict and cooperation among the factions.

Habatsu is an informal group within a party, clearly based on the relationship of patron and dependence. While it fulfills the func-

tions of batsu mentioned earlier, habatsu leaders are expected to
play several concrete roles. Responsible for securing political funds
to support the members of their groups in election campaigns, they
also determine the qualifications of members and, if qualified, help
them in an election by appearing in their districts and otherwise.
Their influence is exhibited not only in elections but also by their
power to distribute political positions, such as committee chairman-
ships, vital official posts, and, above all, cabinet posts. Moreover,
they extend their power to pass legislation that satisfies their constituents. It is notable that political factions within a party usually
insist on their own territoriality and exclusiveness, so much so that
members of the same party rather often view each other as if they
were members of different parties unless they belong to the same
faction. Distance between the uchi and yoso worlds is clearly visible
among factions.

When political influence is exerted, along the line of habatsu,
upon politicians and their constituents, it sometimes has a deleterious
effect. Constituents tend to interpret narrowly what habatsu do for
them as the sole basis for electing candidates, rather than the roles
they play in national politics. Hence, ex-Premier Tanaka, former
head of the most powerfully financed faction in the ruling party, who
was arrested for his part in the Lockheed scandal, was reelected in
1977 by an overwhelming vote of his constituents; they could not see
him in a broad frame of political reference, but only as a man who
had brought them national funds for local improvement and business
prosperity.

In addition to habatsu, there were many other batsu in the
past: the well-known zaibatsu; gakubatsu ("school batsu"); bureaucratic batsu; military batsu, which were influential during the war;
keibatsu, consisting of a network of powerful families built through
marriage as a means of elevating gifted young men; and the like.
Zaibatsu were financial cliques of prewar Japan, which developed as
powerful monopolistic groups of economic power and centered around
the core of extended family relationships. They recruited competent
men from outside their families, however, to promote their business
organizations. All zaibatsu were disbanded by the occupation authorities. The role that gakubatsu have played has also been highly significant in the development of Japanese bureaucracy and business organizations. They are cliques of men who share the same educational
identification, that is, in terms of academic institutions from which
they graduated. These cliques are, again, based on a kin tract and,
even today, exercise strong influence on access to companies and
government bureaus granted to individuals from different academic
institutions, as well as on the promotion of employees. Individuals
of a clique feel that they are bound together for certain common as-

sumed traits, such as superior education and competence, exclusive socialization, and similar outlooks. Such assumed traits and recommendations by one graduate for another serve as a centripetal force creating personal ties between individuals in the same gakubatsu.

Personality and the Group

It is clear from studies of culture and personality that there must be a high degree of fit between the requirements of a social structure and basic personality if a society is to maintain its order and if personality disorder is not to occur excessively. Basic personality refers to adaptive psychological skills and abilities shared by most members of a society—a product resulting from specific institutional forms and social means of coping with the problems of living. What are the major characteristics of Japanese basic personality that are compatible with Japanese social structure? Although some of these characteristics were touched upon earlier, let us give further attention to them.

To constitute an advanced industrial society, Japanese social organizations are required to operate according to functional prerequisites defined by the rational principles of industrialism, including, for example, universalism. While Japanese society is guided by such principles in a variety of respects, it is, however, better characterized as blending them with particularism and relativism, which often take precedence. Of Japanese society, where people see themselves primarily as members of groups, Edwin Reischauer, the noted student of Japanese history, observes in The Japanese that "specific intragroup and also intergroup relationships may reasonably take precedence over universal principles. . . . Ethics may be more relativistic or situational than universal."[25] It is not exaggeration to suggest that Japanese are more situation- and group-centered than peoples of the other industrialized nations in the world.

The strong emphasis upon group and situation centeredness in Japan led Ruth Benedict to believe that the Japanese are shame-oriented. According to her, Japanese behavior is guided by externalized moral criteria rather than internalized ones. While these two types of criteria are often indistinguishable, the analytical difference between them is that the former criteria are defined and controlled by the actor's situation, comprising culturally determined social relations, while the latter criteria are universalistic, as well as immutable, and are internalized on the part of the actor. Such a difference may be better elucidated in terms of the distinction made by David Riesman[26] between tradition direction and inner direction, but as Benedict puts it:

> The primacy of shame in Japanese life means . . . that
> any man watches the judgment of the public upon his deeds.
> He need only fantasy what their verdict will be but orients
> himself toward the object of the others. . . . True shame
> cultures rely on external sanctions for good behavior. . . .
>   A society that inculcates absolute standards of morality
> and relies on men's developing a conscience is a guilt cul-
> ture . . . but a man in such a society may, as in the
> United States, suffer in addition from shame when he ac-
> cuses himself of gaucheries.[27]

The fact is that people in Western societies—where the tradition of absolutist Christianity has been strong—and Japanese both
act according to a blend of both criteria, but the Japanese are more
heavily guided by externalized criteria. It is important, nevertheless, to point out that these criteria, including giri and ninjo, are
not simply social measures of external sanction. Relativistic and
external as they may be, they become a part of one's moral system
that orients him or her in social life. Hence, as Doi observes, a
Japanese's sense of guilt is aroused most keenly when he or she be-
trays the trust of the group, particularly in relationships where giri
is involved and where betrayal could lead to the severing of the link.[28]
According to George De Vos, a specialist in psychological anthropology,

> When shame and guilt have undergone a process of internal-
> ization during the course of an individual's development,
> both become operative regardless of the relative absence
> of external threats of punishment or overt concern with
> the opinions of others concerning his behavior. Behavior
> is automatically self-evaluated without the presence of
> others. A simple dichotomy relating internalized shame
> only to ego ideal and internalized guilt only to an auto-
> matically operative superego is one to be seriously ques-
> tioned.[29]

The emphasis upon group and situation centeredness in Japan
serves as a source both of Japanese motivation to attend college and
also of pressure imposed on adolescents to excel academically.
That is, a feeling of shame is variably aroused on the part of adolescents if they do not pass entrance examinations or if they fail to attend college for one reason or another, since their failure represents
an inability to meet the expectations of the group-centered society
(see Chapter 5).
    Earlier, we examined the psychology of amae as characteristic
of Japanese personality. The Japanese are prone to seek relations

that foster dependence, without which they feel insecure, alienated, and lost; relations of dependence are both vertical—as upon superiors, authorities, and the emperor—and horizontal. A classic example occurred during a historic national crisis in 1873, shortly after the Meiji Restoration, when the emperor's sanction was sought by political leaders of the government who were unable to dissuade frustrated, aggressive exsamurai from withdrawing their plan to invade Korea. The sanction was effective even though the emperor had only nominal power. This sort of cultural mentality prevails today in many dimensions of Japanese life; suitable authorities could be marriage go-betweens, teachers, bureaucratic and corporate section chiefs, and the like, if dependency-seekers can secure their indulgence. Even since World War II, the government has repeatedly attempted to define the emperor as "the moral center" of the Japanese in the postwar curriculum. The reader will find, later in this volume, that such attempts have been in significant measure politically motivated. Nevertheless, they involve a culturally defined motivation related to the psychology of amae.

Although the notion of individuality was introduced to Japan in the postwar era, Japanese have never accepted the Western meaning of the concept, and probably do not fully understand it as specifically related to the context of social relations. They are not socialized to see themselves as distinct individuals with independent views and dispositions. The circumstances of industrialization have brought about radical changes in the institutional pattern of modern living, but not in personal attitudes toward the individual. In Ronald Dore's words, "In a typically Japanese way, the necessary revolution in individual attitudes—a revolution which is only possible through the self-awareness and effort of each individual—is being omitted."[30]

Japanese have placed much less value on individualistic self-realization than Westerners, whose typical ideal has been personal and self-realization apart from family and group. The Japanese sense of personal gratification and achievement is generally developed in relation to groups (including the family and larger groups) that determine the objects of devotion and values that reward personal life and activity. One may get the misguided impression that the Japanese social structure does not place importance on what may be called "instrumental orientation," as opposed to "expressive orientation." Instrumental orientation has been historically emphasized in the context of group, which is also the source of expressive orientation.

> The Japanese sense of accomplishment or achievement
> could be satisfied ultimately only by being defined as rele-
> vant to a sense of self as part of family, or part of some-

thing larger than the individualized self. The sense of
self, for many Japanese, is realized only through repay-
ment of deeply felt obligations, which, if not fulfilled,
give rise to a sense of intolerable guilt. This sense of
loyalty to authority and need to repay obligation stems
from interaction of the child with its parents before there
is any verbalization of an ideology of loyalty beyond the
primary family itself. The emotional impact of life
within the primary family sets the keystone to life's meaning.[31]

Having received such a socialization, Japanese internalize a
high achievement motivation and the capacity for concerted group efforts. The role of the family as a socializing agent is a key to the
development of achievement motivation. During the evolution of
Japan into a complex, modern society, the forms in which a sense of
obligation, guilt, and shame are expressed have undergone modification without reducing the importance of these dimensions of social
relations.

It is obvious by now that socialization for achievement orientation in Japanese society is quite different from that observed in the
United States. The former fosters motivation for excellence and
achievement through the encouragement of dependence and nurture
in the family, while the latter stresses the reinforcement of self-
reliance. The generalization, made by David McClelland in The
Achieving Society, that there is a positive correlation between the
level of achievement motivation and that of socialization for self-
reliance and personal competence does not apply to the Japanese.[32]
Such a contrast between Euro-American and Japanese societies may
cause a quandary, but must be understood in terms of differences in
social and cultural structure. This contrast is also revealed in the
cultural orientations underlying education in these societies. Japanese education reflects the traditional cultural orientation discussed
here; its emphasis is on achievement with a stress on adaptability to
group norms, but not on the development of individuality, which is a
central concern in Euro-American societies. Moreover, Japanese
motivation for achievement and competence, which is the backbone
of its current economic development, ought not be seen simply as a
product of Japanese modernization. That is, as social mobility increased since the Meiji Restoration, one's social success (shusse—
a word frequently used in Japan) for the sake of family and the larger
group was stressed, and the emphasis on achievement motivation was
carried over even from the Tokugawa era when mobility was limited.[33]

The Japanese are hardworking and diligent people, and they exhibit perseverance and toughness of character. Their energies and

devotion are, by and large, channeled into groups, which, in turn, generates personal satisfaction. Yet they are not free from a psychological malaise, which they recognize themselves, resulting from the pressures for uniformity and heavy burdens of duty and obligation—constraints a tightly knit society imposes upon its individuals. Institutional forms of living have changed rapidly, but the moral and social patterns of behavior, on the whole, have altered little. The Japanese have a new bottle for the old wine. This symbolized their mode of cultural persistence and a way of coping with new problems.

CONCLUSION

The primary purpose of this chapter was to present the background for our exploration of Japanese education to follow. The Japanese pattern of adaptation was examined; central to it is the group orientation underlying the structure of social relations in Japanese society. As will be quite obvious in the succeeding chapters, this discussion of group orientation is essential to understanding education in Japan. Although this chapter is not primarily concerned with education, educational implications of the Japanese pattern of adaptation have been mentioned in passing in the anticipation that they will be fully developed later in this volume.

NOTES

1. Marshall Sahlins and Elman Service, eds., Evolution and Culture (Ann Arbor: University of Michigan Press, 1970), pp. 12-13.

2. Talcott Parsons, The Social System (Glencoe, Ill.: Free Press, 1959), pp. 58-67.

3. See Nobuo K. Shimahara, "Cultural Evolution: Technology as a Converging Force," in Social Forces and Schooling, ed. Nobuo K. Shimahara and Adam Scrupski (New York: David McKay, 1975), pp. 26-39.

4. S. N. Eisenstadt, Tradition, Change and Modernization (New York: John Wiley, 1973), pp. 22-25.

5. See Yehudi Cohen, "The State System, Schooling, and Cognitive and Motivational Patterns," in Social Forces and Schooling, Shimahara and Scrupski, pp. 103-39.

6. Francis Hsu, Clan, Caste and Club (New York: Van Nostrand, 1963).

7. See David Riesman, The Lonely Crowd (New Haven, Conn.: Yale University Press, 1961).

8. See Talcott Parsons and Winston White, "The Link between Character and Society," in Culture and Social Character, ed. Sey-

42 / ADAPTATION AND EDUCATION IN JAPAN

mour Martin Lipset and Leo Lowenthal (New York: Free Press, 1961), pp. 89–135; Philip Slater, The Pursuit of Loneliness (Boston: Beacon Press, 1970).

9. See Chie Nakane, Japanese Society (London: Penguin, 1973).

10. Ibid., pp. 90–107.

11. Chie Nakane, Tate Shakaino Ningen Kankei [The human relations of a vertical society] (Tokyo: Kōdansha, 1976), pp. 46–53.

12. See Takeo Doi, The Anatomy of Dependence (Tokyo: Kōdansha, 1977).

13. Takeo Doi, Amae Zakko [Collected essays on amae] (Tokyo: Kōbundo, 1976), pp. 185–92.

14. Quoted in Erik H. Erikson, Identity, Youth, and Crisis (New York: W. W. Norton, 1969), p. 19.

15. Doi, Anatomy of Dependence, pp. 28–35.

16. See Takeyoshi Kawashima, Ideorogī Toshiteno Kazokuseido [The familial institution as an ideology] (Tokyo: Iwanami, 1957); Seiichi Kitano, Ieto Dōzokuno Kisoriron [The fundamental theory of ie and dōzoku] (Tokyo: Miraisha, 1976); Chie Nakane, Kinship and Economic Organization in Rural Japan (London: London School of Economics, 1967).

17. Francis Hsu, Iemoto: The Heart of Japan (Cambridge, Mass.: Schenkman, 1975), pp. 25–99.

18. Kizaemon Ariga, Ariga Kizaemon Chosakushū VII: Shakaishino Shomondai [The collection of Ariga Kizamemon's works VII: problems in social history] (Tokyo: Miraisha, 1969), p. 288.

19. See Hsu, Iemoto.

20. Kawashima, Ideorogī Toshiteno Kazokuseido.

21. Hsu, Iemoto, p. 62.

22. Sachio Okamoto, "Nipponteki Keieimo Keifu" ["The geneology of Japanese management"], in Nippon Keieishio Manabu I [A study of the history of Japanese management I], ed. Masaaki Kobayashi et al. (Tokyo: Yūhikaku, 1976), pp. 253–69.

23. Zbigniew Brzezinski, The Fragile Blossom: Crisis and Change in Japan (New York: Ronald Press, 1970), p. 49.

24. Saburō Yasuda, "On Batsu," Gendai Shakaigaku [Modern sociology] 2 (1975): 187–205.

25. Edwin O. Reischauer, The Japanese (Cambridge, Mass.: Harvard University Press, 1977), p. 138.

26. See Riesman, The Lonely Crowd.

27. Ruth Benedict, The Chrysanthemum and the Sword (Tokyo: Charles Tuttle, 1976), pp. 222, 224.

28. Doi, Anatomy of Dependence, pp. 49–50.

29. George de Vos, Socialization for Achievement (Berkeley: University of California Press, 1973), p. 148.

30. Ronald Dore, City Life in Japan (Berkeley: University of California Press, 1958), p. 393.

31. de Vos, Socialization for Achievement, p. 195.

32. David McClelland, The Achieving Society (Princeton, N.J.: Van Nostrand, 1961).

33. See Robert Bellah, Tokugawa Religion (Glencoe, Ill.: Free Press, 1957).

3
THE EVOLUTION OF
JAPANESE EDUCATION

The dramatic evolution in Japanese education evident since the Meiji Restoration has occurred in response to pressures for modernization. Education had existed before the dawn of Japanese modernization, but its functions in the premodern period were defined in a different frame of reference from the one applied since the restoration. One needs to view the evolution of schooling in Japan as a part of its adaptation to the external and internal social, political, and economic forces of the last half of the nineteenth century. The aims and functions of education were defined in terms of the imperatives of the new state. The evolution of formal education in Japan presents a case supporting a general view that the needs of society take precedence over those of individuals, and this sociological observation is generally applicable to contemporary Japanese education as well. In this view, although individual needs may not be ignored, they are definitely subordinated to the institutional imperatives of society. The degree and pattern of subordination vary, depending upon societies, but the history of Japanese education since the restoration to the end of World War II exhibits a strong emphasis on the subordination of the individual to the state.

Education may be understood in terms of its four major functions: pattern maintenance, integration, political socialization, and "adaptive" competency, as narrowly defined.[1] In other words, education is designed to reinforce cultural patterns and to develop a uniformity of motivational and cognitive orientations of individuals toward society so as to stabilize social integration and the political system; it is also patterned to meet the economic needs of society so that it may survive in a given environment. The Meiji era provides us with a marvelous opportunity to examine these functions, as well as to appreciate the contention that educational reforms generally involve special attention to these functions.

Another unique feature of the evolution of schooling is the development of separation between elite and mass education. Schooling for the elite has been shaped in response to the need of the state to train individuals who will play strategic national and international roles in political, economic, and other vital social institutions directly concerned with the stability of national order and the upgrading of adaptive capability vis-à-vis other societies. Mass education, meanwhile, has emerged to integrate society. Anthropologist Yehudi Cohen speaks eloquently of the types of education:

> Mass education in a civilizational state has to be seen as a manifestation of two cross-cutting principles. The first of these is the civilizational state's need to train an elite who will fill the boundary roles in addition to ruling within the society; this is an adaptive outgrowth of the pressures engendered by the civilization as a network. The second is to establish ideological uniformity throughout the society by eliminating local boundary systems which can serve as the seedbeds of particularistic and antistate symbol systems; this is an adaptive outgrowth of the pressures engendered by the state per se. In other words, elite education is an adaptive response to the pressures generated by a society's participation in a civilizational network; mass education is principally a response to the forces stemming from civilizational and state pressures in juxtaposition.[2]

The Meiji educational reforms clearly reflect our view on the development of separation between elite and mass schooling.

TOKUGAWA EDUCATION AS THE PRECURSOR OF MEIJI EDUCATION

Tokugawa education was composed of a variety of institutionalized practices for ideological indoctrination and the inculcation of competency in certain areas of social life. Because its aims and functions were appropriate to the stateless stage of Japanese social development, Tokugawa education could not serve as full prototype for Meiji education. It was precursory, nevertheless, in that it had offered a wide range of schooling to the Japanese, particularly the ruling class of samurai, during the stable feudal period of two and one-half centuries. The ruling class and privileged commoners had developed a strong awareness of the need for education. Without this awareness and the extensive experience in the institutional practice of education developed during the Tokugawa era, the Japanese could not have embarked upon the comprehensive educational reforms initiated in the Meiji era.

Tokugawa education was largely guided by Confucianism, which had been introduced to Japan around the middle of the first millennium, and was studied most extensively during the Tokugawa period. Providing an ideology that was quite instrumental in maintaining the feudal social structure, Confucian literature also offered rich textual and pedagogical materials. For these two reasons, Confucianism became the major basis for educating the samurai, who constituted 5 to 7 percent of the population.

Although it was a badge of social distinction, education was also a necessity for the samurai, brought about by the need to turn from military to bureaucratic pursuits during the peaceful feudal era. Furthermore, the samurai code required them to cultivate both letters and military training. The education itself was under the tutelage of Confucian-trained teachers, who operated schools and colleges supported by the domains, some of which had started in the early seventeenth century. Toward the end of the Tokugawa era, these domain-supported schools numbered nearly 300. Samurai received training in technical competence related to, for example, reading and writing, character development, and ethical principles for statecraft, with emphasis on filial piety and benevolence.

Meanwhile, education for the common people developed without direct support of the domains, through the institution known as terakoya, or parish schools. Facilities consisted of temples and private homes, and the rudimentary subjects and simplest Confucian teachings were taught by priests, unattached samurai, Confucian scholars, and educated commoners. The Tokugawa shogun encouraged the development of terakoya, and nearly 15,000 common schools existed before the restoration.

Besides terakoya, about 1,500 privately organized boarding schools, diverse in size and training, also existed. Based on the master-disciple relationship found in iemoto, they were commonly called juku, the name that is still used today to designate private schools that prepare students for college and high school entrance examinations. In the early nineteenth century they proliferated rapidly, and many outstanding leaders of the Meiji Restoration received inspiration and training from distinguished juku masters.

As noted earlier, Confucianism was the most influential and eminent source of studies throughout the Tokugawa era. Around the turn of the nineteenth century, however, its influence began to decline, and studies of Japanese literature and Western learning, particularly Dutch language and science, came to receive considerable attention. As a result, the waning feudal period coincided with a growing diversification in literature, learning in general, and widespread literacy.[3]

ADAPTATION AND EDUCATIONAL
REFORMS IN THE MEIJI RESTORATION

Although the turbulence of the Meiji Restoration seemed likely at first to produce a quite different society in Japan, the reader will recall that, despite rapid modernization, profound change has not occurred. That the pattern of Japanese social structure in the anthropological sense—that is, the pattern of social relations—has changed relatively little is evidence that Japanese culture has been a stabilizing and tenacious force in the country's adaptation to changing internal and external environments. Indeed, it is the very tenacity of the culture that has made the social transformation of Japan unique.

Adaptation involves the manner in which people make use of indigenous cultural modes of thought and behavior to cope with new problems. The Meiji educational reforms were typical of this type of adaptation, a pattern guided by traditional cultural orientations. As sweeping economic and political changes began after the restoration, Meiji leaders focused their attention on education as an instrument for modernization. They did not seek a modification of Tokugawa education—no matter how radical—but attempted to identify a new, Western model for Japanese education. This attempt was entirely consistent with their view that Japan must attain equality with the West if it was to respond effectively to the several pressures of Western civilization. In short, through effective education they sought to develop advanced Western technology and science in Japan. They were keenly aware that the industrialization of Japan would be impossible without a generation schooled in contemporary science and technology.

Meanwhile, the Meiji leaders confronted problems that were both external and internal. National integration itself was at stake, and the leaders believed that nation building could best be accomplished by establishing a comprehensive national educational system that would provide the young with cognitive and motivational orientations for national unity.

In the face of the unprecedented national crises immediately before and after the restoration, the Meiji leaders moved swiftly to accomplish exceedingly costly and totally foreign reforms without a sufficient understanding of Western educational systems and adequate planning for the reforms. The result was a dialectical course of trial and error that lasted for nearly two decades, although it eventually produced a national educational system that stood until Japan's defeat in 1945.

The first educational reform was launched in 1872, five years after the restoration. After its collapse, a second reform was introduced in 1879. The third reform, which was already conceived at the

time the second reform came into effect, was completed in 1890 with
the promulgation of the Imperial Rescript on Education. As a result, all controversial reform debates ended until the middle of the
twentieth century. Curiously, the underlying orientation of the third
reform was unmistakably characteristic of traditional Japan, whereas
the structure of the reformed system was Western, reflecting the
typically Japanese pattern of adaptation discussed earlier.

The Fundamental Code of Education

In 1871 the Ministry of Education came into being, empowered
to act on all educational matters. Its Fundamental Code of Education (gakusei) issued in 1872 gave the Japanese, for the first time in
their history, a plan outlining a comprehensive national school system.[4] It was a bold and progressive system, largely copied from
the one then current in France. That system, based upon educational reforms pioneered by Napoleon in the early nineteenth century and perfected under the Guizot Law of 1833, rendered education
independent of the church. Following the French model, the Japanese nation was divided into eight university districts, each to establish a university. Each university district was further broken down
into 32 middle school districts, each one of which was again subdi-
vided into 210 elementary school districts. Elementary education,
four years in a lower division and another four years in an upper
division, was designed to be a unified egalitarian system for which
all children were eligible, regardless of social class (see Figure 3).
The French system represented an administratively centralized order that was appealing to Japanese leaders, particularly those concerned with the development of national order and unity.

Prior to the Fundamental Code of Education, French education
had already been tried independently by pioneers in the former domain of Fukuyama in 1868 and 1870, according to a book on French
education translated into Japanese by a samurai retainer of the domain. It is interesting to note that the work was a major source of
information to the Ministry of Education planning committee that was
preparing the new educational plan.[5] While the committee was studying a model for Japanese education, the Iwakura mission was in the
United States and Europe studying their educational structures and
curricula. One of the members of the mission was Fujimaro Tanaka,
who became first senior secretary of the ministry, one of the most
influential men in the early development of Meiji education; the adoption of the French system, however, was decided by the ministry
while Tanaka was abroad.

Another curious feature of the first reform is its eclectic character. Although the central administration was predominantly French-

FIGURE 3

The School System (Gakusei) of 1872

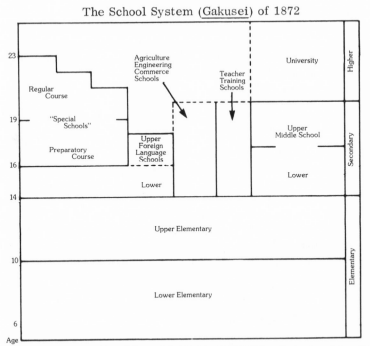

Source: T. Tsuchiya, Meiji Zenki Kyōiku Seisokushino Kenkyū
[A study of the development of educational policies in the first half
of the Meiji era] (Tokyo: Azekura Shobō, 1963), p. 64.

oriented, the curriculum of the elementary schools was modeled after the U.S. system, reflecting the influence of the Iwakura mission,
particularly Tanaka, who had intensively studied education in the
United States and knew the works of Horace Mann and Henry Barnard.

It is notable, too, that the proclamation announcing the reform
plan baldly rejected traditional education and, in turn, advocated a
liberal view:

> Centuries have elapsed since schools were first established,
> but man has gone astray through misguidance. Learning
> being viewed as the exclusive privilege of the Samurai and
> his superiors, farmers, artisans, merchants, and women
> have neglected it altogether and know not even its mean-
> ing. Even those few among the Samurai and his superiors
> who did pursue learning were apt to claim to be for the
> state, not knowing that it was the very foundation of success
> in life.[6]

Furthermore, as Michio Nagai points out, the preamble of the code stressed "the betterment of the daily life of the individual rather than the needs of the State."[7] Both the proclamation and the preamble indirectly denied Confucian ideology as a foundation for Japanese education, the ethical mainstay that had justified the Tokugawa system, and emphasized the place of the individual vis-à-vis the state.

During the period of trial and error, the leaders of the government were preoccupied with the goal of speedily implanting Western education in Japanese soil by copying Western institutional practices and even educational purposes. Although they were audacious, industrious, and devoted in searching for a practical model, their attempt to implant the French system was doomed to failure from the outset. The Japanese simply could not, nor were they willing to, completely assimilate Western practices; moreover, the government that launched the reform could not provide a sufficient financial commitment to implementing it.

Given the tenacity of Japanese culture, the lack of sufficient resources to create rapid change successfully, the absence of people's readiness to accept drastic changes of a foreign nature, and the backwardness of the government's fiscal policy, one might conclude that the Meiji leaders were overanxious to transform Japan in too short a time. Understandably, the fiscal state of the country was very weak in early Meiji years, yet the government had to commit itself to all major issues of the Meiji reconstruction in the political, military, economic, social, and educational spheres. Such a historic situation imposed severe limitations on the government, which prevented it from expending sufficient funds to support the nationwide school system.

In 1873, for example, the government's financial assistance for public education constituted only 12 percent of the total cost. In fact, the government assumed that people should bear the cost even though many of them were still impoverished and unable to assume an extra expenditure. The government's fiscal policies in the 1870s were largely determined by other priorities. The Meiji oligarchy, in which Toshimichi Ōkubo, Takamori Saigō, and Kōjin Kido were central figures, was divided on the issues of expeditions to Korea and Taiwan. While Kido and Ōkubo insisted on expending resources for domestic development, Saigō urged the expeditions. Kido became minister of Education in 1874, but resigned when the government decided to send troops to Taiwan. This incident was followed by the Satsuma Rebellion in 1877, chiefly instigated by Saigō against the Ōkubo government, which created a major national crisis. The government could spend for education only 1 percent of the total expenditure required by the domestic war.

The problem was also related to the direct import of curricula from the West. In addition to the traditional, standard subjects such as reading and writing, children were exposed to totally new subjects: geography, natural history, chemistry, physical education, and singing. In the absence of Japanese texts on these subjects, translated foreign books, including a work of Adam Smith, were widely used at the elementary school level. Apparently, both teachers and children were unable to comprehend foreign materials well. The problem was further compounded by an insufficient number of teachers to meet the requirements of the code.

As a result of these features of the problem, attendance in school did not increase as anticipated (see Table 2). The government and local schools were forced to create various devices, involving both incentive and punishment, to increase attendance. Meanwhile, protests against imposed schooling were rampant in various prefectures; people in villages and towns burned schools and rioted.

Resistance to the government's policy was also exhibited by a trend to revive Confucian education. Baffled by the imported Western

TABLE 2

School Attendance
(in percent)

Year	Boys	Girls	Average
1873	39.90	15.14	28.13
1874	46.17	17.22	32.30
1875	50.49	18.58	35.19
1876	54.16	21.03	38.32
1877	55.97	22.48	39.88
1878	57.59	23.51	41.26
1879	58.21	22.59	41.16
1880	58.72	21.91	41.06
1881	59.95	24.67	42.98
1882	64.65	30.98	48.51
1883	67.16	33.64	51.03
1884	66.95	33.29	50.76
1885	65.80	32.07	49.62
1886	61.99	29.01	46.33
1887	60.31	28.26	45.00
1888	63.00	30.21	47.36
1889	64.28	30.45	48.18
1890	65.14	31.13	48.93

Source: Ministry of Education, Japan's Growth and Education (Tokyo: Ministry of Education, 1965), p. 180.

education, people believed the traditional education provided in
terakoya and juku was more viable and relevant. Consequently, alternative private schools were built here and there. [8]

The Education Ordinance

During the first decade of the restoration, the Meiji leaders,
intellectuals, and progressive activists for both national identity and
Westernization followed a courageous but chaotic course. Unfavora-
ble reactions to the importation of Western civilization led, understandably, to a growing movement for national revitalism, or Japanization. The Education Ordinance (gakurei), issued in 1879 to remedy
the weaknesses of the earlier reform, appeared at the same time that
sentiments for national revitalism were becoming more explicit and
articulate. Nevertheless, instead of responding to nationalistic sentiments, the ordinance reshaped the school system in an attempt to
counter the persistent popular resistance to educational centralization and the rigid imposition of national standards on localities.

Thus, the underlying orientation of the ordinance clearly represented a shift from the centralized French system to the decentralized U.S. structure. Charged with writing the draft of the ordinance, Tanaka invited David Murray, a professor at Rutgers College
whom he had met during his early trip to the United States, to advise
him. Assisted by Murray, Tanaka completed the draft and submitted
it to Hirobumi Itō, the head of the government, for approval. Upon
his approval it was submitted to the genrō (elder statesmen), who, in
turn, modified it extensively.

Tanaka's reform, based on the U.S. model, provided for local
autonomy and established equality and pluralism as a basis for modern education. It included provisions for the election of an education
board in each village and town, for the establishment and maintenance
of schools, and—as a compromise with the prevailing trend to establish private schools as a reaction to the government's Western education—for the establishment of private schools as a part of the compulsory system. Tanaka's emphasis on local control of education, which
in his view represented another compromise, was disastrous, however, for the people interpreted the ordinance to mean that the government had lost interest in education. Subsequently, some schools
were closed, and attendance dropped (see Table 2). The number of
private schools based on the terakoya model more than tripled in
Tokyo the year after the ordinance was issued. Under increasing
pressure from the conservatives and antigovernment activities, Tanaka resigned in 1880.

When the ordinance was issued in 1879, the political climate
was complex and critical. Saigō, Kido, and Okubo, who constituted

the Meiji oligarchy representing the power and prestige of the government to the emperor, had all died within the span of one year. Saigō's clash with Ōkubo and Kido over his insistence on the expedition to Korea and Ōkubo's increasingly dominant role in the government led to the Satsuma Rebellion in which Saigō died, in September 1877. When the Ōkubo government emerged victorious, it was besieged with political and fiscal crises. Kido, who was deeply upset by the conflict within the oligarchy and Saigo's unyielding demand for the expedition, died four months earlier than Saigō. Ōkubo, left alone to rebuild the bankrupt government, was assassinated by Saigō's supporters in May 1878. As the country lost its three most powerful leaders, the sudden vacuum of leadership deeply concerned the emperor. Hirobumi Itō succeeded Ōkubo, but was a vulnerable leader since he lacked Ōkubo's rich experience, power, and prestige.

Another important factor in the background of the ordinance was the Freedom and People's Rights movement, which was formed in 1874 by Taisuke Itagaki, one of the original leaders of the restoration, who had fallen out with his colleagues in 1873. Although the original idea of the movement was drawn from liberal French thought —as its name suggests—its supporters formed a nationalistic and antigovernment group that included frustrated ex-activists of the restoration, former samurai denied participation in the government, and dissatisfied landlords. Toward the end of the 1870s it became an influential anti-Western force, calling for a new national leadership as dissension among the three oligarchs caused them to lose control over national policies. In fact, the movement planned to conspire with the Saigō group to overthrow the government, but the plan was aborted.

Related to these two political factors was the rising influence of Nagazane Motoda, the Confucian lecturer of the imperial court, who was close to the Meiji emperor and enjoyed his complete support. When the three pillars collapsed and restive sentiments against the government increased, Motoda exploited the political climate to strengthen the emperor's influence over the government and headed on a collision course with Itō.

In the same year that the government announced the ordinance, the court issued the Great Principles of Education (Kyōgaku Taishi), emphasizing the revival of Confucian tradition as the fundamental orientation for schooling. Opposing views, represented by Motoda and Itō, were presented regarding the state of the nation and education. The debate between the two men resulted in Motoda's victory over Itō, which, in turn, led to the solid formation of education in Japan along Motoda's ideological line. Thereafter, Japan began to turn away from the pro-Western orientation in education.

In essence, the Great Principles of Education expressed a reaction to Japanese Westernization—to which it attributed the corrosion of traditional morality and social instability—and articulated a cultural revitalism. Motoda advocated a national orthodoxy and opposed the separation between politics and education. He further insisted that the primary goals of education should be moral rather than scientific.

Itō, a former samurai, had been exposed extensively to Western civilization, and presented a Western view of education. To him, social instability and moral laxity accompanied rapid social change, and, therefore, could not be entirely attributed to Japan's Westernization. Itō rejected the Confucian assumption that politics and education were inseparable, and insisted that the development of scientific learning required noninterference by the government. He viewed the creation of a state orthodoxy as regressive. It is clear that the views of Motoda and Itō were diametrically opposed. There is little wonder that Itō favored the ordinance, at least at the time of its issuance. These three political factors, among others, interlaced with each other, and formed the background of the second reform; they made Itō vulnerable and forced him to compromise with Modota's traditionalist position.[9]

The Building of State-Centered Education

The second reform, too, was destined to fail from the outset. It underwent revisions and under the leadership of Arinori Mori, Itō's protégé who became the minister of Education in 1885, the structure and orientation of Japanese education were completely reversed again: from local to central control, from an individual to a state-centered orientation, from a pro-Western ideology to nationalism.

Obviously, nationalistic sentiments were growing stronger, and their proponents sought a national identity compatible with Japanese tradition, as well as political and social stability. Itō's task, meanwhile, was to consolidate the integration of the nation by building a strong government under a new constitution. It led him to the monarchical model of Prussia—the political unification of which was accomplished in 1871 with strong control residing in the central government. In 1882 Itō led a mission to Europe to study political systems to prepare for the drafting of the Japanese constitution. While he rejected U.S. British, and French systems as incompatible with Japan, he espoused the Prussian concept that the state is integrated under the monarch and that education is an instrument of the state. Itō learned from German scholars the philosophical and political rationale for the imperial political system of Japan—the rationale congenial to growing Japanese sentiments. While in Germany, Itō and Mori, ambassador to Britain at that time, held a conference in which they agreed to the Prussian notion of education. Thus, preparations for the constitution and the final educational reform were rapidly proceeding. In 1885 the first Itō cabinet was formed, and Mori was appointed minister of Education.

Mori issued a series of new ordinances in 1886 to develop a uniform system of elementary and higher education. His reform was perfected with the Imperial Rescript on Education. The constitution was established in 1889, and the Rescript was promulgated a year later. Fusing elements of Confucian ethics and Shinto statism—as well as a modern orientation toward learning—into the imperial frame of the state, the Rescript delineated the purpose of education and the responsibilities of the citizen in the new state. It served as the fundamental ideological frame of modern education until 1945.

The Rescript represented a resurgence of traditional ideologies associated with Japanese and Chinese learning that were influential in the first years of the Meiji era. These elements had been countered by a Western-style liberalism emphasizing scientific training and a progressive political philosophy, and consequently, the advocates of Confucianism, Japanese learning, and Shintoism had been pushed into the background until the end of the 1870s. It also represented both a continuity of the cultural tradition and a synthesis of diverse ideologies that hinged upon the early history of Meiji. [10]

Yet, another aspect of Mori's reform had a lasting effect on the development of Japanese education. Following the Prussian model, Mori established a dual system of schooling that separated the training of the elite from that of the masses. Nevertheless, these differential trainings shared the philosophy that they were not primarily for the growth of the individual per se, but for the state. Schooling for the masses was intended to develop the uniformity of cognitive and motivational orientations instrumental to the continuity of the state; therefore, Mori regarded teacher training as particularly crucial. Prospective teachers were trained by strict militaristic rules, and all were required to live in dormitories so that they might be constantly under rigid supervision. Their socialization under such uniform and stern conditions was thought to be essential to promote the development of a pattern of behavior and the internalization of the national ideology, both of which were perceived to be vital to the maintenance of national order.

In contrast to teacher training, university education for the prospective elite provided an atmosphere of freedom and creativity. Yet, as the ordinance on university education stated, the aim of the imperial university was to teach and research academic matters essential to the state.

The School System

Mori laid the foundations of the school system of imperial
Japan through a series of ordinances issued in 1886, a year after he
had become the minister of Education. Although Mori's reform was
subjected to minor changes in later years, its basic structure remained unmodified until Japan's defeat in 1945 (see Figure 4). In
1908 compulsory education for six years finally became a full reality.[11]

Japanese higher education was based on a dual system consisting of the academic track and the nonacademic, technical track. With
regard to education for the elite, the underlying principle of selection
in the exclusive academic track was based on competition, not on
birth. Those who pursued the elite course were required to pass
highly competitive entrance examinations to win the privileges available at higher levels of the academic track. Therefore, free mobility
was provided through open competition. After universal elementary
education for six years, the track led to middle school for five years,
higher school for three years, and university for another three years.
Admissions to the national higher schools (a total of 32) from middle
schools were most strenuous, since the higher schools were largely
designed to be preparatory for the universities. Avenues to university education for graduates of the higher schools were differentiated
in terms of the order of their exclusiveness, ranked as follows: seven
imperial universities (plus an additional imperial university each in
Taiwan and in Korea), 12 single-faculty, government universities, and
25 private universities. Graduates of the imperial universities, particularly Tokyo Imperial University, filled strategic positions in the
government bureaus.

As we have already seen, the government paid special attention
to normal schools in terms of indoctrination in loyalty and patriotism.
While the teacher trainees, prospective indoctrinators of elementary
and youth schools, were required to live in dormitories and receive
military training, their expenses were entirely covered by public
funds. In his reform, Mori's first priority was to establish the imperial universities as the primary training ground for national leaders. His second priority was given to training teachers, since he regarded it as one of the most strategic sources for nation building.
What was stressed in teacher training was not reflective intelligence,
but a particular kind of character. For example, Mori's ordinance
on normal schools stipulated that teacher trainees possess special
common personality traits, for example, obedience, dignity, and
benevolence.[12]

Meanwhile, provisions were made for those unable to aspire
to the higher schools. Most notable was the establishment of techni-

FIGURE 4

Japanese Educational System Prior to 1945

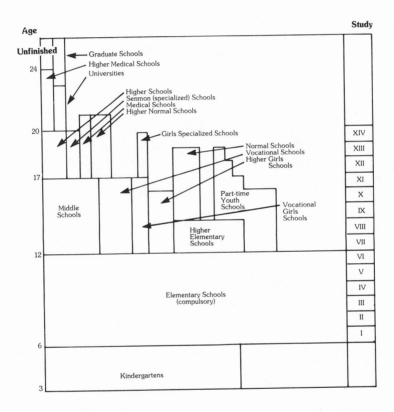

Source: Compiled by the author.

cal institutes (senmongakkō) to provide three to five years of terminal, college-level education. These were equivalent to the higher schools in some respects, but different in training and prestige. Admission to the institutes required a middle school diploma and passing the entrance examinations. The majority of these institutes absorbed highly competent youth who were trained in the technical areas of industry, medicine, and commerce. The rest offered specialties mainly in agriculture, fisheries, and pharmacy. By 1900 these technical institutes, including public and private schools, produced more than eight times as many skilled students as the imperial universities, but in terms of occupational allocation the dual structure of higher education was also clearly defined. Those who completed the academic track moved into prestigious professions and government bureaus, whereas graduates of the technical institutes were generally allocated to less prestigious technical and semiprofessional jobs. [13]

As to educating women, most women were not expected to pursue the above tracks excluding normal schools—a reflection of the traditional attitude toward women in Japan—although there were exceptions. Typically, their curriculum differed after the third year of elementary education. Girls of privileged families attended secondary-level schools for women called kōtō joggakō for four to five years of instruction. Unlike the middle schools for men, however, these institutions did not emphasize academic studies.

The youth schools (seinen gakkō) were created in 1935. Briefly, their chief purpose was to train great numbers of youths to be workers and potential soldiers. The duration of the training varied, ranging from two to seven years, on both a part-time and full-time basis. Those unable to advance to the middle school or its counterpart for women received training at the youth schools. Before World War II, 75 percent of the youth in Japan, including the students attending higher elementary schools, were enrolled in the youth schools. That was the culmination of education for the masses. It should be borne in mind, however, that despite the dual structure of schooling in Japan the first six years of elementary education were based on a universal, single track. The ramifications of tracking began only after the sixth common year.

Finally, we must note that private schools played a highly significant role in the evolution of Japanese education. Except for the elementary level (as well as the youth schools), private schools contributed to the education of a large number of adolescents and youths. They enrolled more students in the categories of technical institutes and universities than the institutions supported by the government. This trend continues to the present time, as will be seen later.

As shown earlier, the Ministry of Education, originally established in 1871, was especially significant in the development of education in Japan. The ministry was the highest authority in the centralized system of education. As such, it had direct or indirect control over all schools, both public and private, in the nation in the areas related to, for example, educational policy, textbooks, teacher certifications, entrance qualifications, programs of study, academic calendars, salaries, budgets, and many other vital aspects of educational administration.

ADAPTATION AND THE MODERN
EDUCATIONAL SYSTEM

What we have seen here is a case of modernization; the notion of Westernization by itself does not accurately characterize the process of nation building and the evolution of education in Japan. Adaptation is a dual process: both specific and general. Japanese education was differentiated and upgraded based on Western models, but its underlying orientation since 1886 was indigenous to Japan.

Adaptation involves a utilization of traditional cultural orientations attempting to solve emerging problems from either internal or external sources. Another factor of adaptation is the changing structural conditions of life—institutional changes—that affect people's patterns of response to problems. In other words, changes in the structural conditions of life determine to varying degrees the pattern of adaptation. Analytically, cultural and structural conditions (institutional arrangements) are different, but they influence each other; that is, they interact with, and frequently produce modifications, in each other. In speaking of cultural ecology, which refers to a creative, adaptive process, Julian Steward offers the concept of "cultural core," that is, the constellation of features closely related to subsistence activities and economic arrangements. While recognizing the functional interdependence of all features of culture, he emphasizes the role of the culture core, which reflects the structural conditions of life: "changes are basically traceable to new adaptations required by changing technology and productive arrangements."[14] Steward sees technology and productive arrangements—the culture core—as primary factors for culture changes.

As a result of institutional changes in the most vital spheres of life, including those of technology and productive arrangements, Japanese education underwent an enormous transformation. But that transformation occurred in a culturally prescribed way. In the early years of the Meiji, educational reformers appear to have ignored Japan's cultural capacity to accommodate radical changes produced by the introduction of cultural and social practices foreign to Japan; this resulted in failure for their reforms. As we have seen, in the

educational system the cultural orientations alien to the Japanese
were replaced by primordial Japanese orientations. Yet the educational system's structure was not so much a product of Japanese innovation as it was a synthesis of Western models, particularly of
centralized French and Prussian structures.

It would be reasonable to assume that one of the cultural conditions for the monarchical model sought by Itō and his colleagues as
the basis of modern Japan is directly related to the Japanese concept
of group. At a time of social instability and chaos, the Japanese attempted to search for an object of dependence that would bring about
integration and order in their society. During the years of great
transition, they lost the object of amae and were helpless. Socialized
in the group environment, the Japanese, particularly the Meiji leaders, may have felt too insecure and vulnerable to risk taking the
initiative in building a political system the sovereignty of which
would rest on individual Japanese. Such a government would have
been too heavy a burden for the dependence-oriented Japanese to assume. As seen in contemporary Japan, however, the group concept
functions quite differently in a more stable situation. It tends to maxi-
mize individuals' participation in decision making and other organizational activities, as in the ringi system discussed in Chapter 2. It
also protects individuals as members of a group. The decision-making process in organizations tends to be slow, but the decisions that
emerge reflect a group consensus.

An understanding of the transition period in the evolution of
Japanese education requires a brief return to the Meiji era in order
to examine the biography of Arinori Mori,[15] founder of modern Japanese education, and elucidate his orientation toward the object of de-
pendency. Mori was born in 1847, the son of a samurai family in the
Satsuma domain at the tip of Kyushu. He was a brilliant activist, and
an astute observer of social transformation in the late Tokugawa era,
who developed a deep sense of crisis about the future of Japan. He
could not ignore the presence of armed, destructive, steam-powered
ships of the British navy off the Satsuma shore. At the age of 19, he
went to England to study science and mathematics, the foundations of
which, he thought, were essential to building a Japanese navy. By
the time he returned from England he had become a "revolutionary."
In 1869, when he was only 23 years old, he advocated, before a group
of 376 councilmen, that the exsamurai's practice of wearing swords
be abolished. As the sword epitomized the samurai and symbolized
his exclusive status, this was a most radical view at that time. So
radical was it that it subsequently led to the assassination of his
strongest supporter, Seigorō Ono.

In the following year, Mori was dispatched to the United States
as Japanese consul. When he visited New York, he emphasized the

importance of Japanese Westernization and the viability of adopting English as the first language of the Japanese. He also urged a group of Japanese students studying in the United States to marry American women to "improve the Japanese race" before returning to Japan. He further held that "progress is impossible without revolution" in Japan. Upon returning from the United States in 1873, he formed— in collaboration with Yukichi Fukuzawa, the most liberal and noted spokesman of Western civilization—a progressive group of sophisticated intellectuals and political leaders of Western orientation in order to inspire a "fresh civilizational" atmosphere in Japan. His radical position was also characterized by his insistence upon equality between husband and wife, as well as contractual marriage free from traditional constraints. In fact, Mori entertained a contractual marriage with a Japanese woman, though divorce soon followed; later, he confessed a deep regret about such marriages. Subsequently, following the most traditional practice, he married a daughter of Tomomi Iwakura, one of the most distinguished leaders of the restoration.

Within a half decade, however, Mori's ideological outlook gradually moved toward conservatism. By 1879, when he was dispatched to England as Japanese consul to revise the treaty with Britain, he had moved away from Fukuzawa and the ardent advocates for the establishment of a popular national parliament. At the time he met Itō in Germany, he was in complete agreement with Itō's conservative view, based on the Prussian political philosophy that advocated a monarchical state. Mori's view, which was often more conservative, was expressed as follows: "Subject . . . is the word [used] in reference to the emperor. In relation to the emperor, the subject has responsibilities and only limited status but should not have rights."[16] Therefore, Japanese citizens, in Mori's opinion, had no rights vis-à-vis the emperor and were subject to him without limit. For him, the emperor was the object of national devotion and the source of unity of the nation, and it was that view upon which Mori's educational reform was based. In 1889, a year before the Imperial Rescript on Education was promulgated, Mori was assassinated by a Shintoist fanatic; he was then only 42 years old.

Reflecting upon Mori's unusual and colorful career, one may see him as what Robert Lifton calls a "Protean" individual, that is, capable of assuming different forms. In one respect Mori's life suggests a contemporary Japanese zengakuren (student organization) student who starts out as a radical and ends up supporting the capitalist establishment without a sense of contradiction or inconsistency; this is a typical pattern of transformation of many young radicals in Japan today. Lifton points out one general historical development, among others, as being of special importance for creating "Protean man":

It is the . . . sense of what I called historical, or psychohistorical dislocation, the break in the sense of connection
men have long felt with vital and nourishing symbols of
their cultural traditions—symbols revolving around family, idea systems, religions, and the life cycle in general.
. . . One perceives these traditional symbols as irrele-
vant, burdensome, or even inactivating, and yet one cannot avoid carrying them within, or having one's self-process profoundly affected by them. [17]

There is little doubt that Mori was suffering from a sense of
psychohistorical dislocation experienced in the late Tokugawa and
early Meiji periods. His final solution, to resolve the break in his
sense of linkage with the vital symbols of the cultural tradition, was
to return to the tradition itself and, particularly, to seek the emperor as the symbolic object of dependence.

POSTWAR EDUCATION

During the period since the Japanese defeat in 1945, Japanese
education has undergone drastic transformation similar to the one
experienced during the early Meiji period. The prewar system of
education for the imperial state was replaced by a new one, based on
the U.S. model, which emphasized decentralization of educational
control and the development of individual growth. This paralleled
the Meiji educational reform initiated by the Education Ordinance.
Furthermore, just as the early Meiji reform was replaced by a state-
centered system modeled after the Prussian educational system, the
central orientation and the structure of educational control in the new
postwar system was also superseded by a stress on the uniformity of
individual motivation and development, as well as the centralization
of power: group-oriented characteristics more indigenous to Japanese society. One of the most significant differences between the
two reforms, however, is that the Meiji reform was initiated by Japanese, whereas the postwar reform was imposed on the Japanese by
the United States. The shift from the U.S. pattern of educational
practice toward a more Japanese pattern was completed within 15
years. In order to understand that shift, it is examined here with
attention to the pattern of Japanese adaptation. Political and ideological interpretations of the transformation have been offered thus far,
but such interpretations have ignored Japanese culture and the distinct orientations that prescribe shapes of change in major institutional
systems. The following discussion will serve to elucidate the pattern
of Japanese adaptation.

Postwar Educational Reform: An Overview

World War II finally ended when Japan accepted the Potsdam
Declaration on August 4, 1945. The foundations of prewar education
in the imperial state were entirely uprooted, and in the last half of
the 1940s Japanese education changed radically, under the supervision of the Allied powers as a consequence of the enactment of five
new educational laws: the fundamental law of education (1947); the
school education law (1947); the school board law (1948); the law on
public teachers (1949); and the social education (adult education) law
(1949).

Actually, the postwar reform started in 1946, on the basis of
the report of the United States Education Mission to Japan submitted
to General MacArthur, supreme commander for the Allied powers,
but prewar education was discontinued immediately after the Japanese surrender. As indicated in the Potsdam Declaration, the ultimate goal of the occupation policy of the Allied powers was to eradicate all superstructures of Japanese ultranationalism and to transform Japan from a militaristic totalitarianism to a democratic system. Japanese military forces and all organizations that supported
the war were disbanded, and, in order to eradicate the education that
had served the war as one of the most effective agents for nurturing
nationalism in the minds of youth, MacArthur issued orders in 1945
regarding the educational system, the examination of teachers and
educational officials, the abolition of the government's support of
Shintoism, and the prohibition of the instruction of prewar moral
education (shūshin), Japanese history, and geography, through which
the indoctrination of ultranationalistic and militaristic ideology had
been practiced.[18]

A comprehensive reform of Japanese education was, however,
designed and initiated by the U.S. mission headed by George Stoddard,
and it was a revolutionary innovation transplanted into Japanese society (see Figure 5). The report of the mission consisted of proposals
comprising six categories: the aims and content of Japanese education; language reform; administration of education at the primary and
secondary levels; teaching and the education of teachers; adult education; and higher education.

The most innovative features of this report were the following
recommendations. First, it emphasized administrative decentralization and greater local control. Second, it proposed a new single-
track school system consisting of an elementary school education for
six years, middle school education for three years, high school education for three years, and higher education. It recommended that
elementary and middle school education, covering a total of nine
years, be compulsory. Education was to be tax-supported, coedu-

cational, and tuition-free. This proposal became a model for the creation of the 6-3-3-4 system, which came into full operation in 1949 under the school law.

Third, it introduced the concept of individuality into the curriculum. A curriculum, the mission suggested, should consist not only of an accepted body of knowledge but also take into account the physical and mental activities of pupils and their differing abilities and social factors. Fourth, it stressed the creation of greater opportunities for liberal education at higher levels; this proposal led to the later, new developments in college education. Fifth, it recommended that the written language be reformed; as a result, Roman characters were introduced and the written language was simplified to a great extent.

Sixth, it suggested two more important innovations: the advancement of adult education and the improvement of the education of teachers. It suggested that adult education expand through parent-teacher activities, extension classes for adults, the opening of schools to a variety of community activities, and the use of public libraries. The mission also recommended that traditional teaching methods that emphasized memorization and "a vertical system of duties and loyalties" should be changed in order to foster independent thinking, the development of personality, and democratic citizenship. It further proposed in-service education for teachers and the reorganization of teacher education at the college level.

In order to renovate Japanese education according to the framework proposed by the mission, the Education Reform Committee was organized in the Ministry of Education in 1946. This Japanese agency had played one of the most innovative roles in changing Japanese education.[19] The origin of the committee can be traced back to a Japanese committee appointed to aid the education mission. After the completion of the occupational reform, it developed into a central advisory agency of the Ministry of Education—the Education Reform Council—which initiated various innovations in education. The council was further transformed into the Central Council of Education, in which role it functioned as a permanent council.

The committee accepted the recommendations of the mission as the basis for formulating the outlines of the five education laws.[20] Again, the committee emphasized, as expected, the growth of individual personality, academic freedom, equality of education, general education as a universal nine-year compulsory program, coeducation, adult education, and democracy in school administration. In carrying out the postwar education reform, the Ministry of Education was assisted by the Civil Information and Education Section (CIE) of the Office of the Supreme Commander for the Allied powers. The CIE offered constant guidance to the Education Reform Committee, as well

FIGURE 5

Postwar Educational System

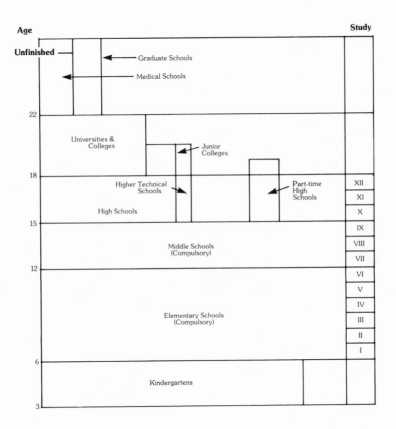

Source: Compiled by the author.

as to other educational organizations of the Ministry of Education and the school systems. Under the guidance of the CIE, a variety of new programs was carried out to reorient Japanese teachers and educational leaders. One such program was an institute for educational leadership, held in Tokyo and other large cities throughout Japan.[21] Devoted to the reeducation of those educational leaders directly involved in educational innovation, the institute introduced U.S. educational theories and practices in such fields as educational administration, educational principles, teaching methods, guidance, educational psychology, correspondence education, college extension courses, school library, and adult education.[22]

Progressive education, the predominant influence in the United States in the 1930s and 1940s, was directly introduced to Japan; teaching methods and curricula practiced in Japan in the late 1940s were derived directly from progressive education. The pedagogical theories of leading U.S. progressives exerted significant influence upon formative Japanese education. While the core curriculum was studied and attempted rather extensively, the educational process also emphasized problem solving and the child's self-activity, interest, freedom, and self-expression. Club activities, homeroom, and guidance also attracted considerable attention as new concepts of extracurricular activity.

The historic reform designed by the United States Education Mission required a revolutionary change in Japanese philosophic orientation. Experimentalism, with which John Dewey's philosophy was generally identified, was the most influential underlying orientation of the new education in Japan. A major problem confronted by progressive college professors and other leaders in the postwar education, therefore, was to translate experimentalism, developed on foreign soil, into the radically different matrix of Japanese culture. Teachers were exposed to concepts of experimentalism under the guidance of visiting U.S. educators and Japanese scholars. Subsequently, it is claimed that the majority of Japanese schools, particularly at the elementary school level, came under the influence of progressive education before 1950.[23]

By 1950, Japanese educators were beginning to express their impatience with the transplanted progressive education, since they were discovering that it did not work in the Japanese culture. In the early 1950s, pedagogical criticisms against progressive education were raised by a host of Japanese scholars. These negative reactions toward progressive education were growing in an emerging social and political situation, which had affected the course of Japan's history. In this sense, events during the early 1950s may be said to be as significant as those during 1945-50 in the development of Japanese postwar history. The Korean War, which broke out in 1950, had a crucial impact upon Japanese politics and economy. Politically, it helped give rise to the Japanese Defense Force in 1952, six years after the Japanese constitution had renounced military forces. In 1951, the San Francisco peace treaty was concluded between Japan and the Allied powers, and Japan's political independence was restored. Events in those years had thus contributed to restoring Japanese confidence not only politically and economically but also psychologically. In the realm of pedagogy, that short period was marked by reactions against the passive acceptance and uncritical application of American teaching methods and theories. Experimentalism came under heavy criticism for the first time in 1952.[24]

It was also in 1952 that the Ministry of Education began to consider an extensive revision of the social studies curricula at the elementary and secondary school levels, in order to improve instruction in geography, history, and moral education; the revised curricula was announced in 1955. In the same year, the ministry revealed a plan to revise comprehensively the entire curricula at the elementary and middle school levels, and the revision was announced in 1958. This was followed by the announcement of the high school curricular revision by the Ministry of Education in 1960. Those events marked a definite departure from the early postwar, experience-centered education and a shift to a more traditional, subject-centered education with focus on the continuity of Japanese culture, structured instruction, and transmission of a body of abstract knowledge.[25] Methodologically, the uniformity of cognitive and motivational orientations of the students, as well as the teachers, began to be stressed again; teachers employed behavioristic conditioning to impart skills, knowledge, and attitudes. Thus, during the course of the 1950s, the original orientation of early postwar education disappeared from most schools. Japanese education had quickly adapted to the demands of the political, economic, and social institutions of Japan—institutions central to the culture core. Thereafter, the fundamental orientation of Japanese education has not greatly changed up to the present time.

Moral Education

The development of moral education in the postwar period also exhibited that pattern of adaptation by which the nature of schooling changed in response to the needs of political and other institutions of Japanese society. Moral education represented a twofold problem. First, the Ministry of Education was concerned with the diffuseness in the relationship of the individual to the state, which occurred as a result of the war and the new Japanese political system, and it de-

manded a clear definition of the relationship. Second, moral education served as an instrument by which the state strengthened its control over schooling in the nation. The introduction of moral education, and its continuance through the present time, has a symbolic,
more than a substantive, significance. It is symbolic in the sense
that it represents the power of the state over antistate forces; it is
not substantive as much as one might expect because it has consistently been treated as a dispensable area of education. Available
evidence shows that the time allocated to moral education has, more
often than not, been used for examination preparation and drilling in
major subjects.[26]

Exploring the provenance of postwar moral education will aid
the understanding of its peculiar position. Intellectuals and politicians, reflecting both a divergence and a resurgence of ideologies in
postwar Japan, debated moral education at length in academia and in
the national Diet. In 1957, after a half dozen years of controversy,
the Ministry of Education decided to incorporate moral education into
the elementary and middle school curricula as a separate subject,
and it was taught as an independent instructional area for the first
time in 1958. In order to appreciate the resurgence of moral education, it is necessary to examine the historical background that allowed
its reestablishment, despite the extreme controversy that surrounded
it in the postwar period.

As mentioned above, prewar moral education (shūshin) and the
Imperial Rescript on Education were two pivotal means of fostering
moral character in the Japanese. Policy during the occupation clearly
called for abolishing the Rescript; thus, the national Diet, accepting
the policy of the Allied powers, annulled the Rescript in 1948. To
many conservative Japanese, however, this meant spiritual and
moral subversion.

Reflecting a deep national concern over moral education, Prime
Minister Shigeru Yoshida, the head of the majority conservative party,
announced shortly after assuming his position in 1949 that an educational statement (kyōiku sengen) on morality should be prepared to
replace the Rescript.[27] He insisted that, in view of postwar moral
dislocation, a new educational orientation toward the moral basis of
life must be considered. Yoshida's call for an educational statement
on morality not only disturbed intellectuals, educators, and progressive politicians but also caused a deep suspicion that it might be a
means for controlling freedom of thought, as the Rescript had been
designed to do.

Although Yoshida's proposal was, for a while, in danger of being aborted because of public attacks against it, the appointment of
Teiyū Amano as minister of Education in 1950 revived an active reconsideration of moral education. Amano was the first minister of

Education to emphasize moral education in the postwar period. He intended to introduce moral education as an independent subject fashioned after the pattern of social studies and prewar moral education.[28] As justification, he argued that the introduction of moral education would provide a reorientation for Japanese children and youth toward the individual, the state, and the symbolic nature of the emperor. In his view, "The moral center of the state is the emperor, who is an object of Japanese citizens' affection, but by no means the center of power."[29] The Japanese, he felt, no longer realized that the state is the matrix and the foundation of the individual. Furthermore, he maintained that essential ideas stated in the Rescript were still valid and could serve as moral criteria, although he rejected the notion that those precepts be presented as moral criteria in the form of the Rescript.

No sooner had Amano's view been made public than representatives of the education committee in the Diet, as well as other progressive politicians and intellectuals, attacked it as reactionary and promoting the revival of Japanese nationalism. Nevertheless, Minister of Education Okano, who replaced Amano in 1953, supported Amano's viewpoint by emphasizing the cultivation of patriotism through effective instruction in geography, history, and moral education. In turn, Shigeo Ōdachi, the successor to Okano, similarly advocated education for patriotism, thus agreeing ideologically with Okano and Amano. Interestingly enough, he also declared that the basic ideals of the Rescript and the fundamental law of education (which aims to cultivate an attitude toward peace and the growth of the individual) were not contradictory. Maintaining a conservative ideological position, the Ministry of Education, under the leadership of the minister who was a political appointee, thus had endeavored continuously to introduce moral education.

It is important to point out that liberals did not oppose moral education itself, but were persistently opposed to state control of it. They also recognized that many Japanese suffered from a vacuum in their moral lives, owing to an unprecedented change in the Japanese value system. The nature of moral education, however, was viewed quite differently by conservatives and liberals. The conservative approach was to attempt to fill the vacuum with norms defined within the context of traditional Japanese culture, whereas the liberal approach was to impart "democratic" values.

In the early 1950s spokesmen for political liberalism, mostly university professors, attempted to develop a counterproposal for moral education free from state control.[30] Their positions was represented in a view expressed by Bantarō Kido, for example, who argued that the purpose of moral education should be the realization of the dignity and rights of each individual and the creation of a new social order.[31]

In the second half of the 1950s, moral education continued to be a source of heated controversy among educators, scholars, and politicians while the Ministry of Education was formulating a concrete plan for it. As evidence of the nature of the controversy, one should note the great number of articles, theses, and books on methodologies, purposes, and problems of moral education that were published during those years.[32] Arata Osada, who represented a strong progressive position, opposed the separation of moral education as an independent subject from the whole dynamic configuration of the child's experience. He maintained that moral education should be carried out by way of "guidance," which helps the child, in a holistic way, to develop a moral orientation. It is meaningless, he argued, to teach moral education as an intellectual body of precepts compiled in artificially isolated subject matter.[33]

In the midst of the debates on moral education in 1957, the Ministry of Education decided to set up a separate program for instruction in moral education at the elementary and middle school levels. Shortly after the decision had been made, the Japan Pedagogical Society, whose membership consists of college and university professors, and the Japan Teachers Union (the powerful so-called Nikkyōso) protested vehemently, but their protest did not alter the decision of the ministry. Contrary to the fear of the liberals, however, the framework of moral education presented by the ministry did not suggest a revitalization of traditional prewar moral education, but consisted of moral considerations of social and individual life. In the course of developing the rationale for moral education, the Ministry of Education modified the conservative views represented by the ministers in the early 1950s. Nevertheless, the implementation of moral education meant a victory for the ministry, since it constituted an extension of state power into the control of education.

EDUCATIONAL ADMINISTRATION

Parallel to the significant changes in curricula and moral education that took place after Japanese independence, a drastic alteration occurred in the pattern of educational control. Lay and local control of education, which had lasted for only a few years, was replaced by a pattern of centralized control that eliminated the public election of school board members. Through such an alteration the state regained control, to a great extent, over localities and, in turn, localities lost their power to control education. Subsequently, the centralization of power became firmly established. The reader is reminded again that, although this alteration was not an exact replication of the Meiji reform, there is an interesting parallel between the Meiji and postindependence reforms.

Interpretations of the centralization of power in education have been offered from a political point of view; some of them are quite plausible,[34] but let us look at it from a cultural point of view. As discussed earlier, the Japanese have a tendency to relinquish their individual rights and responsibilities to the group and are willing to accept subordination of the individual to the group. They are concerned more with the group as a whole than with each individual, and they tend to consider themselves in terms of the centripetal force of the group. Given this cultural attitude and pattern of behavior, Japanese are likely to be congenial to centralization of activities in various institutional spheres, the political, economic, and social, as well as the educational. The alteration of educational control thus reflects Japanese cultural orientation. The state capitalized on the growing conservative atmosphere in the 1950s and the centripetal pattern of Japanese culture in order to gain more control over schooling.

In this regard, two legislative measures have particularly increased the state's power over schooling. The first measure, introduced in 1954, involved the establishment of "political neutrality" of education. It was called "a temporary measure concerning the maintenance of political neutrality of education in all compulsory schools," and it was intended to control the political activities of teachers, particularly the Japan Teachers Union, which was a politically oriented and powerful group, as well as antistate activities in public education. The other legislative measure, enacted in 1956, concerned the organization and operation of local educational administration; commonly known as the new school board law, it was a revision of the school board law of 1948. Both measures were drafted and passed in the Diet shortly after the transition from the formative to the stabilizing period of Japanese postwar history, and both, particularly the new school board law, effectively consolidated central control of educational administration.

A comparison of the new school board law of 1956 with the previous school board law of 1948 will demonstrate how control of education came to be centralized. The concept of a school board was introduced into Japanese education by the United States Education Mission in 1946. On the basis of its recommendations, about 10,000 school boards, organized throughout Japan by 1952, served as the new institutions of educational administration.[35] Because the organization and functions of school boards were unfamiliar to most Japanese, five years were necessary after the passage of the first school board law in 1948 to establish school boards in all prefectures, cities, and local communities. Obviously, creating school boards caused a revolutionary change in traditional Japanese education.

The school board law of 1948 was meant to achieve three goals. First, the school board was established to decentralize power. Its essential objective was to bring about a radical modification in the traditional bureaucratic system of education. Second, public election of school board members was adopted in order to reflect local needs in educational policy. It was an endeavor to fulfill the democratization of educational administration. Third, the law stipulated that the school boards were to function independently of other administrative authorities.

The school board law of 1956 introduced three principal changes. The most significant modification was the appointment of school board members by mayors or governors, rather than their election by the public. The underlying principle of the public election of school board members, as stated in Article 10 of the fundamental education law was that the members must be directly responsible to the citizens and free of illegitimate control by any other authority. This principle was modified to a great extent when school board members became appointees. With respect to the members of a prefectural school board, since 1956 the governor has been authorized to appoint them, and their appointments require the consent of the prefectural assembly. In cities and towns, mayors must follow the same procedure as the governor. The prefectural superintendent, however, is appointed by the prefectural school board, and his or her appointment requires approval of the minister of Education. The superintendent of schools at the city and town levels is similarly appointed by the school board, which appointment requires the approval of the prefectural school board.

The second principal change was the reinforcement of the uniformity of educational standards determined by the Ministry of Education, which controls policies of the prefectural and the local school boards. In contrast to the 1956 law, the 1948 law allowed for mutual independence of each school board at all levels with respect to policy decisions. According to the new law, the Ministry of Education and the prefectural school boards not only give administrative guidance but also impose educational standards upon the local school boards.

The third major change altered the right to appoint public schoolteachers. Under the old law, teachers were appointed by each local school board, whereas, under the new law, the board has the right only to submit confidential recommendations on appointments to the prefectural school board, which makes the final decision on appointments.

CONCLUSION

At the outset of this chapter, we referred to the functions of education in terms of integration, political socialization, "adaptive" competency (economic function), and pattern maintenance. The introduction of moral education and the two legislative measures discussed above are understood in terms of the state's attempts to consolidate social integration. The motivation for introducing controversial moral education was based on the perception of those in strategic positions in the educational and political systems that a higher degree of uniformity in children's motivational orientations was necessary for the state. The two legislative measures, on the other hand, gave the state more power to control teachers' activities and divergence at the local level, as well as to increase the state's ability to impose its imperatives upon the entire national school system.

The state's concern for stronger political socialization was presented in terms of the revision of the social studies curricula, particularly history and geography, and in terms of the legislative measure that attempted to neutralize public schoolteachers. The comprehensive curricular revision announced in 1958 was addressed to the need for greater adaptive competency, that is, the need to upgrade the ability of Japanese youth to learn the skills and knowledge demanded by the nation's rapid economic growth in the last half of the 1950s. These functions of education—integration, political socialization, and adaptive competency—are part and parcel of the educational process in general, but those particular legislative and curricular revisions highlight the functions of schooling.

Upgrading adaptive competency and intensifying political socialization and integration, on the other hand, were accomplished in a culturally prescribed way; that is, the Japanese pattern of educational change, as in other institutional activities, is, to a great extent, determined culturally. Therefore, the changes that were introduced are by and large compatible with the central orientation of Japanese culture. As it has been noted repeatedly, Japanese culture emphasizes centripetality, uniformity, the group (the state included), and motivation for high achievement and competency for the sake of the group. These particular dimensions are significant in the transformation of schooling in both the postwar and the Meiji eras. In turn, education reinforces these aspects of the cultural orientation—referred to earlier as a function of pattern maintenance—as will be seen in the next chapter.

Finally, with reference to the general pattern of change in schooling since the Meiji Restoration, the reader may have been struck by the remarkably similar patterns of transformation exhibited in the early Meiji and postwar reforms. At the time of the restoration in 1868 and following the Japanese defeat in 1945, the Japanese tradition was shaken and Japan had virtually no alternative but to accept Western solutions. On both occasions crises occurred in Japan's relationships with the West, and its political transformations were equally drastic. Nevertheless, one of the important differences between the two is that the restoration was the result of an internal political transformation, though it was stimulated by external civilizational forces, while Japanese "democratization," as conceived by the Allied powers, was unconditionally imposed upon the nation.

Early Meiji reformers actively sought to adopt French and U.S. educational practices as a way to modernize Japanese education. By 1866, however, the liberal French orientation toward schooling and the U.S. stress on decentralization of educational administration were both replaced by the Imperial Rescript on Education and a state-centered system of schooling. The postwar educational reform, on the other hand, was imposed by the United States Education Mission and accepted by the Japanese. It emphasized the participation of citizens in education, decentralization, individual growth, experience-centered teaching and learning, and the elimination of authoritarianism and ultranationalism.

By the end of the 1950s, those emphases gave way to a new orientation: a greater degree of uniformity, state control, traditional subject-centered teaching and learning, and behavioral conditioning. It took 15 years to consolidate the permanent educational system in the Meiji period after the Fundamental Code of Education was introduced in 1872. Similarly, it took 15 years to complete the building of the foundations of present schooling after the visit of the United States Education Mission to Japan in 1946. (The comprehensive curricular revision of 1958 was implemented at the elementary school level in 1961, at the middle school level in 1962, and the high school level in 1963.) Of course, there are numerous differences between the present system and state-centered Meiji schooling. One major difference is that education now takes place in a democratic political system—although the degree to which democracy is exercised is debatable—whereas Meiji schooling was defined within the framework of a monarchical, nationalistic, political structure. Nevertheless, these similarities provide further evidence in support of the contention here that broad changes in education are culturally guided and that Japanese schooling reflects the Japanese pattern of adaptation.

A final word relative to elite and mass education: Unlike the Meiji reforms, the postwar reforms have consistently emphasized a single-track system. Although the postwar educational system has a linear track structure, there has been, however, a diversification of tracking within the system, at the high school level, into an academic course and a vocational course. Postwar elite and mass education are discussed extensively in the following chapter.

NOTES

1. These technical terms are derived from Talcott Parsons' analysis of four functional variables. See Talcott Parsons and Gerald M. Platt, The American University (Cambridge, Mass.: Harvard University Press, 1973), pp. 1-32.

2. Yehudi Cohen, "The State System, Schooling, and Cognitive and Motivational Patterns," in Social Forces and Schooling, ed. Nobuo K. Shimahara and Adam Scrupski (New York: David McKay, 1975), p. 125.

3. For more details on Tokugawa education, see Ronald Dore, Education in Tokugawa Japan (Berkeley: University of California Press, 1965); "Education: Japan," in The Political Modernization of Japan and Turkey, ed. Robert E. Ward and Dankwart A. Rustow, pp. 176-204 (Princeton, N.J.: Princeton University Press, 1964); John W. Hall and Richard Beardsley, Twelve Doors to Japan (New York: McGraw-Hill, 1965), pp. 384-426.

4. Extensive studies on the evolution of education in the Meiji era are presented in Tokiomi Kaigo, Kyōiku Chokugo Seiritsushino Kenkyū [A study of the development of the imperial rescript on education] (Tokyo: Tokyo University Press, 1965); Tadao Tsuchiya, Meiji Zenki Kyōiku Seisokushino Kenkyū [A study of the development of educational policies in the first half of the Meiji era] (Tokyo: Azekura Shobō, 1963); Buichi Horimatsu, Nippon Kindai Kyōikushi [Modern educational history of Japan] (Tokyo: Risōsha, 1959); Michio Nagai, "Westernization and Japanization: The Early Meiji Transformation of Education," in Tradition and Modernization in Japanese Culture, ed. Donald H. Shively (Princeton, N.J.: Princeton University Press, 1971), pp. 35-76; Michio Nagai, Kindaikato Kyōiku [Modernization and education] (Tokyo: Tokyo University Press, 1969).

5. Nagai, "Westernization and Japanization," p. 52.

6. Quoted from ibid., p. 53.

7. Ibid., p. 54.

8. See Horimatsu, Nippon Kindai Kyōikushi.

9. Nagai presents a concise interpretation of this period in "Westernization and Japanization" and Kindaikato Kyōiku.

10. See Kaigo, Kyōiku Chokugo Seiritsushino Kenkyū; Horimatsu, Nippon Kindai Kyōikushi.

11. See Hall and Beardsley, Twelve Doors to Japan, chap. 9.

12. Horimatsu, Nippon Kindai Kyōikushi, pp. 147-51.

13. Ikuo Amano presents an excellent analysis on the roles of the technical institutes in Kyūsei Senmon Gakkō [The technical institute] (Tokyo: Nikkei Shinsho, 1978).

14. Julian Steward, The Theory of Culture Change (Urbana: University of Illinois Press, 1972), p. 26.

15. See Nagai, Kindaikato Kyōiku, pp. 173-90.

16. Ibid., p. 184.

17. Robert Lifton, "Psychocultural Perspective," in Educational Reconstruction, ed. Nobuo Shimahara (Columbus, Ohio: Charles Merrill, 1973), p. 70.

18. Tametomo Mitsui, "Shin Kyōikuno Handō" [Reaction of new education], in Kindai Kyōikushi [Modern history of education], ed. Tokiomi Kaigo and Toshiaki Murakami (Tokyo: Seishin Shobō, 1959), p. 266.

19. Shogo Ichikawa, "Kyōiku Kihanhō" [Fundamental law of education], in Kindai Kyōikushi, Kaigo and Murakami, pp. 255-56.

20. Kazuo Kobayashi, Noboru Toyosawa, and Shiro Hoda, Kindai Nippon Kyōikuno Ayumi [Development of modern Japanese education] (Tokyo: Rossosha, 1960), p. 130.

21. Takashi Ota, "Shinkyōikuno Hatten" [Development of new education], in Kindai Kyōikushi, Kaigo and Murakami, p. 260.

22. Ibid., p. 262.

23. Ryūichi Nasuno, "Sengono Kyōiku" [Postwar education], in Kyōikushi [History of education], ed. Seiichi Miyazawa (Tokyo: Tokyo Keizai Shinpōsha, 1965), pp. 335-38.

24. See Akira Mori, Keikenshugino Kyōiku Genri [Educational principles of experimentalism] (Tokyo: Kanko Shobō, 1952).

25. See Hisao Yanai and Akira Kawai, Gendai Nipponno Kyōiku Shisō [Educational thought of modern Japan] (Tokyo: Reimei Shobō, 1963), pp. 319-35.

26. See Nobuo Shimahara, "A Study of the Enculturative Roles of Japanese Education" (Ed.D. diss., Boston University, 1967).

27. Kenji Funayama, Sengo Nippon Kyōiku Ronsōshi [Controversial history of postwar education] (Tokyo: Tōyokan, 1963), p. 272.

28. Teiyu Amano, The Asahi Shimbun [The Asahi newspaper], November 26, 1950.

29. Funayama, Sengo Nippon Kyōiku Ronsōshi, p. 276.

30. Ibid., pp. 268-305.

31. See Bantarō Kido, "Minshushugito Dūtoku Kyōiku" [Democracy and moral education], Kyōshitsu [Classroom], vol. 6 (1950).

32. Funayama, Sengo Nippon Kyōiku Ronsōshi, pp. 268-305.

33. See Arata Osada, "A Critique of Shūshin Subject Reintroduced," Sekai [The world], November 1957; idem, "A Critique of Moral Education and Its Weakness," Sekai, February 1958.

34. See, for example, Tokimomi Kaigo and Masao Terasaki, "Sengo Kyōikuno Kentōto Saihen" [Examination and reconstruction of postwar education], in Kyōiku Kaikaku [Educational reform], ed. Tokimomi Kaigo (Tokyo: Tokyo University Press, 1975), pp. 241-80.

35. Kobayashi, Toyosawa, and Hoda, Kindai Nippon Kyōikuno Ayumi, p. 130.

4
THE COLLEGE
ENTRANCE EXAMINATIONS

Having discussed, in the preceding chapter, the evolution of schooling in Japan from the Tokugawa era to the present, this chapter will focus narrowly on one phase of contemporary education: instruction for the college entrance examinations. The college entrance examinations warrant our extensive attention because they exemplify perfectly how education reflects the Japanese pattern of adaptation and responds to cultural and social antecedents. The entrance examinations are a focal matter of the most critical concern for students, parents, and teachers, and, in large measure, they also determine the general orientation of schooling in Japan. Therefore, our examination of this single element offers us a rich opportunity to understand not only its particular functions and problems but the general tendencies of education as well, and it will become abundantly clear that one cannot fully comprehend Japanese education without understanding the entrance examinations and their effects. Our inquiry into the subject will lead to a greater insight into Japanese education. Specifically, this chapter considers how schooling is oriented toward the entrance examinations; Chapter 5 presents detailed case studies that further elucidate and support the generalizations formed here.

PROBLEMS OF PREADULT SOCIALIZATION

Society can function because its members' behavior is predictable and subject to regulation; each society develops a social system, consisting of a network of patterned behavior, in order to perpetuate itself. It also establishes a mechanism for regulating behavior at different levels of age, according to the degree of social and physical maturity. Although this mechanism varies widely, contingent upon the extent to which a society is differentiated and complex, the primary concern of every society remains the same: social integration.

Various social activities are institutionalized, and each individual is socialized to maintain social integration.

Socialization of the preadult is always a concern of great importance in both relatively simple and highly complex societies. Particularly crucial is the transition from preadult to adult status, which occurred at a comparatively early stage of physical and social maturity in previous agrarian and simple societies. Initiation rites were extensively practiced in order to mark the social significance of the transition as perceived by both the initiators and the initiated. In describing the initiation rites of aboriginal Australian tribes, Arnold van Gennep points out, for example:

> These ceremonies last from the tenth to the thirtieth year. . . . In some tribes the novice is considered dead, and he remains dead for the duration of his novitiate. It lasts for a fairly long time and consists of a physical and mental weakening which is undoubtedly intended to make him lose all recollection of his childhood existence. Then follows the positive part: instruction in tribal law and a gradual education as the novice witnesses totem ceremonies, recitations of myths, etc. The final act is a religious ceremony and, above all, a special mutilation which varies with the tribe and which makes the novice forever identical with the adult members.[1]

In contrast, the initiation of preadults, including adolescents and youth, in industrialized societies is a prolonged process. While the initiation into adult status is not as drastic as it was among the Australian tribes, the postponement of adult status for adolescents and youth has created social tension and psychological constraints for them, problems often attributed to a "generation gap." Variably imposed on preadults, a "moratorium" defers their full-fledged participation in society for many years—twice as long as the time required for most of the tribal Australians. In various societies, this period can last for 18, 22, and even 25 or more years. The period of preadult moratorium is devoted to education, an institution in which most preadults participate exclusively. Consequently, physically mature preadults are deprived of full opportunities to grow psychologically and socially when their pattern of institutional participation is limited. The preadult moratorium is a by-product of the contemporary industrial social structure in general, and prolonged schooling is employed as a rite of passage to adult status.

S. N. Eisenstadt discusses the processes of transition in what he terms "particularistic" and "universalistic" societies.[2] The former is usually a kinship-based society, emphasizing particularist,

ascriptive, and role-diffused social relations; the latter is essentially
a society that employs generally universalist, role-specific, and
achievement orientations toward social relations and activities in institutions other than the familial and kinship institutions.[3] The com-
monality between these two societal patterns becomes manifest when
we observe that early socialization in the family, regardless of the
type of society, tends to reflect the character of the kinship-oriented
society; parents and children commonly maintain and enjoy the satisfaction of expressive needs, rather than instrumental ones, in the
framework of ascriptive and particularistic social relations.

In the case of a particularistic society, the transition from
preadult to adult status is relatively smooth. The orientations of
both family and society being nearly identical, the extension of familial identification and solidarity into society is both logical and easy.
Nevertheless, as it was noted, such societies emphasize the ritual
significance of transition in order to detach the novitiate from childhood associations and, in turn, to impart a certain cognitive map of
the adult world.

In sharp contrast, universalistic societies impose a great deal
of the conflict inherent in the transition upon adolescents because extending familial orientation into society is not feasible. Nonfamilial
institutions function according to instrumental orientations that stress
achievement and universalism, whereas familial institutions are, in
large measure, guided by expressive orientations.

As children grow older, they are gradually introduced into an
instrumental world that divests them, to a significant degree, of the
expressive basis of social relations and activities. The instrumental
world broadens the scope of instrumental relations and segregates
the expressive relations from them. It tends to impose on them a
stronger element of contingency relative to the regulation of roles and
rewards as it replaces secure, stable, and particularistic boundaries
of familial groups with unspecified universalistic relations. Generally, the most influential instrumental world, to which children and
adolescents are extensively exposed, is the school and its environment.

As in other complex societies, the Japanese school represents
an instrumental world, and we can view Japanese education as a
uniquely intensive and unusually pressured preparation for the passage
into the adult world. Figure 6 compares group-centered Japanese
society and individual-centered U.S. society and suggests the uniqueness of the intense Japanese preparation for the passage to adult
status.

In Japan, pressures for personal achievement peak around the
age of 18, when preadults take the college entrance examinations.
Covert pressures for the examinations generally start around the

FIGURE 6

Social Pressure for Individual Achievement in Japan and the United States

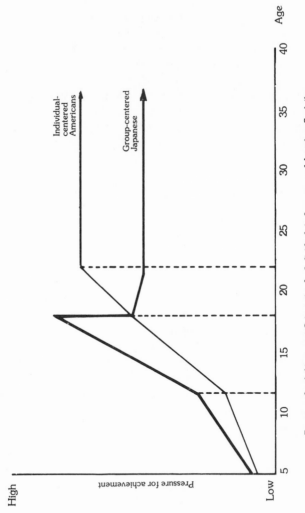

Pressures for Achievement Orientation for Individuals in Japanese and American Societies.

Source: Compiled by the author.

ages of 12 or 13, however, via high school entrance examinations, success in which can eventually provide superior preparation for the college entrance examinations. As shown in Figure 6, pressures for individual achievement to pass the entrance examinations intensify in the years of adolescence. Once access to college has been attained, these pressures diminish drastically and, after graduation from college, they remain stable on a lower plateau.

When college graduates obtain employment, they find the familiar pressure for individual excellence rapidly eroding in the face of a demand for group achievement. As pointed out earlier, the excellence and imperatives of the group often take precedence over the individual's personal achievement and needs in Japan. Within Eisenstadt's frame of reference, Japan is a universalistic society, but its emphasis on the group's precedence over the individual involves significant particularistic elements. Above all, what is most interesting is that the emphasis on universalistic and achievement orientations during the adolescent years gives way to group orientations, which tend to be particularistic. Therefore, it is reasonable to assume that the strong pressures for individual achievement in adolescence are equivalent to those pressures in the rite of passage described by van Gennep.

In comparison, pressures for individual achievement in the United States increase progressively through the college years and remain on a high plateau. They are continuous, unlike the discontinuous Japanese pressures. Hence, U.S. citizens have to compete with each other constantly in their centrifugal society. "One's gain is another's loss" is the "name of the game" throughout a typical American's life, whereas a Japanese tends to be content with the protection provided by his or her group. Nevertheless, typical college-bound Japanese adolescents suffer from far more uniformly imposed demands for surpassing others and social and psychological constraints than typical American high school students in the academic track.

In short, the regulation of role allocation in Japanese society has so developed that it requires a high degree of individual competition in the adolescent years—a type of competition for access to certain social resources, especially institutions of higher education. Since such competition is not designed to promote lasting individual creativity, intellectual development, or other similar qualities, its functions may be best understood as the regulatory constraints—in the form of selection—that Japanese society chooses to impose upon adolescents and youth.

In addition to culturally designed, intense experience, another vital characteristic of the rite of passage is the development of a certain cognitive and motivational map, promoted through the rite of passage, that serves as the primary basis of motivational and cognitive activities in the later years of life.[4] This is a crucial feature of Japanese preparation for the college entrance examinations, and we will explore it thoroughly in our discussion of schooling for the entrance examinations, below.

SCHOOLING FOR THE COLLEGE ENTRANCE EXAMINATIONS

In the early 1960s anthropologist Ezra Vogel studied city life in Tokyo, paying special attention to Japanese entrance examinations as the gateway to the status of a "salary man," an expression commonly used in Japan to refer to a white-collar worker. As he described the situation at that time,

> No single event, with the possible exception of marriage, determines the course of a young man's life as much as entrance examinations, and nothing, including marriage, requires as many years of planning and hard work. . . . These arduous preparations constitute a kind of rite de passage whereby a young man proves that he has the qualities of ability and endurance necessary for becoming a salary man.[5]

Vogel's study took place immediately after the comprehensive curriculum revision at the elementary and secondary levels had gone into effect, and this passage describes what he called the "infernal entrance examination" situation 15 years ago. Yet, even today, the Japanese college entrance examination (CEE) is one of the most tenacious sources of tension in contemporary Japanese life. Pressures for the socialization of adolescents and shaping secondary schools to meet the requirements of the high school and college entrance examinations have become a common source of chronic anxiety for students, parents, and teachers.

As discussed earlier, post-World War II education in Japan consists of elementary education for six years, secondary education—composed of middle and high school education—each for three years, and college education. Only the first nine years of schooling at the elementary and middle levels are compulsory. In 1975, 38.4 percent of the 1.6 million eligible youth (those who had reached 18 years of age) entered colleges, and the total enrollment of Japanese college students amounted to a little more than 2.1 million (see Table 3).

Approximately 800,000 applicants take the CEE every year from late February through March. There is particularly intense competi-

TABLE 3

Japanese Universities and Colleges: Student Enrollment, 1975

	Number of Institutions	Male	Female
National university and college	81	279,881	77,891
Prefectural and city college	34	36,304	14,576
Private university and college	305	1,049,639	275,791
Two-year college (national, prefectural, city, private)	513	48,658	305,124
Technical school (private and national)	n.a.	72,219	736
National school for special education	n.a.	0	1,976
Total	933	1,486,701	676,094

n.a.: data not available

Source: Ministry of Education, Wagakunino Kyōiku Suijun [The educational standard of our nation] (Tokyo: Okurasho Insatsukyoku, 1976), pp. 222-27, 285.

tion among those applicants who seek admission to the national universities. Academically able applicants tend to concentrate upon these schools, which are less costly and generally considered more prestigious and better financed than the private institutions. Average rates of competition, expressed as the number of total applicants divided by the number admitted, at the national institutions in 1974, for example, were as follows: 8.3 in humanities; 6.8 in social sciences; 5.3 in natural sciences and engineering; 11.6 in medicine and dentistry; and 4.8 in education.[6]

Among the private institutions, although a few are outstanding, the majority rank lower than the national universities. Competition for admission to the private institutions is equally high, however, because each applicant takes examinations at three to four different institutions and sometimes in different fields within the same university.

Despite such competition, only 30 percent of the total applicants were not admitted to college in 1975. The intense competition reflects the comparative rankings of the universities, in that the applicants compete most fiercely for admission to the universities with the highest prestige. The competition is heightened even more because many applicants (nearly 40 percent in 1974, excluding those for the two-year colleges) consist of what are called rōnin students (the term formerly denoted the lordless samurai)—high school graduates who devote a year or more at home or at private preparatory schools to prepare exclusively for the CEE for particular colleges because of having failed to gain admission in a previous year. The existence of a large number of rōnin students is peculiar to Japanese society and suggests that youth regard admission to particular colleges as especially crucial. It goes without saying that the pressure for such posthigh school preparation for the CEE increases the psychological and financial stress on the students and their families.

The CEE carries the greatest weight in deciding admissions to colleges. It alone determines admissions to the national and other publicly controlled colleges, since such other kinds of relevant information as high school scholastic records, teachers' recommendations, and aptitude are little considered, although the submission of carefully prepared high school reports is required. This reflects a Japanese cultural orientation in which individual characteristics are not considered to be as essential as the standard of the group. The reader will recall that the Japanese are inclined to disregard personal uniqueness and to submerge individual identity in a large group to which they belong. Therefore, it is the criteria of a group to which individual identity is subjected. Probably, this orientation is "unconsciously" applied to the evaluation of college applicants, but it determines the weight of the entrance examination. The most prevalent and explicit justification by university and college professors who evaluate the qualifications of applicants, is that high school records, aptitude, and other related information exhibiting personal characteristics of the applicants, are too "subjective" and unreliable a basis on which to make an "objective" judgment of each applicant.

Thus, the applicant has no alternative but to concentrate upon preparing for the CEE, which is given only once a year. In addition, during the examination period, the applicant is forced to cope with accumulated pressures that culminate in enormous tension during the examination itself. The applicant's tension is heightened because

in the popular mind, universities are ranked in a strict hierarchy of prestige, secondary schools are ranked in terms of the number of students they can place in prestigious institutions, and graduates are judged by many employers and others in terms of the university, and faculty of a university, into which they win admission through the examination system, rather than in terms of what they know and are able to do. Thus there is a general belief that a student's performance in one crucial examination at about the age of 18 is likely to determine the rest of his life. In other words: the university entrance examination is the primary sorting device for careers in Japanese society.[7]

Many private colleges follow the criteria for admission established by the national and other publicly controlled colleges, although other variables, such as the ability of the applicant's family to contribute financially, often become important factors. The financial contribution is very important to private medical schools in particular. In 1976, for example, there were only two private medical schools in the nation that did not require financial contributions as a condition for admission. Among those who were admitted to the private schools of dentistry, 99 percent made such contributions. The average contribution to the private medical schools per person was $84,000, and more than 5 percent of those admitted contributed over $150,000 each. Scandals involving acceptances of unqualified applicants contingent upon large, mandatory, and covert contributions are not rare, especially among the new, private colleges, which require large sums for their operation.[8]

The CEE has a powerful effect upon secondary and even elementary education. The very orientation of secondary education is defined by the pressures of the CEE, which imposes a particular framework upon the socialization and schooling of adolescents, according to which their cognitive and motivational orientations to education are developed. In other words, a majority of adolescents are conditioned to view schooling as truly relevant when it promotes preparation for the CEE, and as only marginally useful when it does not contribute to their ultimate goal—university admission. Obviously, adolescents experience a great deal of self-denial and lack intrinsic motivation for learning. It is within this framework that most nonvocational high schools, constituting two-thirds of all high schools, serve as preparatory agents for the CEE by orienting their entire educational processes toward its demands.

Meanwhile, in the middle schools, education has become increasingly aimed at preparing for the high school entrance examinations. A common assumption is that the degree of academic competitiveness at a given high school ultimately determines the rank of the college to which its students can gain entry. This assumption clearly leads to competition for admission to high schools that are highly ranked academically. Therefore, most middle schools are invariably oriented toward preparing students to compete successfully for entrance to high schools.

ADAPTATION AND EDUCATION IN JAPAN

At nearly all high schools (excluding the vocational high
ols), teaching methods and curricula are designed largely to
t the requirements for the CEE. Hence, they have been turned
into "cram systems" in one way or another. Many schools, for example, adopt a system where text-based teaching in major subjects,
such as mathematics and English, is shortened and completed by the
end of the second year, or early in the third year, in order to devote
the remaining time to CEE drilling. Drill books, consisting of examination questions given in the past, are often used in place of
texts. In addition, most students, particularly seniors, are required to take a number of exercise tests, including several tests
designed by particular schools expressly for the CEE, a half dozen
mock entrance examinations (usually called _moshi_ in Japanese) given
by private corporations, and term and midterm tests. Most of these
tests, other than term tests, are taken only to improve the ability of
the students to take examinations.

Such examination-centered schooling is often criticized by the
Japan Teachers Union (Nikkyōso), the largest and most powerful national teachers organization. The union has attacked the distortion
of secondary education, at the cost of personal, social, and intellectual maturity, in a voluminous report published in both Japanese and
English.

> As has been explained, [the] present day system of con-
> ducting entrance examinations for admission to universi-
> ties has aggravated [the] entire phase of Japan's educa-
> tion, particularly upper and lower secondary education,
> and even primary and kindergarten education. . . . Many
> plans have been worked out with an aim to improve the
> situation, particularly regarding subjects of examinations.
> Such improvements, however, are far from effective in
> solving the problem, because they only help to divert the
> people's attention from the very cause of the problem.
> . . . The present entrance examination system should be
> abolished, and universities, as an organic part of youth
> education, should be open for all young people who desire
> to enter them and are considered as qualified. Considera-
> tions should be given not to select a few for admission but
> how to prepare most appropriate university education for
> all persons who are qualified. University reform must be
> performed from this standpoint.[9]

Yet, most union teachers not only acquiesce in the current
orientation of schooling but reinforce it by responding to examination
pressures. Underlying such a contradiction is the overwhelming fact

that the reputations of schools and teachers are largely determined by their success in preparing students for entrance examinations. Pressures from parents and the general public for drilling students are exerted constantly. Moreover, many union teachers commonly engage in private tutoring, "moonlighting," for students preparing for entrance examinations.

Let us look back again at the early 1960s, in order to provide some historical perspective. The following description is taken from the author's research in 1964.

Above all, a passive reinforcement of learning is emphasized through frequent tests which, in turn, are aimed, to a large extent, at preparation for high school and college entrance examinations. Even at lower grade levels, education is conducted through drilling and out-of-school tutoring to prepare children for kindergartens and compulsory schools that require entrance examinations. By and large, Japanese formal education is universally geared to the examination system, generating a particular motivational pattern, shared by children, parents, and teachers, that supports and reinforces drill-learning. In Kagawa Prefecture, this motivation is being further developed by the incentives provided by National Achievement Tests and Kagawa Achievement Tests.

Discussing the examination system and its influence upon the nature of educational programs, Kando, principal of Tōzai Middle School, stated that the criteria for college entrance examinations determine not only the educational content of high schools and earlier levels of education, but also methods of teaching and learning. High school entrance examinations, in turn, influence the basic nature of preparatory education at the middle school level. The kind of education offered at the elementary school level is affected by the examination pressures imposed upon middle schools. That the frame of expectations for college entrance examinations determines earlier education to a significant degree may well be viewed as a general manifestation of the dominance of essentialist orientations in Japanese education. None of the informants interviewed denied Kando's observations. The ideal model, aspired to by a large number of teachers and parents, is, as related by Kando, to send their children to the best kindergarten in local communities, then to a Fuzoku (meaning university affiliation) elementary school, then to a Fuzoku middle school (both affiliated with Kagawa University), then to Takamatsu High School, which is considered to be the most reliable path in Kagawa Prefecture to Tokyo University. Teachers, parents, and students referred to the excellent reputation of Takamatsu High School and its highly disciplined preparatory training.

An anecdote related by Superintendent Kurono reflects the orientation of this school. His nephew was called to the office of his teacher at Takamatsu High School, where the teacher said to him: "You look unusually energetic and full of blood. Look at your friend. His face is pale. Do you know why? He studies very hard until late at night. You should study like him until you also become pale!"[10]

This description demonstrates a continuity of examination-oriented schooling and supports Vogel's general observation quoted earlier.

It is also worth noting that numerous private tutoring services, tutoring schools that operate in parallel with the elementary, middle, and high schools, and college preparatory schools (all generally called juku) exist today in order to respond to examination pressures. According to a survey conducted by the Ministry of Education,[11] for example, there are nearly 50,000 juku in Japan offering services to middle and elementary school students. The survey reports that about 27 percent of all sixth graders and 38 percent of all middle school students attend juku. In the urban areas with populations of more than 100,000, nearly 50 percent of the middle school students go to juku. So intense is the demand that 60 percent of juku have been established since 1966, although their growth has also been promoted by private educational industries and retired teachers, as well as moonlighting teachers (17 percent of the juku teachers), who have capitalized upon the potential demand for preparatory and sometimes compensatory schooling and tutoring. The juku, in their turn, further stimulate the competition among students. Like new, private colleges, many juku wax and wane and are essentially businesses. Chūnichi Gakushū Juku in Nagaya, for example, catering to elementary and middle schoolchildren, had expanded phenomenally in a few years and went bankrupt in 1977 (incurring debts of $12 million). It was a huge chain organization, just like a large supermarket, that had 700 branches in the nation.

Furthermore, a large proportion of high school students, about the same as the middle school students, attend juku after school and on Sundays to receive examination drilling. The scale of these juku varies from mammoth preparatory schools accommodating more than 10,000, available in every large city, to small ones for a half dozen students. Large juku have full-time instructors and handsome dormi-

tories for rōnin who come from distant towns and cities. Some of
them have staffs that conduct nationwide exercise examinations and
also publish successful drill books.

Following a similar orientation, a number of publishing firms
specialize in drill books, magazines, tests, and references related
to the entrance examinations. These published materials occupy
probably a quarter of the bookshelves in a typical Japanese bookstore.
Apparently, the more these firms can create anxiety on the part of
students and their parents, the more materials they can sell.

Another effect of the CEE is the formation of a hierarchy of
high schools. As alluded to above, the number of students that high
schools are able to place in universities with good reputations determines the high school's rank. Hence, high-ranking schools are selective and admit only those students with good scholastic records and
excellent examination skills. The quality of teaching staff and the
school environment have relatively little influence on ranking. Every
prefecture and major city has a hierarchy of high schools determined
solely by this criterion.

Moreover, ambitious families all over the nation attempt to
send their children to the most competitive private high schools,
which can provide them with a gateway to Tokyo University. Such
high schools are ranked, with national Fuzoku and other public high
schools, according to the same criterion. Ten such high schools in
order of rank, indicating in parentheses affiliations and the number
of students admitted to Tokyo University in 1977, are the following:
Kaisei (private, 123), Azabu (private, 106), Kyōikudai Fuzoku at
Komaba (national, 86), Rasaaru (private, 86), Musashino (private,
62), Shōnan (prefectural, 61), Eikō Gakuen (private, 59), and Nishi
(prefectural, 54). It is significant that these top ten high schools,
mostly private, control access to the best university in the nation by
monopolizing more than 36 percent of the total applicants admitted
(2,283).

In 1977, 92.6 percent of the middle school graduates entered
the high schools. Yet the way middle schoolteachers influence who
goes to which high schools is revealing and also reinforces the ranking order. Senior students in the middle schools take prefecturewide,
mock high school entrance tests (high school moshi) five to eight times
a year. These tests are either recommended or required by middle
schoolteachers, who need the students' data to determine the level of
performance in tests. The results of each test, which are translated
into T-scores, are sent to participating schools. After repeated
moshi, teachers assume that the level of a student's performance has
become so predictable that they can safely decide the rank of the
high school to which he or she may aspire. Hence, most teachers
use the results of moshi to identify the appropriate high schools for

their graduates. This practice has resulted in a pattern of apparent polarization in high school education, in which academically able applicants concentrate upon admission to high-ranking schools, and relatively incompetent applicants have no other choice but the low-ranking schools.

CULTURAL AND ECONOMIC
CONDITIONS FOR CEE

Why is Japanese schooling singularly oriented to examination requirements, particularly the CEE? Why is competition for CEE so ferocious? A variety of factors contribute to the intensification of the CEE pressures, the most influential ones being cultural and economic factors.

Cultural Factors

The Japanese cultural orientation has been discussed in Chapter 2 and in parts of Chapters 3 and 4. It is necessary, however, to return to some aspects of that earlier discussion, at the risk of redundancy, in order to relate them directly to the CEE.

It is a paramount need of the Japanese that they not only belong to a group but also become permanent members, so as to establish a lasting identity and, in turn, to receive lifelong protection. This need is most effectively met by lifelong employment, generally practiced by private corporations and government institutions at different levels. Recall that the Japanese group is characterized by motivational uniformity, inclusiveness, hierarchy, and exclusiveness vis-à-vis other groups. Such characteristics generate centripetal forces in social relations, solidifying and keeping individual members within the boundary of a group. Hence, Japanese are often permanently locked into given organizations. This has led to a relative lack of interorganizational mobility on the part of individuals and, consequently, to the evolution of Japanese social stratification by institutions rather than by individuals; in other words, individuals lack horizontal mobility in Japanese society.

Returning to the problems of the CEE, the group orientation of Japanese culture serves as a primary motivational force that drives Japanese adolescents to compete fiercely in the CEE. The CEE sorts out adolescents to place them in institutions of higher education that vary greatly in the access to work organizations they can provide for graduates. Hence, applicants tend to concentrate on universities and colleges that guarantee them access to the firms and governmental institutions that rank highly in the Japanese social stratification system. Since Japanese favor lifetime employment in such organizations, whether or not they are able to secure employment in these organizations immediately following university graduation becomes highly crucial to their social mobility. From the viewpoint of an organization, it is vital for job applicants to be very recent graduates, since they are expected to be enculturated into the organization from the bottom of its hierarchy.

Access to large private firms and governmental institutions is determined not only by the level of a young person's education but, more important, by the reputation of the university from which he or she graduated. In other words, major employers regard the level of institutional prestige as a major criterion for judging the qualifications of job applicants. It is interesting to note that university prestige is associated with the rating of entrance examinations regardless of students' performance at their universities.[12] Hence, qualifications for employment in such organizations are often determined at the point of entry into universities via the CEE.

Major employers also use the level of prestige as a criterion when recruiting at universities. This employment practice is called shiteikōsei. According to a recent survey, 35 percent of the sample of major employers subscribe to shiteikōsei to recruit applicants for office personnel.[13] Still another survey indicated that 300 major firms depend in varying degrees on this employment practice.[14] Sixty-five universities are often patronized by these major firms, including seven formerly imperial universities, two nonimperial national universities, and two large private universities, these being regarded as the most prestigious in Japan. These eleven universities, particularly Tokyo University, also serve as the major source of graduates in elite fields, such as politics, business, medicine, law, and academia.[15]

It is evident that admission to these prestigious universities, and other patronized universities, is vital to students if they are to gain access to groups of their own choice—work organizations with security and prestige. Once applicants are admitted to these universities, university education is relatively easy since, unlike the extremely rigorous entrance examinations, it does not generally require rigorous training. After students enter universities, they are more often than not treated as if they are members of exclusive groups; their status is secure, and they fear neither competition nor demands for academic work. A guarantee of graduation in four years is implicit; universities consider it their social responsibility to graduate those they admit. Undoubtedly, this is a reflection of the cultural orientation discussed earlier. Thus, the most intense competitive pressure in the life of a Japanese ends forever with the CEE.

Economic Factors

Economic variables also greatly influence the CEE, but they must be considered within the framework of the Japanese cultural orientation. The proportion of eligible youth who currently attend institutions of higher education has increased enormously in the past 20 years. In 1960, a few years after Japan had restored economic stability following the devastating destruction of economic and social life during World War II, only 10.3 percent of the eligible students were admitted to college; in 1965 the percentage rose to 22.7; in 1970, to 24; in 1975, to 38.4.[16] Japanese per capita income, meanwhile, has risen constantly: $458 in 1960; $1,000 in 1967; $1,887 in 1970; $4,400 in 1975.[17] In the late 1960s, in terms of GNP, Japan surpassed West Germany and took a position second to the United States among non-Communist nations. Certainly, there is an unequivocal correlation between Japan's economic growth and the growth of college enrollment.

Income differentials among males in the first year of their first employment for three groups—college, high school, and middle school graduates—are given in Table 4. Although the intervals among these indexes have been considerably narrowed in the 15 years between 1960 and 1975, the college graduate has an undoubtedly greater advantage over the other two groups. In terms of longitudinally computed career income, when the index for the college graduate is held constant at 100, the indexes of the high school and middle school graduates are: 71.4 and 61.5 in 1966; 73.9 and 66.7 in 1970; 77.2 and 69.2 in 1974.[18] What these statistics demonstrate is that the differentials in initial incomes among the three groups are, by and large, reflected in their career incomes.

With regard to the allocation of jobs, a majority of college graduates are predominantly employed in white-collar office, engineering, and managerial functions. In 1975, 51 percent of these jobs were allocated to college graduates, whereas 48.3 percent went to high school graduates. Nearly 75 percent of the blue-collar jobs in the primary and secondary industries were allocated to high school graduates, while the rest were largely allocated to middle school graduates.[19]

In short, it is advantageous from an economic point of view for Japanese youths to receive higher education if they can afford it, since college education is a means for social mobility. The current trend is toward a progressively greater number of families being able to afford sending young sons and daughters to college as long as they can win admissions. The economic variables referred to here help to explain the sharp rise in college enrollment and, in turn, the competitive pressure for college admission. When the Japanese economy was

TABLE 4

Index of Income Differentials among Males in the First Year
of First Employment

	College	High School	Middle School
1960	100	62.4	45.2
1965	100	71.8	57.2
1970	100	75.8	63.7
1975	100	84.0	69.4

Source: From Makoto Asō and Morikazu Ushiogi, eds., Gakureki Kōyōron [The utility of academic credentials] (Tokyo: Ūhikaku,
1977), p. 139.

growing at a rapid pace in the 1960s and early 1970s, higher education responded to the demands of industries to expand. The number
of four-year colleges and universities increased 71 percent in the 15
years between 1960 and 1975, reaching a total of 420, and the number
of two-year colleges grew from 280 to 513, an increase of 83 percent.

Despite the mushrooming of institutions of higher education in
one and a half decades, there are currently about 30 percent more
applicants than these institutions can admit. This surplus of applicants, however, is not a major variable in accounting for the fierce
competition in the CEE. A more influential factor, therefore, must
be sought in the orientation of Japanese culture, particularly the
group orientation.

CONCLUSION

Turning once again to the pattern of Japanese adaptation—which
involves Japanese group orientation—it is now evident that the CEE
is a powerful means employed by this society to determine individual
group membership. A unique aspect of Japanese society, as an advanced industrial nation, is that once one's group membership is established, transfer to another group is by no means easy because of
the salient centripetal, hierarchical, and exclusive orientation of the
Japanese group. Therefore, it becomes a matter of great concern
for individuals to gain access to a group—a work organization that
will provide them with lasting security, social identity, and status—
as early as they are qualified to seek membership.

The CEE is a central mechanism that is perpetuated to respond to the cultural imperatives of the Japanese group. The intensity of competition for the CEE must be accounted for by a number of factors, the most significant ones being cultural and economic. Above all, the cultural factor is the more inclusive and influential variable.

NOTES

1. Arnold van Gennep, The Rites of Passage (Chicago: University of Chicago Press, 1969), pp. 74-75.
2. See S. N. Eisenstadt, From Generation to Generation (New York: Macmillan, 1971).
3. The sociological terms used are widely employed by sociologists and anthropologists. For their definitions, see Talcott Parsons, The Social System (Glencoe, Ill.: Free Press, 1959), pp. 58-67; Talcott Parsons and Edward Shils, eds., Toward a General Theory of Action (Cambridge, Mass.: Harvard University Press, 1951), pt. 2.
4. For a related reference, see Yehudi Cohen, The Transition from Childhood to Adolescence (Chicago: Aldine, 1974).
5. Ezra Vogel, Japan's New Middle Class (Berkeley: University of California Press, 1965), p. 40.
6. Ministry of Education, Wagakunino Kyōiku Suijun [The educational standard of our nation] (Tokyo: Ōkurashō Insatsukyoku, 1976), pp. 218-19.
7. Organization for Economic Cooperation and Development, Reviews of National Policies for Education: Japan (Paris: OECD, 1971), pp. 88-89.
8. Asahi Shinbun (Asahi daily newspaper), February 1977; also series of articles in June and July 1977.
9. Japan Teachers Union, How to Reform Japan's Education (Tokyo: Japan Teachers Union, 1975), pp. 123-24.
10. See Nobuo K. Shimahara, "A Study of the Enculturative Roles of Education" (Ph.D. diss., Boston University, 1967).
11. Asahi Shinbun, March 12, 1977.
12. Japanese Recruit Center, "Gakurekini Kansuru Kigyōno Iken Chōsa" [Survey of corporations' opinions on educational credentials] (Tokyo: Nippon Rikurūto Center, 1975), p. 19.
13. Committee for Economic Development, "Kigyōnai Shūgyōshano Gakurekini Kansuru Chōsa" [Survey on employees and educational credentials in corporations] (Tokyo: Keizai Dōyūkai, 1975), p. 20.
14. Japanese Recruit Center, Shūshoku Jānaru [Journal on employment], February 1971, pp. 17-43.

15. See also Hiroshi Mannari, Bizinesu Eriito [Business elite] (Tokyo: Chūōkōronsha, 1974); Masaaki Takane, Nipponno Seiji Eriito [Political elite in Japan] (Tokyo: Chūōkōronsha, 1976).

16. See Ministry of Education, Wagakunino Kyōiku Suijun, pp. 214-15.

17. See United Nations, Statistical Yearbook (New York: United Nations, 1976).

18. For further details, see Ministry of Labor, Rōdōhakusho [Labor White Paper] (Tokyo: Ōkurashō Insatsukyoku, 1960, 1965, 1970, 1975).

19. Makoto Asō and Morikazu Ushiogi, eds., Gakureki Kōyōron [The utility of academic credentials] (Tokyo: Uhikaku, 1977), p. 138.

5

SOCIALIZATION FOR THE COLLEGE ENTRANCE EXAMINATIONS: THREE CASE STUDIES

In order to shed light upon the discussion of schooling for the CEE, this chapter presents three case studies that will examine different aspects of the process of socialization for the CEE. The schools chosen for the case studies and discussion are significantly different from each other, so that we can consider differential aspects of the problem of CEE-oriented socialization. While these high schools do differ from each other, notably in the methods they use to socialize students, the concerns of students and parents with the CEE are common. Although these case studies represent the particular problems of these high schools to an appreciable degree, they will illuminate the process of schooling at the high school level in general and problems involved in it. The socialization of students at each high school is described in detail so the reader can understand its concrete process and problems, and make his or her own generalizations about them. The names of the various schools mentioned have been changed to maintain their anonymity.

SAIGŌ HIGH SCHOOL

The first school to be described briefly is "Saigō," a ten-year old prefectural high school with an enrollment of 1,100 students, located outside the city limits of Nagoya, Aichi Prefecture, and fourth largest city in Japan (population, 2 million). It is one of five schools the author studied. Established in 1968, it has beautiful suburban surroundings that were primarily agricultural until about ten years ago. In the past ten years these surroundings have rapidly changed into a bedroom suburb of Nagoya, where a large proportion of the residents commute for work; agriculture is still the occupation of the rest of the people. The socioeconomic background of the school varies from working to middle class, but, regardless of social classes, practically all parents are concerned with their children's social mobility and, therefore, with their access to college education. Parents have confidence in the manner in which their sons and daughters are prepared for the CEE by Saigō, whatever method of preparation it may employ. Most of them are so dependent on Saigō that they encourage their children to follow their teachers' guidance under any circumstance.

Saigō has the best audiovisual and other learning laboratory facilities in the entire prefecture. It enrolls students from Nagoya and its neighboring communities who come from approximately the fiftieth percentile of their respective middle schools; thus, they were rejected by the more competitive prefectural high schools in Nagoya. Teachers at Saigō characterize many of its tenth-grade students as lacking the basic cognitive skills essential to their grade level and especially lacking a habit of sustained learning when they first enter the school. Teachers admit that many students at Saigō suffer from feelings of inferiority, which have developed in competitive middle school socialization and were heightened upon rejection by the prefectural high schools in Nagoya.

Despite the caliber of its students, every year Saigō places 95 percent of its graduates in various colleges, one-third of them in local, national universities. In sharp contrast to the high percentage of rōnin on the national level, only 8 percent of the senior students at Saigō become rōnin as a result of Saigō's special effort to reduce rōnin. It has outdistanced other recently established schools in the prefecture in securing relatively good placements, and it is beginning to challenge more traditional and competitive schools in Nagoya.

Group Training

The unique characteristic of this school is its continuous emphasis on the development, through various formal and informal activities, of certain attitudinal, cognitive, and behavioral patterns on the part of students. This socialization is deliberate and intense, stressing a break from the past so that students may reorient themselves toward new goals. It involves a few major events, the description of which will highlight its significance.

Since its inception, Saigō has been launching unique programs in which students are trained for three years to develop a pattern of disciplined behavior. The school emphasizes self-denial, strict conformity to the group, endurance, prompt response to external expectations, and acceptance of teachers as the source of moral and academic authority. A social studies teacher at Saigō suggests that their underlying principle is the "Confucian ethic." These programs are part of what is called group-oriented seikatsushidō—the intense socialization previously noted. Saigō contends that its students can be trained through these programs to meet CEE requirements. Saigō is now seen as a model for over 60 recently established public high schools in the prefecture. It is also judged nationally to provide a unique direction for high school education, and thus teachers and administrators from all over Japan visit Saigō every year to observe its educational program.

Group training begins from the first day of attendance for the tenth-grade students. On the first sunny, spring day in April, 350 tenth graders, all wearing identical white caps, line up on the athletic ground of the school. They are divided into groups of about 40, the leaders of which were selected to coordinate group activities. These new Saigō students are unfamiliar with the training but appear quite anxious, since many of them have heard rumors about what some of them identified as "Spartan education." The group leaders are told how to give commands to their groups in order to move them from one position to another. It is quite difficult and somewhat embarrassing for the appointed leaders since they have never commanded groups in this fashion before. Under the supervision of teachers and senior students, all tenth graders participate for a day in a strict physical training program that requires swift and precise coordinated movement and quick response to authority, as in military training. Formations of movement change quickly from one to another, but, in a while, they are repeated. Because individual error is regarded as the responsibility of the entire group, both group leaders and participating members are tense. Subsequently, this training forms the model for various athletic contests, club activities, and other kinds of events. Visitors to the school are invariably impressed with the orderliness, promptness, and control of behavior the students show.

The tenth-grade students undergo the most intense four-day "initiation ritual," called genpukushiki by teachers and students (the term originated in the Nara (646-794) and Heian (794-1185) periods, during which twelve-year-old boys participated in a rite of passage signifying their new status as adults). It is conducted during the summer, before the tenth-grade students develop sufficient sensitivity to teachers' expectations. Students spend these days with their teachers and one or two PTA members in a distant mountainous area in Nagano Prefecture, staying in local inns at night, in order to facilitate the internalization of the teachers' expectations and the development of disciplined group behavior. Before this event, however, three days are devoted to preparations at the school. Thus, both participating teachers and students have to disrupt their summer vacations during the seven days needed for this particular ritual.

This program is an extension of the aforementioned physical training program, but is more intensive and "shocking," involving more varied activities, such as mountain climbing, campfire building, temple visiting, and group living. Students are punished when they are not orderly and obedient. Punishments include admonition, pushing, ridiculing, and "rabbit hopping" (students are told to hop like a rabbit for a period of time). Each day begins very early in the morning, when teachers whistle to signal all students to get up. Students are required to line up immediately on the specified assembly area without any opportunity to take care of personal needs. Teachers stress promptness and punctuality.

The first day begins with strenuous mountain climbing after an early breakfast. Students have already been told of the rules they are expected to observe while climbing. Individual students are not allowed to drop out of their group, no matter how difficult it is to keep pace. What matters is how long each person can persevere. There should be no relaxed, picnic mood. All students are dressed identically, and their uniforms and sneakers have only two colors: white and black. While climbing, towels cannot be hung sloppily over the shoulders since, according to the rule, they must be contained in a certain place. Boys and girls are not permitted to chat with each other and are in completely separate lines; such chatting is considered distracting and not conducive to the morale of the group. They are emphatically told that simplicity, dedication, singlemindedness, and uniformity are of most vital importance to them.

When they return in the afternoon, they line up again in the assembly area for the principal's admonition and reflective comments by other teachers. After a strenuous day, the students receive a special dinner. When dinner is almost over, several boys and girls are still in the dining room, however, with a couple of stern-looking teachers. They have not eaten the salmon bones, and the teachers insist that they must finish them. One girl is weeping from embarrassment, while the others are reluctantly chewing the hard bones. Subsequently, they will be told to write letters of apology to the teachers and to bring them to the teachers' offices.

The second and third days are devoted to visiting temples and, again, to mountain climbing, and the fourth day's climax is campfire building. On this particular occasion, both teachers and students are unusually relaxed, boisterous, and there is no punishment for behavior judged excessive according to the Saigō standard. Students are relieved and even amused to see their teachers so unpretentious and friendly. Teachers, meanwhile, insist that both the sternness and the relaxation of tension are necessary to socialize their students.

Teachers admit that most tenth-grade students become docile, obedient, and persevering, as well as very sensitive to the group norms imposed upon them through this training, even though prior to the experience many had resisted the stern, foreign socialization.

These students did not receive such unyielding socialization at their middle schools. In fact, Saigō students acknowledged that they remained scared, restless, and nervous for at least most of the first year at the school and that they were always alert throughout the three years lest they be called to the faculty office for admonition. Students are concerned that individual failure to meet the faculty's expectations may cause terrible embarrassment, since not only individuals but entire groups are often punished.

Application of Group Training

The teachers apply the fundamental orientation of the aforementioned training in the classrooms, and discipline the students to develop a habit of sustained learning. Since the senior year (twelfth grade) is most crucial for the CEE, most of the 350 senior students are expected to receive hoshū (supplementary drilling) nearly every day for one hour before the regular morning class and for two hours after the regular afternoon class; this is an intensive group exercise not seen at prefectural schools in Nagoya.

During the humid midsummer, Saigō conducts a condensed cramming session for the senior students during four days and three nights at the school, where the students must live and sleep; this is the last major event in Saigō's intense socialization. The summer season for seniors is the most critical period for CEE preparation. Over the summer, they are expected to examine all examination subjects at least once, so they may begin to utilize drill books in the fall to cover a wide range of examination topics and questions. Most senior students at Saigō are nervous and insecure when the last summer arrives, since they are not confident about how well they can review their previous studies. Meanwhile, they often meet superior students, former classmates in their middle schools, who appear formidable to them since they are far more advanced in their preparations. A majority of the seniors in Nagoya are enrolled in what they hope will be their last condensed summer sessions at juku. Every student and his or her mother begin to feel the intensified competition and increased anxiety. Generally, Japanese mothers are much more extensively involved in the socialization and education of their children than fathers, who are not at home during the day.

It is at this time that the Saigō cramming session is offered. Teachers explain that its major objective is to build the student's habit of concentrating on study for many hours and enduring difficulties related to such concentration. The session requires the participants to rise at 6:00 in the morning and to retire at 11:30 at night. There are recess periods after lunch, in the midafternoon, and after supper. Outside catering services are used to get meals for the participants to free them from any housekeeping chores. During the session, teachers constantly patrol classrooms and assist students when they need guidance. Otherwise, the participants are expected to make their own schedules for four days and to concentrate on their CEE preparations. Most students are able to concentrate on the first day, but from the second day on a fair number of them become distracted because of fatigue and inability to continue concentration. While teachers are present, however, they either pretend to work or attempt to study. Though they are, to varying degrees, aware that this session is designed to assist them for the CEE, some of them cannot help feeling that they are forced to study by teachers and parents.

Whether or not this is actually effective, teachers consider it important to the students' success in the CEE. After all, they devote time and effort to their students without monetary or other self-serving rewards. Many extracurricular activities, including the "initiation ritual" in Nagano, hoshū, and the summer sessions, are all voluntary services provided by dedicated teachers.

In addition to these events, which have a significant influence on students, Saigō offers many other extracurricular activities involving other grade levels: a four-day excursion for the juniors to Tokyo, Kyushu, and other distant places; schoolwide events, including chorus, soccer, volleyball, baseball, and athletic competitions; winter physical training, commencement ceremonies, and a graduation party for the seniors; and club activities, in which a majority of sophomore and junior students participate on a regular basis. In other words, a visitor to the school cannot help but receive the impression that Saigō students are extensively involved not only in preparation for the CEE but in these extracurricular activities as well; such activities are part and parcel of Saigō group-oriented socialization.

The summer cramming session and hoshū are not part of the prefectural schools in the city. Unlike many students at those schools who attend juku, few students at Saigō go to juku. Group-oriented hoshū appears sufficient to fulfill the function of juku for the students at Saigō.

Dependence and Extrinsic Motivation

Saigō students are not only strictly guided by their teachers but are also motivated to depend upon them. Faculty members expect their students to study as intensely as those at schools in Nagoya. A study profile of an above-average male senior obtained three months prior to the CEE reveals this phenomenon well. The student got up at 6:30 A.M. and reached school at 7:30. From 7:45 to 8:30 he received morning hoshū (four times a week), followed by regular morning class at 8:50. Classes ended at 3:10 P.M., and were followed by afternoon hoshū (twice a week) from 3:40 to 5:00; he returned home by 6:00. After supper he began study at 8:00 and continued until 1:00 in the morning. In his senior year, the student took four term tests and eleven exercise examinations given by private corporations and Saigō; test scores were periodically posted on a bulletin board.

In order to make CEE preparatory studies effective, Saigō, as do other schools, divides students at the beginning of their junior year into different tracks: the humanities and social sciences group for private universities and colleges; the same categorical group for national universities; and the natural science and engineering group for both private and national universities and colleges. Each group has optional courses that stress particular subjects central to the framework of that group's examinations. Most senior students take nationally administered moshi five or six times a year, as do many students elsewhere. The student referred to above took five such tests given by three different corporations. Saigō emphasizes cramming by repeating the same texts over and over again, but it also uses drill books extensively during hoshū.

A majority of the students at Saigō appear to be extrinsically motivated to prepare diligently for the CEE largely because of external pressures exerted by their group, teachers, parents, and the mass media. The mass media play somewhat of an important role, in that they constantly transmit to adolescents the message that they will not become respectable, mature members of society without a college education. Hence, mass media help to compel adolescents to conform, and they constitute a force for extrinsic motivation. On the other hand, despite the vital role of hoshū in preparing for the CEE, it is interesting to note that many students complain about it, though they never dare to express complaints to teachers. They continue to participate in it so that they may not betray the expectations of their group, particularly of their teachers. Teachers, meanwhile, are proud that, in response to their expectations, their students are amenable and superior to students in other new prefectural schools; obviously, they are aware of group rivalry among high schools. Saigō's faculty is effectively applying the group orientation inherent in Japanese culture to schooling for the CEE, particularly as it underscores the conformity of motivational orientation and the inclusiveness of group members. Although group pressures are exerted on students at Saigō for CEE preparation, it is the sole burden of each student, not his group, to pass the CEE. In other words, individual achievement is a primary determinant for access to college.

According to teachers at Saigō, given the average academic qualities of their students and the wishes of nearly all parents that their children attend college, Saigō's approach to training students is probably most conducive to achieving the students' goals of winning college admission. In fact, the parents interviewed are more or less pleased with the socialization and hoshū provided by the school. Nevertheless, one teacher reported that a few parents often object to Saigō's socialization. The faculty at the school is also aware that the Japan Teachers Union and some intellectuals in Nagoya frequently criticize it for its "authoritarianism."

Meanwhile, Saigō teachers are expected to work much harder than faculties in most other schools. They arrive at the school by 7:30 in the morning and leave after 6:00 in the evening. While much of their time is committed to regular teaching, hoshū, and socialization activities, they frequently meet late in the afternoon to coordinate their activities. Most of their spring and summer vacations are also devoted to hoshū, the summer initiation program, the summer cramming session, and planning. One of the factors most crucial to the operation of Saigō, according to the director of academic affairs, is the homogeneity of the teachers' attitudes toward education at the school. Therefore, he says, teachers often gather after school and during vacation periods for dinner and drinks to promote a group feeling. When new teachers are appointed, they are taken to a distant inn or hotel overnight where they are "initiated" into the Saigō group— that is, become acquainted with its group orientation and expectations.

Saigō has a reputation in the Nagoya area for conducting "Spartan" schooling, forcing students to study without due consideration for their individual characteristics and motivations. The other two high schools studied in Nagoya provide more relaxed environments. Group-oriented socialization, as emphasized by Saigō, is absent from these schools. Whether or not Saigō's schooling is typical, it elucidates one response to the pressures of the CEE.

UMIGAOKA HIGH SCHOOL

"Umigaoka" is a prefectural high school and presents a sharp contrast to Saigō in many respects. Common to both high schools, however, is the manner in which their reputations are determined; it is a reflection of the perceptions of parents, teachers, and students with regard to the ability of these high schools to place their graduates in prestigious universities.

Umigaoka has long been regarded as the most prestigious school in Nagoya, as well as in Aichi Prefecture; it has enjoyed a national reputation as a competitive "preparatory" school for the CEE. In contrast to the attractive, modern buildings and spacious suburban environment of Saigō, Umigaoka, having an enrollment comparable to Saigō's, is situated in a crowded, urban environment with a mixture of commercial establishments and private homes existing side by side. Its students are accommodated in old-fashioned, wooden, three-story buildings; it was originally established as a school for foreign languages in 1874, early in the Meiji era, two years after the Fundamental Code of Education had been promulgated, and it became the first middle school in Aichi Prefecture in 1876. As mentioned earlier, middle school was the most important strategic stage for young men who sought the academic track leading to higher school, for it drilled them for fiercely competitive entrance examinations for the higher schools. When the postwar education system came into operation in 1948, it became a prefectural high school.

Umigaoka's reputation in the postwar period reached its apex around 1967 when it placed 70 graduates in Tokyo University, 35 in Kyoto University, the second most prestigious university in the nation, and 156 in Nagoya University, one of the seven former imperial universities. Around that time, most schools in Nagoya could place only a few in Tokyo University. Nearly 200 middle schools in the entire prefecture had competed to place one or two students in Umigaoka. The general socioeconomic background of the Umigaoka students was upper-middle to lower-upper class, and it remains, by and large, the same at present.

In the early years of the postwar period, from 1948 to 1956, what is called a "local school-district system" (shōgakkusei) had been implemented in Aichi Prefecture. Following the recommendations of the United States Education Mission, this system emphasized decentralized schooling and limited access to schools to local residents within a given district. Under the regulations of the system, adolescents in only two wards of Nagoya were permitted to attend Umigaoka, if admitted, and therefore had greater access to this high school than they did under the prewar middle school regulations. Nevertheless, because of its prewar reputation as an academically competitive middle school, parents all over the prefecture tenaciously sought their children's admission to Umigaoka. In some cases, families temporarily moved to the district to legitimate their children's access to the school, while, in other cases, children alone moved to live with relatives in the district for the same purpose. In still other cases, adolescents' residences were established only on paper through manipulation. Whatever the case, it is evident that parents all over the prefecture perceived Umigaoka to be a key for gaining access to prestigious universities. Consequently, apartments and rooming houses were built around the school to accommodate the demands for temporary residence.

Under the local district system, however, Umigaoka was not competing equally with top private high schools that were not constrained by residential restrictions. It placed, for example, only eight graduates in Tokyo University in 1955. Its reputation was in decline, while competitive private schools were admitting only top graduates of the middle schools in the prefecture. In general, top students were inclined to look to private schools more than to Umigaoka.

Schooling at the secondary level in other prefectures was similarly under the regulations of the school district system. But in the first half of the 1950s, prefectures began to replace the local district system with a "large school district system" (daigakkusei), a prefecture-wide system free from internal residential restrictions.* This move coincided with a changing political climate which led to the passage of the school board law of 1956 that, as mentioned, emphasized centralized control of education. In Aichi Prefecture, a large-district system superseded the local district system in the same year the school board law passed, two years prior to the announcement of the comprehensive curricular revision at the elementary and secondary levels in 1958.

Again, various changes in Japanese education in the 1950s, including a modification of residential restrictions, reflected a radical shift from a generally American educational orientation—emphasizing decentralization of educational control—to a Japanese orientation, which stressed the centralization of schooling. It was argued that this shift was part of the pattern of Japanese adaptation. While the large-district system denies a number of local residents access to educational institutions in their locality, it permits a concentration of homogeneous students in high schools through prefecture-wide competition among applicants: a phenomenon determined not by geographical, but by competitive boundaries. A Japanese orientation toward centripetality is clearly evident in this phenomenon. Some teacher-informants regard this system as rewarding merit rather than ascription (residence in this case) and as compatible with Japanese cultural orientations.

School Grouping and the CEE

Subsequent to the establishment of the new system, Umigaoka began to regain its reputation as the most prestigious high school in

---

*Many prefectures replaced the small school district system with the large school district system in the late 1950s and the early 1960s. There were also variations reflecting both systems, which

the prefecture. By 1960, a hierarchical pattern of high schools in the city emerged, determined by the competitive placement of students in top universities. This hierarchical pattern had developed further and rigidified until the early 1970s, with Umigaoka at the top and a few schools at the bottom. Middle schools in the prefecture had helped reinforce it by placing their students according to an accepted notion of the high school hierarchy. Toward the end of the 1960s, its development was not only a source of widespread public complaints, but it also became a political controversy. The public criticized Umigaoka in particular for its "elitist" policy, which emphasized selectivity and discriminated against a majority of the students in the prefecture despite being a public school. Such criticisms were also raised, to a degree, against several other prefectural schools in Nagoya that were attempting to emulate Umigaoka.

Subsequently, such complaints led the prefectural board of education to adopt a gakkōgun (school grouping) system, involving 15 prefectural high schools in Nagoya, whereby the placement of applicants in those schools would be equalized relative to their academic qualities, as a matter of policy. The system consists of 15 units, each of which comprises two schools (see Figure 7). For example, X and Y (schools) constitute Unit I while Y and Z, Unit II. The applicants admitted to Unit I are equally divided into X and Y without allowing for personal preference and those accepted by Unit II, into Y and Z. Thus, Y accepts students from both Units I and II.

The concept of group is at work in this system. The responsibilities for the excessive hierarchy were attributed to all 15 high schools in the city. Instead of requiring changes in the individual high school admissions policies, the grouping system was imposed upon all schools. This represented a typical Japanese group approach to the problem. In other words, schools were not expected to take independent initiatives to remedy the problem, since the high school hierarchy was perceived as a relative phenomenon representing the differential positions of the schools in a common, group, frame of reference. It was probably anticipated that it would be impossible for group-oriented Japanese and institutions to ameliorate the problem on an individual basis. The school-grouping approach, therefore, was accepted by all prefectural schools in the city.

A gakkōgun system was first developed in Tokyo and implemented in 1967, when Tokyo was baffled by a concentration of superior students in a small number of prefectural schools that monopolized ac-

---

were called "a middle school district system" (chūgakkusei). In the case of Aichi Prefecture, the entire prefecture is divided into two large school districts.

FIGURE 7

Gakkōgun System in Nagoya

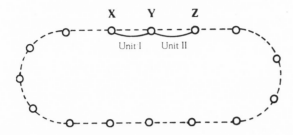

Source: Compiled by the author.

cess to the prestigious universities. As a result, the reputations of
Hibiya High School, the most challenged and envied school in Tokyo,
and of other schools in a similar category have steadily declined as
many top students have sought admission to private and national
schools unaffected by the gakkōgun system, rather than to tradition-
ally outstanding prefectural high schools. A new hierarchy of prefectural schools, however, has evolved within the new system, the
original purpose of which was to minimize it. Meanwhile, capitaliz-
ing upon the new gakkōgun policies, contending private and national
schools have successfully replaced the positions of Hibiya and its
equivalent public schools.

The gakkōgun system in Nagoya was implemented in 1973 for
the first time, and it had as significant an effect upon the 15 high
schools as it had in Tokyo. It has contributed to creating a more
balanced distribution of applicants among the 15 schools in terms
of academic and test performance. This has led to the decline of
Umigaoka and a few other top schools in the hierarchy, and, in turn,
to the rise of Chikusa, a ten-year-old school, and several other
schools. Now, Umigaoka must accept applicants above the eightieth
percentile in their respective middle schools, instead of those above
the ninety-eighth percentile, as it did prior to 1973.

In the light of those changes, Umigaoka's primary concern,
though often implicit, is to regain its traditional position within the
gakkōgun system and, particularly, to cope with Chikusa's challenge.
In fact, there are perceptions commonly shared by middle school
teachers, students, and parents that Chikusa has overtaken Umigaoka.
Some Umigaoka students envy their former peers attending Chikusa
who, in their view, are more rigorously drilled. Furthermore, results of Chūtō tests and moshi (mock entrance examinations)—given
by independent, private corporations eight times a year and taken by
more than 95 percent of all ninth graders in the prefecture—recently

indicated that Chikusa applicants tend to perform better than Umigaoka applicants. Because of these perceptions and test results, increasing numbers of teachers and students, as well as parents, favor Chikusa over Umigaoka.

In this connection, it is important to note that, in the year the gakkōgun system went into effect, many top students applied to Tokai High School, a top private preparatory school, rather than to Umigaoka as they had during the period of the local district system. Ninth-grade teachers and parents, as well as juku teachers, constantly monitor every piece of information relevant to high school admission to determine which high school would provide the best chances for gaining access to top universities. Such monitoring is so widespread a practice that it has contributed to the formation of a new hierarchy of high schools within the gakkōgun system. Everyone is aware that, like stocks, high schools are in a competitive "market."

Drilling Strategy

This competitiveness concerns teachers at Umigaoka. The director of academic affairs at the school still insists that its primary task is to "instruct talented students," to use his phrase, who can be admitted to prestigious universities. He and other teachers are resentful of the gakkōgun system because, in their view, it was designed to "destroy" Umigaoka. Now he sees a clear polarization of student quality. The school must accept applicants from Units I and II under the gakkōgun system, students from Unit I consisting of Umigaoka and another school which is considered the least examination oriented in the system. These students are inferior to those from Unit II, which comprises, incidentally, Umigaoka and Chikusa. Faced with this problem, the policy of the school, according to him, is to orient instruction and drilling to the superior students at the expense of the other students and to teach them 20 percent above what is required in the manual of the course of study. At faculty and committee meetings in which Umigaoka's policies for the CEE are discussed, the director plays a dominant role and keeps the faculty well informed of the relative position of the school vis-à-vis other high schools in the city. Computer printouts describing the results of the aforementioned Chūtō tests, their detailed analyses and interpretations, comparative descriptions of CEE results, results of moshi for the CEE given by private corporations, and results of moshi prepared by the school—as well as correlational analyses of these factors—are periodically prepared and presented to the faculty by the director.

Given the heterogeneity of student quality, the director and his supporters are interested in implementing ability grouping in order to make CEE preparations more effective. They refrain because they fear accusations of "discriminatory education" by parents, union teachers, and the public in general. Thus, Umigaoka has not proceeded with ability grouping. In the director's view, ability grouping would benefit both academically superior and inferior students. But, in the Japanese group, members disfavor attempts to introduce centrifugal forces separating one individual from another. While they are actually stratified within the group, they commonly entertain the notion that the groups are all-inclusive. Therefore, Japanese are very sensitive to even an insinuation of separation and discrimination, and this psychology applies to Umigaoka and most other high schools in the nation. This is one of the primary reasons why ability grouping in Japan is avoided at all levels of education.

The polarization of education at Umigaoka is reinforced by its policy to instruct 20 percent above the requirement and by its condensed cramming. Text-based teaching in such major subjects as mathematics and English is terminated by the end of the junior year in order to devote the senior year to more intensive drilling for the CEE, for which drill books are commonly used.

Polarized education at the school affects juniors and sophomores as well as seniors. An average junior student interviewed during this research is a case in point. He aspired to study at Tokyo University when he was in the fifth grade; thereafter he studied hard, as he was encouraged to do by his parents and teachers, and attended juku in order to insure his admission to Umigaoka. In his junior year, he attempted to study more diligently than ever; it was his established schedule to study from about 8:30 P.M. to 1:00 A.M. every day, focusing on reviewing major examination subjects. In order to maintain this schedule, he decided to participate in the archery club—nearly 50 percent of all sophomores and juniors join various clubs at Umigaoka—instead of the rugby club, which he really liked partly because he was physically qualified for such a sport. The main reason was that rugby would have exhausted him and interfered with his study. Eventually, he withdrew from the archery club to devote more time to study.

The problem this student had was that he could not keep up with the pace of instruction; his diligent study notwithstanding, he constantly fell behind. Though he spent a lot of time reviewing examination subjects, he could not concentrate on that alone. He felt he would not be qualified to take the CEE for either Tokyo or Nagoya universities. He participated in a summer cramming session at a juku, but did not benefit from it. Having lost confidence in himself, he harshly blamed himself instead of teachers and faster peers. He confessed sadly that he did not know how to improve his study. Meanwhile, he was aware that his mother still had a high expectation for him, and encouraged him from time to time. He rarely spoke to his father about his academic performance since he was afraid of his father's reactions. His feelings of ambivalence grew steadily, and he hoped that the teacher would slow down so that he could comprehend what was covered every day at school. When he got bad examination results he was no longer as disappointed as he had been. In a word, he was a victim of Umigaoka education.

In contrast, a sophomore interviewed exhibited an aggressive outlook and prefers competition; obviously, he was a beneficiary of the school's policies. To begin with, he was an ambitious, brilliant boy. When he was a ninth grader, he received the highest scores in Chūtō tests in his school. He attended Kawai Juku, the largest private preparatory school in Nagoya, which enrolls about 15,000 students of different ages, from 5:00 P.M. to 7:00 P.M. three times a week. He studied drill books from 8:30 P.M. to 12:00 P.M. every day. He often used a timer in order to determine how many questions he could correctly answer in a given period of time. He was able to engage in other activities as well. In the eighth grade, he served as president of the student government (seitokai) of his school. Early in the ninth grade, he received the first prize for his English composition in a citywide contest, and also won a gold medal in a prefectural contest for his composition (in Japanese) on taxation; the composition was later entered in a national contest. He was also the leader of the school chorus.

His test results at Umigaoka, up to the time of the interview, had not been good in his view. He felt he had not been disciplining himself well, so he decided to quit the judo club, and he attended Kawai Juku and another juku simultaneously. Disappointed that he could not receive as much stimulation as he originally expected from his classmates, he felt he had to be an "individualist," driving himself rigorously. In the current CEE system, he said, competition and the survival of the fittest are the foremost rules. Therefore, in order to surpass others, according to him, he had to "study limitlessly and memorize everything." His parents agreed with his view. His aspiration was to study medicine at Tokyo University.

The Umigaoka policies may have worked well in terms of placing students in Tokyo University. There was an increase of students (excluding rōnin) admitted to the university in 1977 as compared with 1976, which meant to the school that it had begun to regain its tradition.

In contrast to Saigō, Umigaoka has a far more relaxed orientation toward the notion of authority and the manner in which individual students prepare for the CEE. Bright students are expected to challenge teachers. The school does not offer hoshū and related programs, other than prolonged, intensive drilling during the class period. Students are expected to make their own plans for CEE preparation; nearly 50 percent of the students at the school either participate in condensed juku programs in the spring or summer or attend juku on a yearly basis. About 50 percent of the students become rōnin, having failed to pass entrance examinations in the first year. These differences between the two schools may be related in part to the differential socioeconomic backgrounds of the schools.

Despite constant examination pressures, Umigaoka students were known for their political activism in the 1960s. They had developed the most active student government in the prefecture. Student unrest at the school peaked in 1969, reflecting the widespread unrest among college students in the nation and abroad. Umigaoka's unrest was motivated by students' opposition to the extension of the Treaty of Mutual Security and Cooperation with the United States signed in 1960 and intensified by a Ministry of Education policy prohibiting the political activities of high school students. Students at Umigaoka, supported by union teachers, defied the orders of the principal and the prefectural superintendent of schools and held a series of school-wide student assemblies for five days, suspending all class participation and culminating in an unprecedented off-campus demonstration. This activism ended in the 1970s. While a small group of students still defies the principal's authority on political grounds, a teacher observes that they are individually helpless and need teachers' support for CEE preparations.

Selection of College

The primary criterion for students' determination of their preferred universities and specialities is performance in the moshi given by the school. At a meeting in late spring, teachers inform all senior students of the criteria for the selection of universities, and in the late fall they meet with parents. In a tense atmosphere, teachers present charts illustrating the categories of universities and colleges in rank order, along with the results of moshi and correlations between the two, so that both students and their parents may know which category of universities they are likely to be qualified for. In addition, most students get information about universities and colleges from two indirect sources: they rely heavily on the voluminous books on universities and colleges published by several companies and they acquire information offered by teachers, peers, parents, brothers, sisters, and other relatives. University personnel never visit the school to inform students and teachers of their institutions and programs, and few students have opportunities to visit the universities. The only exception here is that private colleges in the vicinity do in-

vite teachers to hotels, or other suitable places, to give them information about their programs. Given the absence of opportunities for
visitation and conferences with university personnel and professors,
students must inevitably rely on books and are likely to be attracted
to high-ranking institutions as described and evaluated therein.

In December final decisions must be made regarding applica-
tions. Umigaoka holds a series of three-party conferences involving
a homeroom teacher, a student, and a parent. The teacher spreads
on the table the records of the student's test scores, including those
of moshi, and a university ranking list published by Kawai Juku. This
list correlates those scores with university ranks. Such a conference
is described as follows in the author's notes:

> This conference involves a son and his mother. He is in-
> terested in studying chemistry at Nagoya University or at
> Nagoya Institute of Technology. His scores in chemistry
> and English are low, however, and he is in only the fiftieth
> percentile at Umigaoka. The teacher tries to find other
> schools of technology in the vicinity, including Gifu School
> of Technology, the ranking of which may correlate with
> his scores. The boy's father is opposed to his son's at-
> tending a college outside the Aichi area and also to his
> becoming rōnin. This limits choices. Aichi School of
> Technology is another possibility, suggests the teacher.
> Meijō may be good also, but it is getting more difficult
> to be admitted. Meanwhile, the teacher restudies the
> student's T-scores in moshi and the ranking list to find
> out if Aichi School of Technology is in the range of his
> scores. The student does not like Aichi and Meijō. His
> current score is 45. Turning attention to Nagoya Uni-
> versity's chemistry department again, the teacher says
> his score must be improved to 57 to be admitted. The
> teacher insists that the student and his mother must be
> realistic about his choices of college. Then he suggests
> the school of economics at Nanzan University and the
> school of agriculture at Nagoya University. Following
> the suggestions, the mother asks what kind of occupation
> her son can obtain after graduating from the school of
> agriculture. The teacher replies that they will have to
> think about it in the future. The time allowed for the con-
> ference is about to expire. Thus, the teacher's final sug-
> gestions are as follows: the first choice is the school of
> agriculture at Nagoya University; the second, Nagoya
> School of Technology; and the third, the school of econom-
> ics at Nanzan. Because the student is not allowed to become

rōnin next year, and because of his scores in moshi, the
teacher suggests that is the best strategy. The mother
asks the last question: if her son spends an additional year
as rōnin, would he be able to aim one rank higher? The
teacher assures her that all he has to do is to study
harder.

The conference just described is rather typical for a majority
of students, whereas top students define their career goals more
clearly and identify universities of their preference better. But, in
general, it is apparent that the applicant's aptitude is not sufficiently
taken into consideration in deciding his or her university and special
field. Many students are content if they are accepted by universities
in high ranks, regardless of the academic specialties to which they
are admitted. What concerns them most is the university's reputation
as perceived by people in general. Yet, there is also a ranking order
of specialties, which places medicine at the top, followed by law, science, engineering, literature, education, and, at the bottom, agriculture. A widespread tendency is for applicants with very high scores
to choose medicine and applicants with low scores to apply for agriculture.

Role of Tannin

In the face of such pressures, one might anticipate suicides and
dropouts. Both Saigō and Umigaoka have had no suicides in recent
years. In Saigō, three students recently transferred to other schools,
but no one dropped out in 1976-77. In Umigaoka, only two or three
students in every grade drop out each year, and some of these are
brought back through teachers' personal efforts. Generally most high
schools are inclined to cover up dropouts and cases of delinquency,
for such problems are thought to reveal the failure of the schools, not
of the individuals.

When problems occur, a homeroom teacher assumes a central
role in dealing with them. Tannin, the Japanese term for homeroom
teacher, may describe his or her expected role better than the role-
specific, American notion of homeroom teacher. They serve as
"pseudoparents," as phrased by one teacher, the overseers of the
classes assigned to them. Their roles as head of their groups are
diverse and include teaching, drilling, and counseling, as well as
many other functions. Tannin not only supervise their groups at
school; they also visit students' homes and summon their parents to
their offices if there are cases of dropping out or delinquency. They
are expected to protect their groups and assume responsibility for

problems faced by their students because they are members of their groups. This is a general cultural expectation applied to all rural, suburban, and urban schools, though there are variations in the pattern. Therefore, tannin exercise a great deal of influence over their students and their parents, who, in turn, rely on them for personal, familial, academic, and, above all, CEE problems.

A case in point was a senior student at Umigaoka who did not have enough credits to graduate in 1977. Her tannin pleaded that she be permitted to graduate, for failure to do so that year might become a social stigma that she would bear for a long time. He insisted that the faculty treat her with ninjo (see Chapter 2); furthermore, he did not want to see any failure in his group. This problem was discussed until 9:00 P.M. at two faculty meetings. Half of the faculty supported him, and the other half opposed. Finally, the principal, baffled by the deadlock, presented a compromise plan: the student would retake the final examinations and be permitted to graduate if she passed them. Subsequently, it was reported, she did graduate that year.

The diffused role of tannin and this particular incident reflect the Japanese group orientation and pattern of adaptation. Once one is admitted to a competitive high school, such as Umigaoka, through entrance examinations, graduation is almost guaranteed, regardless of performance. Hence, the most crucial matter is to gain access to the school, to a group.

FURŌ HIGH SCHOOL

The two high schools considered above differ remarkably in student population, history, and socialization. One is a new school with a heavy emphasis on rigid socialization oriented toward the CEE—a school attempting to catch up with traditional high schools in Nagoya. The other is an "elite" school, the concerted efforts of which are to place its graduates in prestigious universities.

"Furō" differs yet again from the two schools described above. It is a national school having a smaller enrollment, about 400 students, attached to the Faculty of Education at Nagoya University. It became an attached high school (often called Fuzoku) in 1952, though its history began long before that date as one of 17 high schools affiliated with national universities in the nation.

The statement of Furō's purposes reads as follows:
While this school offers high school education in harmony with the mental and physical development of students, it aims to conduct and test studies on educational theories and practice within the framework of educa-

tional policies of the Faculty of Education, Nagoya University, and, additionally, to provide students of Nagoya University with opportunities for practice teaching. . . . To be more concrete, it intends to promote a growth of personality with individuality and rich mind.

Genuine and Spurious Purposes

Unlike Saigō and Umigaoka, this school does not provide students with intensive drilling for the CEE. According to Furō's faculty members and as indicated in the above statement, it is intended to be an "experimental school" where research and experiments are to be conducted; therefore, it should have a heterogeneous student population. Students admitted to Furō are of two kinds: graduates of Furō Middle School, which is also attached to Nagoya University, and graduates of other middle schools. Most of Furō Middle School's graduates are automatically admitted to the high school, though they are formally required to take the entrance tests. Applicants from other schools are chosen by lottery and are then screened further by elementary tests. Graduates of Furō Middle School constitute two-thirds of the total enrollment of Furō High School; they had been admitted to the middle school by means of a lottery. Furō's students display a wide range of academic performance. The socioeconomic background of the school is largely middle class. It is situated within the central campus of Nagoya University, one of the more prestigious universities in the nation. Nearly all Furō graduates advance to college in one way or another. Since it is attached to a top national university, there is some, if not very genuine, sense of pride exhibited to the outsider on the part of the Furō faculty, who have formal relations with the faculty of the university. (After all, Furō's principal is elected from the members of the Faculty of Education by the Furō faculty.)

The status of an attached national school is peculiar; for example, since it is under the control of the Ministry of Education, it is not directly subjected to immediate local pressures of the kind exerted on prefectural high schools. Because of the prestige of the universities with which national schools are affiliated, they can attract competent teachers. Therefore, some faculties have elected to make their schools less examination oriented, as in the case of the attached schools of Nagoya and Tokyo Universities. In many other cases, however, national schools have ignored their explicit, official purposes and have become highly selective and ferociously competitive CEE-oriented schools. High schools attached to Tokyo Kyōiku and Tokyo Gakugei universities are the best examples.

The high school of Tokyo Kyōiku at Komaba, for example, placed 123 students, excluding rōnin, out of a total of about 160 seniors in Tokyo University in 1975. Its students are recruited first for the lower secondary level from all over metropolitan Tokyo. One out of eleven ambitious and most rigorously drilled sixth graders can pass the entrance examinations. Once admitted, they can automatically advance to the upper secondary level, to which about 40 outside students are also admitted through equally competitive entrance examinations. From the kindergarten level, these sixth graders have been infused with the singular goal of passing the entrance examinations. Despite such an elitist orientation, the school's statement of purpose is very little different from the Furō statement. Its vice-principal appears to have more influence on its education than the "absentee" principal, a professor of the university. He spoke proudly of its education, whereas an art teacher interviewed at the school was highly critical of the "distorted" socialization at the school, an obsession with Tokyo University, and the drilling of students on examination subjects. An overwhelming majority of parents, according to the teacher, are concerned only with their children's test scores.

Furō could have become such a selective school had it screened its applicants through highly competitive entrance examinations. In the past there were opportunities to transform it into an exclusive high school. The last occasion was the year the gakkōgun system came into effect. Faced with the contingencies and unpredictability of the new system, middle schoolteachers had guided top ninth-grade students to apply to Furō and the aforementioned Tōkai High School. Consequently, Furō received very able students although they were chosen by lottery and simple entrance tests. In the following year, however, middle school teachers elected not to place their top graduates in Furō, as it became apparent to them that Furō was much less rigorous than the prefectural schools bound by the gakkōgun system; it was devaluated in the academic "exchange market."

The head teacher of Furō is bitterly critical of "market-oriented" middle school teachers and their exclusive emphasis on three examination subjects—English, mathematics, and Japanese—at the expense of the others. In Aichi Prefecture, the students applying to prefectural high schools are tested on these three subjects. Combined with the test scores, school reports are considered for admission. The consequences, according to him, are grave, since students' competence in the other areas is unduly neglected.

At Furō, which is relatively free from criticism against CEE-oriented schooling, every teacher interviewed spoke of the dominant pattern of Japanese schooling at the secondary level in terms of two concepts: tatemae and honne. These two terms were used most frequently in conferences, interviews, and informal conversations during the present research.

Tatemae refers to "formal," "overt," "explicit," "public," and "spurious," whereas honne refers to "actual," "covert," "implicit," "intended," and "private." These terms correspond to yoso and uchi worlds (see Chapter 2). Japanese more often than not behave and think in terms of a continuum comprising dichotomous polarities, such as tatemae and honne. These dichotomies are usually tolerated and often taken for granted. Just as yoso and uchi worlds are a function of the Japanese group orientation, tatemae and honne express two aspects of such an orientation. Outside a group its members represent its tatemae, its formal and spurious position, as in the case of the aforementioned national high school in Tokyo. Within a group, however, its members behave according to the actual, covert, honne level. Therefore, in looking at Japanese organizations, one needs to understand two distinct levels of institutional policies and activities. Although these dichotomous levels of behavior and perception are present, to some extent, in any society, they are distinctly recognized and accepted without a deep sense of contradiction and ambivalence in Japanese society. In other words, where the genuine is expressed, the spurious is always expected.

Furō's head teacher criticizes Japanese secondary schools for their education at the two levels, and this criticism can be applied to Saigō and Umigaoka as well. Saigō's statement of purpose is "to educate students so as to develop their own goals and study diligently." "Be witty, generous, and resolute" is the school motto. Meanwhile, Umigaoka's explicit aim is "to conduct a whole-person education [education aimed to foster the total, complete growth of an individual] according to the basic spirit articulated in the Japanese constitution and the fundamental law of education" and "to develop an individual's whole competence . . . in harmony with the entire society's pursuit of happiness and prosperity."

A manifestation of the contradiction between the two levels is further seen in the results of Furō's survey: 44 percent of the parents and 33 percent of the students at Furō supported an educational program that emphasized basic, scholastic competence and healthy personality growth, whereas only 11 percent of the two groups stressed schooling oriented toward the CEE. As a Furō social studies teacher stated, it is obvious that the former responses emphasize tatemae while the latter, honne. An English teacher at the school also paid special attention to what he called "the double structure of Japanese culture," seen in terms of tatemae and honne, as related to instruction for the CEE. To most Japanese students, he said, English is a relevant and important subject only because it is one of the subjects most stressed in the CEE. In fact, it is taught largely to meet examination requirements, not to build primary competence in its application; but this is not the formal purpose of teaching English. A

former physics teacher at Furō, who is now the principal of a prefectural high school outside Nagoya, suggested that to speak publicly
of drilling students for the CEE—at the expense of education delineated
in the Ministry of Education's manual of the course of study—is taboo.
Therefore, he admitted that his public speeches and comments are
made only at the tatemae level, though they are quite opposite to his
honne views.

Thus, Furō is constrained by the tatemae-honne dichotomy.
Whereas it is allegedly an experimental school with an emphasis on
research, there is little evidence that research is the focus of this
school. Based on comparative data, no significant difference is observed between Furō and the two other schools in terms of individual
teachers' research studies and any other kinds of projects. Commonly, each school publishes rather impressive monographs every year.
Besides, there is little evidence that the faculty members of Nagoya
University are actively involved in studies and experiments at Furō;
rather, the relationship between the faculties of the university and
Furō appears to be somewhat strained. In fact, one sees only limited
reciprocity between the two. Such relationships, it appears, also
constrain the role of the principal, chosen from the university faculty,
vis-à-vis the Furō faculty. Some teachers at Furō openly admitted
that Furō is not an experimental school, as publicly claimed, and alluded to the absence of reciprocity between the two faculties.

Meanwhile, Furō offers a comparatively relaxed environment
for its students, and instruction is not as exclusively geared to CEE
requirements as at Umigaoka and Saigō. This is a main source of
frustration and anxiety on the part of many students who must compete with their peers in other competitive schools to gain access to
universities of high standing. Top ninth grade students at Furō Middle School often contemplate applying to prefectural high schools, instead of advancing automatically to Furō High School. Interestingly,
teachers advise these students to consider this alternative, but, as
most students are not confident they can pass the entrance examinations, they eventually withdraw their plans. In many cases, their
parents are more anxious and pressure them to consider alternatives.

Given the above characterization of Furō, one can judge that,
as an institution, it responds neither to the tatemae expectation to be
an experimental school nor to honne pressures generated by parents
and students for CEE schooling. While Furō teachers insist that they
intend to offer "normal" high school education, they are concerned
with the lack of their commitment to either of the above expectations.
Its actual policies are diffuse, and Furō suffers from the resulting
ambivalence.

Precedence of CEE Preparation

The examination of students' perceptions of Furō and how they cope with CEE pressures reveals a common, real problem for nearly all Furō students who plan to attend college. Although none of the students interviewed supports the current CEE system, CEE preparation—in their view and in those of their parents—should take precedence over a high school education defined by some members of the Furō faculty and in the manual of the course of study issued by the Ministry of Education. They are caught between the honne and tatemae worlds—between the real and the ideal—and they face a dilemma resolved in favor of honne and the real.

The world in which high school students live requires them to sacrifice their pleasures, spontaneity, and sparkle for examination success. No senior students interviewed at Furō and the other two schools had opportunities to date or to go to movie theaters during the senior year, except probably once during the summer. A main reason is obviously that they have no time to spend on leisure. Though they are interested in such experiences and in the opposite sex, they must sublimate those interests until they enter college. A female senior discussed how much she was constrained by CEE pressures. She felt quite guilty when she stayed at school until late in the afternoon chatting with boys, or when she slept for more than seven hours even during the weekend. She was obsessed by feelings that she was wasting time and falling behind, and as a result her tension led to sporadic, nervous stomachaches. A male senior related his experience as well. Although he was able to work on drills for a sustained period of time, continuous concentration on study day after day was difficult even for him. Consequently, he often sat in contemplation, as in Zen meditation, for a while and washed his face with cold water; sometimes, he wrote poetry or sang aloud before returning to study. Feelings of guilt and anxiety were aroused when he could not solve drill problems or when he slept a whole night due to fatigue. Another student spoke of conflicts with his parents that surfaced from time to time as a result of their dissatisfaction with his slow CEE preparation. For example, he went home late every day for a week when he was preparing for a school festival. This irritated his mother and badly upset his father. He and his parents argued for hours. When the student insisted, "You should look at me as a person who needs occasional leisure and must grow, not as a boy studying just for the examinations," it fell on deaf ears. Study profiles of students, including both top and average ones, show that most of them are not very different from those obtained at the two other schools.

Yet Furō students commonly feel inferior to students in the prefectural schools in the city for at least two reasons. Since most students at Furō are not drilled for the high school entrance examinations, they lack a disciplined attitude toward the examinations and the tense atmosphere of the examination-taking experience. Besides, Furō does not prepare them sufficiently for the CEE. When they meet former classmates from the elementary schools and compare each other's high schools, they are often disappointed, for their counterparts are well advanced in their preparations for the CEE; they undergo a similar experience when they attend juku. In fact, their disappointment is supported by an objective reality: Few Furō graduates are admitted to Nagoya University despite the close attachment between the two institutions.

It is estimated that nearly 50 percent of the students at Furō either participate in short-term juku programs or attend juku regularly. Some of the reasons for attending juku are peculiar and should be noted. A bright junior student attends Kawai Juku every Sunday from 9:00 A. M. to 2:00 P. M. in order to get accustomed to the examinations and competitive atmosphere missing in Furō. She belongs to a select entrance examination group, as opposed to less competitive groups. In order to maintain her status in this group she must keep her test scores high. Tests in English, mathematics, and Japanese are provided by the juku. At every session, tests on these subjects are given for 50 minutes each and subsequently discussed. Test scores are later sent to her parents by mail. In addition to attending Kawai, she receives tutoring at home twice a week with her friends.

Many students at Furō appreciate the close, cooperative relations students have with each other in a relatively relaxed environment, unlike in the prefectural schools. They view their teachers as competent and friendly, but they are disturbed by the absence of competitiveness and rigorous socialization at the school. Like students, parents are critical of Furō for the same reason but accept the knowledge that their complaints would not change the Furō policies. The faculty, however, are not entirely insensitive to the honne world of students and parents. Instruction in major subjects in the senior year tends to be oriented toward CEE requirements. Faculty members admitted that teaching is influenced and even distorted by external demands. Yet even this is not enough for students and parents. In short, a clearly visible pattern of students' adaptation to Furō policies is that they do not depend on the school for drilling, but on their own study at home and juku, where they receive drilling, stimulation, and competition.

FUNCTIONS AND DYSFUNCTIONS
OF THE COLLEGE ENTRANCE EXAMINATIONS

To summarize our discussion of the three case studies, despite the differences among the three high schools, students invariably confront the externally imposed social and cultural pressures for the CEE. They follow differential patterns of socialization imposed upon them in one way or another, but they are conditioned by common examination pressures to develop similar motivational and cognitive orientations toward the CEE. Though these case studies reveal unique aspects of each school, various problems discussed in the studies can be generalized. They are universal problems that high school education and adolescents in Japan confront today. Given our analysis of schooling for the CEE in Chapter 4 and the three case studies in this chapter, we can now present further generalizations on the functions and dysfunctions of the CEE.

Social and Political Functions

The CEE serves as a major sorting device for social placement; it is a rite of passage required for adolescents at the age of 18 to secure future membership in certain groups via colleges. The permanent placement of individuals in given organizations provides those individuals with security and lasting social and personal identification. At the same time, the CEE contributes to the stability of Japanese society, which rests on social stratification by institutions rather than individuals. Despite the tensions it creates for adolescents, parents, and teachers, the CEE is an acceptable device, since it reinforces the Japanese cultural orientation with its emphasis on the group and provision for future group membership.

By implication, the CEE contributes to political stability. It determines, to a great extent, a narrowly defined motivational and cognitive framework within which adolescents' activities (learning) are legitimated. Such a framework is conducive to the development of students' conformity in motivational and cognitive activities. From the viewpoint of controlling people within a given political system, conformity is a crucial factor since it fosters a convergent and cohesive force. Hence, one of the chief reasons for the perpetuation of the CEE may be that it serves, indirectly or covertly, the needs of the Japanese political system. In fact, the CEE has never become a major, controversial political issue in the postwar era, even though the cyclical tension it generates every year is one of the main sources of anxiety in Japanese life. Individuals are expected to deny their divergent needs and interests and to be diligent and obedient, clinging to the hope that self-sacrifice will be rewarded when they gain access to colleges. Since the demand for self-sacrifice is imposed upon adolescents during their crucial, formative years (between the ages of 13 and 18), its effect is great; during these years adolescents internalize the cultural, technical, and economic ideology of Japanese society.

Intensive drilling contributes to the inculcation of basic knowledge at both the elementary and secondary school levels. Japanese students are diligent and disciplined.

The CEE has created social conditions for (1) the mushrooming of tutoring and preparatory services that provide thousands upon thousands of school teachers, retired teachers, and college students with opportunities for part-time employment and a significant source of supplementary income and (2) the development of private profit-oriented educational institutions (juku) and industries that have made millions of children the consumers of their services—drilling, drill books, exercise examinations, and magazines.

The CEE places a high value on achievement. It promotes adolescents' orientations toward achievement, although that orientation recedes after they gain access to universities and is blended with an ascriptive orientation of organizations when they gain membership in them.

Dysfunctions

Japanese secondary education suffers from a dualism of educational purposes. While overt purposes of education stated in the manual of the courses of study, the official guidebook issued by the Ministry of Education, emphasize each student's personal, social, and intellectual maturity, actual curricula and teaching are designed to respond to the requirements of the entrance examinations. Similarly, extracurricular activities are subjected to such requirements. Hence, in the actual processes of schooling, little attention is given to students' needs at their current levels of maturity. Students are more interested in examination techniques than in substantive learning and growth. The emphasis on conformity in motivational and cognitive orientations, required by the entrance examinations, suffocates students' potential creativity and diversity of interest—that is, development of their individuality.

Contrary to the assumption that the CEE provides all adolescents with a fair opportunity for open competition based upon the criterion of achievement, the CEE gives undue advantage to students who have received intensive and costly drilling in taking examinations. Therefore, it discriminates against the economically disadvantaged.

The CEE does not uncover latent abilities of adolescents—particularly the disadvantaged and those who are not adept in taking examinations—that may be stimulated and developed later. Hence, it is an arbitrary device for social placement, rather than a pedagogical instrument.

Coupled with the above point is the rigidity of the Japanese social structure, which does not allow horizontal mobility. This is a pattern of mobility that does not encourage individuals to seek work opportunities that contribute to the maximal development of individual potentials. The CEE amounts to an institutional expression of the inflexible social structure and, thus, reinforces it by serving as a central mechanism for determining adolescents' future memberships in work organizations via colleges.

The CEE requires undue sacrifices for adolescents and their families. Students are expected to regard diverse interests and activities as illegitimate. Their legitimate activities must be centered around the requirements of the entrance examinations. They are subjected to drilling and passive absorption of knowledge at school and juku day and night. Families of college-bound adolescents often organize their activities to fit the examination-centered needs of children, at the cost of other members' interests and needs. In particular, the economic cost for rōnin children, drilling, and attendance at juku constitute a large amount of family expenditures.

AN ALTERNATIVE: OLD WINE IN A NEW BOTTLE

In order to ameliorate distortions resulting from the college entrance examinations, in 1971 the Association of National Universities and Colleges (Kokudaikyō), an organization of the presidents of the national institutions of higher education, proposed an alternative approach to the conventional CEE. Its original proposal outlined two-step entrance examinations to be taken primarily by applicants for the national institutions (excluding applicants for 305 private colleges). Subsequently, an ad hoc committee was constituted to design a new structure and new procedures for entrance examinations. Based on its recommendations, which were endorsed by the Ministry of Education, the Association decided to implement the two-step examinations beginning in 1979.

Unlike the current CEE prepared by each institution, the first examination will be prepared and administered by the College Entrance Examination Center, operated under the supervision of the association, for all national universities and colleges as well as for other publicly controlled colleges interested in participating in the uniform examination. The examination will cover all seven major subjects, and will try to evaluate the high school achievement level of applicants. The second entrance examination will be prepared by each institution, and will be designed to select applicants on the basis of their test performance. Depending upon colleges, the number of subjects will range generally from two to four, and interviews with applicants will also be conducted.

It is claimed that the two-step examinations will provide applicants with opportunities to be tested twice instead of once, as in the current practice, and to be evaluated comprehensively. According to the association, these entrance examinations will lead to a fair selection of applicants and, hence, to the "normalization" of high school education. The association assumes that the results of those two examinations will be used by colleges to decide admission. Yet, a recent survey indicates that 60 percent of the institutions participating in the first common examination are planning to use its results to screen applicants eligible for the second examination, rather than to obtain data on the high school achievement level of applicants for the purpose of deciding admission.[1]

In the view of the association, the two-step approach represents an improvement over the current CEE, but high schools are reluctant to admit such improvement. To begin with, the views of high schools are hardly reflected in the association's decision to implement the two-step examinations, since high schools have never been invited to take part in shaping them. High schools all over Japan were briefed on it, but were never encouraged to present counterproposals. In this respect, high schools view the two-step approach as an arbitrary imposition upon them. Second, they fear that this approach would impose a double burden upon high school students, since they must prepare for two types of entrance examinations to gain admission to national universities. The National Association of High School Principals, prefectural associations of high school principals, and high school guidance teachers have frequently issued protests over the implementation of the two-step approach. They have requested that the second examination be eliminated and, instead, that high school reports be used. They have charged that Japanese universities and colleges are self-serving and insensitive to the "infernal" examination pressures imposed upon adolescents and the distortions of high school education they have created. Third, since the two-step examinations do not involve private institutions, it is argued that the lack of uniformity in entrance examinations will make it difficult for high school students to prepare for them. Nonetheless, the dates for the two-step examinations are firmly set, and high schools have no alternative but to acquiesce.

The nōken test, somewhat similar to the first examination, was given to college applicants on a nationwide basis from 1963 to 1968.

It was proposed by the Central Council of Education, an agency advisory to the Ministry of Education, and a governmental corporation was subsequently created to implement it. It was short-lived, however, for universities and colleges did not use it fully, and they eventually ignored it.

Japanese universities and colleges generally insist on their exclusive right to screen applicants by the examinations and criteria they establish individually—a territorial right to determine membership. They deny, by and large, the reliability of the high school reports of applicants, as mentioned earlier, with the claim that these reports lack objectivity. Once applicants gain admission to college through rigorous examinations, however, they are treated inclusively as members of groups immune to competition and rigorous, objective evaluation. The characteristics of the Japanese group referred to earlier are, without exception, attributable to Japanese academic institutions. Critical screening is required when group membership is extended to new members. Therefore, student transfers from one college to another are very difficult and rare. Again, this phenomenon reflects the rigidity of the Japanese social structure when horizontal mobility between different social organizations is limited. Given these backgrounds, the success of the two-step examinations is quite uncertain.

CONCLUSION

It should be clear to the reader by now that the CEE is the most critical rite of passage for adolescents. It requires intense experience, self-denial, durability, the ability to accept psychological mutilation, and, above all, the resilience to accept a certain cognitive and motivational orientation to the society. In other words, it demands the highest degree of individual motivation to excel in a culturally prescribed frame of reference. One of the primary functions of the CEE is the sorting and stratifying of individuals—a vital and final phase in the process of adolescent socialization.

The CEE is only one of the many problems of Japanese education. Yet, since it has such an enormous effect upon education at the secondary and even elementary levels, as well as upon the process of socialization outside, its critical analysis can shed light upon the general orientation and policy of Japanese education. The CEE has been a central focus of Japanese education for years, and an understanding of it is most crucial if education and socialization in Japan are to be fully appreciated.

It is argued, too, that the CEE can be better understood in the framework of Japanese adaptation, a theme that has rarely been dealt with in current literature and research. The CEE is an expression that the group takes precedence over the individual; in other words, the sacrifice or socialization one undergoes because of the CEE is taken for granted by the group. Hence, all are motivated to accept whatever requirements are imposed upon them. The exclusiveness of a group vis-à-vis other groups leads to an emphasis on the most careful selection of new members.

Given the cultural orientation of the Japanese, one may wonder if there are effective alternatives. The current CEE may be superseded by another set of admissions (that is, membership) requirements; but in the view of most researchers such requirements would likely be just as rigid as the CEE.

NOTE

1. Asahi Shinbun (Asahi daily newspaper), May 3, 1977.

6

THE IMPACT OF
ECONOMIC FORCES ON
EDUCATION

In Chapter 3, we discussed the functions and evolution of Japanese education, noting particularly the pattern of adaptation. In Chapters 4 and 5, we considered how the cultural and sociological imperatives of Japanese society have defined contemporary socialization preparatory for the college entrance examinations. This chapter focuses upon the 1960s and explores the economic forces that have shaped educational policies.

Throughout the history of Japanese education, the state has used education as a political and economic instrument. This notion of schooling generally applied in the Meiji era, as well as to the prewar and postwar periods. In other words, the major functions of schooling are defined by the political and economic imperatives of the state, but the manner in which they are shaped is culturally prescribed. The general pattern of Japanese adaptation has served as an overall framework within which education functions. This was clearly seen early in the Meiji and postwar periods.

To review the early postwar period briefly, it was the Korean War, begun in 1950, and Japanese independence in 1951 that together served as a radical turning point in Japanese educational policies. Reference was made to the legislative measure of 1954 on the political neutrality of compulsory education; the school board law of 1956; the curricular revision of social studies, in which the inclusion of moral education had a special political significance; and the announcement of the comprehensive curricular revision at the elementary and secondary school levels. Plans for these measures and curricular changes had been initiated and debated several years prior to the dates they became officially effective. The Korean War and Japanese independence had both direct and immediate impacts upon those changes. In short, education was promptly accommodated to the political climate of the 1950s.

The focus of education in the late 1950s and 1960s, however, changed toward the training of the human resources required by the expanding economy and emerging industrial structure; the state and industries looked to education as a way to meet new challenges. As mentioned earlier, the Japanese economy had regained its prewar level by 1955 and, thereafter, underwent an unprecedented, continuous expansion through the 1960s. During that period, the economic demands of industry significantly determined educational policies. Throughout the period the private economic and public political systems fused, enabling the state to undertake policies that directly enhanced the development of corporate institutions and, subsequently, corporate profits. Describing another context, J. K. Galbraith speaks to the Japanese situation:

> The industrial system, in fact, is inextricably associated with the state. In notable respects the nature corporation is an arm of the state. And the state, in important matters, is an instrument of the industrial system.[1]

CORPORATE POLICY RECOMMENDATIONS

This chapter examines the influence of private industry on the development of educational policy, and the collaboration between the state and the growing capitalist system of Japan. In so doing, particular attention is given to the educational recommendations that originated with industrial and government advisory agencies.

The most influential agency, representing major economic organizations in Japan, is the Federation of Employers Association (Nikkeiren), the major role of which is to coordinate business strategy in labor-management relations. Another agency, the Committee for Economic Development (Keizai Dōyūkai), functions to stimulate business thinking and to incorporate it into the planning of high economic strategy. These two corporate agencies, which periodically recommend educational policy, are vital business organizations; along with the Federation of Economic Organization (Keidanren), they constitute a powerful private body that represents the unified voice of Japanese business and collaborates with the government in developing major business strategies.

The most significant of the governmental counterparts is the Central Council of Education (Chūkyōshin), which was originally organized in 1953 and is a permanent advisory body to the minister of Education. Its role is to make recommendations to the minister on vital educational policies, including legislative measures, curricular revision, and similar policy matters. Its members are appointed by the minister to whose influence they are likely to be amenable. In fact, members of the Japan Teachers Union and other academic associations that are critical of government policy have never been appointed to the Central Council. Therefore, although it is a highly influential agency, it does not represent a wide spectrum of educational views. Another body that makes periodic recommendations to the government is the Economic Council (Kaizai Shingikai), which reflects corporate interests.

Early Recommendations

In the 1950s the Federation of Employers Association (FEA) made several recommendations to the ministry. As early as 1952, shortly after independence, it submitted to the government a memorandum in which the FEA expressed a highly critical view of the postwar educational system implemented just a few years earlier.

> In the new educational system which started after the war, there were fundamental and sweeping reforms of the nation's traditional educational structure, content, and methods. But since these reforms were performed hastily and even without preparation for them, and, furthermore, ignored our nation's circumstances, recently there are a number of criticisms against various failures resulting from the new system. Looking at the future of the nation, we, the employers, feel urgency for reconsidering the system. [2]

While this reflected a resurgence of the pattern of Japanese adaptation, FEA was particularly critical of high school education, with its emphasis on common academic studies and citizenship, and of the general curriculum required at the college level. It urged the Ministry of Education to increase the number of vocational high schools and to revise high school curricula to reflect the needs of the industries. At the same time, it urged a "fundamental" review of postwar higher education to improve studies in special fields that had direct relevance in industry.

In 1954 FEA issued another recommendation intended to reinforce its earlier memorandum. [3] It criticized contemporary education for being incongruent with the demands of industry and reminded the Ministry of Education of the need for increased training in engineering and science at the college level and for the differentiation of higher education. It also proposed new technical schools: five-year technical colleges fusing vocational high schools and two-year colleges and six-year vocational high schools composed of middle vocational high school training. The report characterized the technical colleges as crucial to training the middle-range experts and labor needed in industry.

In 1956, FEA issued another statement and although its recommendations were not new—being simply restatements of FEA's earlier position—they were couched in a new international context.[4] By 1956, business strategists had begun to see Japanese industries not in terms of domestic economic reconstruction, but rather as a means for industrial and economic expansion into a wider international sphere of competition, and, to this purpose, Japanese industries were urging the government to provide more trained labor in specialized fields:

> Recent scientific and technological progress in advanced nations is phenomenal. In preparation for the second industrial revolution involving remarkable developments of nuclear and electronic industries and other technological fields, each nation is systematically training engineers and experts with a sense of urgency. . . . If Japan does not develop systematic training of engineers and experts in the midst of its epoch-making economic growth in order to attain further progress in industrial technology, our industrial technology will lag day by day far behind the international level. This will result in our failure in competition with other nations.[5]

Thus, FEA anticipated greater demands for skilled human resources in industry in order to continue national economic development, as well as to involve the country in the development of Southeast Asia. This was a new vision that Japanese industries entertained of their international economic role.

In response to FEA's repeated demands for improvement and expansion of training in science and engineering, in 1957 the Central Council of Education issued a series of recommendations titled "On Policies to Promote Education in Science and Engineering."[6] Its preface was similar, if not identical, in intent to the FEA's, emphasizing Japanese industry's initiative in the world market and the promotion of international competition. The statement stressed more rigorous and extensive training of students and an improvement of competence in science and mathematics at the college level. It also urged a greater degree of collaboration between academic institutions and private industries and recommended the establishment of five-year technical colleges, as the FEA had proposed. With respect to secondary and elementary education, the document called for more systematic and thorough instruction, particularly in mathematics, science, and Japanese.

In turn, in order to reinforce the Central Council's recommendations, FEA issued yet another statement. [7] One notable suggestion
was that the 6-3-3, single educational system be abolished and replaced by a dual system, similar to the prewar structure, in which
vocational and academic students would be separated into different
tracks from the beginning of middle school through high school. In
FEA's view, this system would be more efficient and would better
promote the development of individual aptitude. This recommendation
is especially significant, for it shows FEA crudely pressing for an
education that was rather one-sidedly suited to economic and industrial efficiency. FEA's new educational vision was further articulated
in 1960, in its brief statement on the establishment of technical colleges. [8] In this statement, FEA maintained that the personnel structure of the corporate system was commonly pyramid-shaped. According to FEA, middle-range skilled resources were critically lacking
and must be supplied by technical colleges. The statement implied
that the entire educational system ought to be pyramidal, to reflect
the industrial structure, and that duality in an educational system is
efficient and rational.

The government's responses to pressures from private industries, the Central Council of Education, and other related groups resulted in three significant events. First, in late 1957, the Ministry
of Education announced a plan to expand programs in science and engineering. Second, it announced comprehensively revised curricula
for the elementary and middle schools in 1958 (see Chapter 3) and,
shortly after, for the high schools. Although in significant part a
cultural reaction to U.S. education transplanted to Japan, the curricular revisions were also a patent and positive response to the economic and political pressures to rebuild the curricula to augment Japan's response to the emerging and potential economic and political
imperatives on both the domestic and the international scenes. Third,
the higher technical school (kōtō senmongakkō) was finally established
in 1962, after being delayed by repeated legislative failures of the
government. The higher technical schools were five-year schools,
composed of training equivalent to the high school and two-year college levels, and independent of those schools. Thus, a partial dual
system became a reality in response to FEA's demands. Although
the government originally intended that the new technical schools
would replace the two-year colleges, relentless opposition by groups
who supported the continuance of the colleges caused the abandonment
of that plan. In 1975 the number of higher technical schools reached
65, most of which were financed by the government. Probably, nothing better elucidates Galbraith's general observation, cited earlier,
than the establishment of Japan's higher technical schools.

Meanwhile, private industries were not merely concerned with
"manpower" training and other economic imperatives; they also faced

the issue of political stability. The political situation from the late 1950s through 1961 was characterized by a mounting crisis as a result of a continual confrontation between the Kishi conservative government, which attempted to ratify the Treaty of Mutual Security and Cooperation with the United States, and the nationwide, unified forces that obstructed the ratification. The confrontation led, in 1960, to political chaos, the resignation of the Kishi cabinet, and the assassination of Inejirō Asanuma, head of the Japan Socialist party, by an ultranationalist fanatic.

At that time, the Committee for Economic Development (CED) called for stronger cooperation between academic institutions and industry:

> The economic sector [the private industries] has promoted cooperation between academic institutions and industries in order to facilitate the modernization of management and technology. The Committee for Economic Development regards as serious the recent student protest movement at the national Diet and elsewhere and believes that it is urgent for the economic sector to endeavor to attract students to the capitalist camp on the basis of a continual effort for the cooperation. For this purpose, we are making a concrete plan to review it in a broad perspective including the political dimension.
>
> Thus far the economic sector has regarded cooperation between academic institutions and industries as a way of promoting technical and management education to produce successors of the industries. . . . One of the reasons why the committee views the cooperation from a broad perspective is the following. . . . In order to develop a healthy democracy, the middle stratum [of the nation] with good intelligence must grow as a stabilizing social force. Particularly, the student bracket is expected to grow as the nucleus of the middle stratum. [9]

CED's position was especially significant because it regarded cooperation between the two spheres both economically and politically and believed that such cooperation would necessarily have a positive political effect upon the private industries as well as on the political order of the society. Furthermore, its view implies that capitalism and democracy are equivalent.

Recommendations in the 1960s

The 1960s were characterized by a phenomenal expansion of the Japanese economy, which had an enormous domestic and international

impact. Personal income was doubling every seven years, and growing Japanese industry required more and more skilled human resources. In fact, Japan had become one of the leading trading nations
in the world, and its efficient adaptation to the world economy became
more urgent. Consequently, both private industries and the government demanded even more of the schools.

Let us first examine the implications of a policy to double personal income—the central political and economic strategy employed
by the government in the 1960s—noting particularly the "Report on
the Long-Range Educational Plan Oriented toward the Doubling of Income," prepared by the Economic Council. [10] The government's plan
to double income had already been initiated by the Kishi cabinet in
1959, but had stalled in the political crisis that arose over the security treaty. Following the collapse of the Kishi administration in late
1960, the Ikeda cabinet took a decisive step in launching a policy to
double income within a decade.

The tone of the introduction to the council's report was similar
to the one in FEA's earlier recommendations. The report itself,
however, described technological evolution as an immediate problem
to be dealt with through "the educational training to develop human
competence"; it urged an increase of specialists in engineering and
science, as well as related experts, and, at the same time, a retraining of employees. The council was optimistic about the income
policy in view of the fact that Japan's economic growth in 1959 had
been 16 percent.

In order to accomplish its goals, the council estimated broad
changes in the labor force in various categories of work organizations.
Taking the 1956–58 level of the labor force as the base line, the council estimated that by 1970 human resources in secondary and tertiary
industries would increase by 56 and 42 percent, respectively, while
human resources in primary industries would decrease by 30 percent.
Those changes required an increase in employable labor by 70 percent. The council also estimated that personal income would increase
270 percent by 1970.

Such drastic changes in the Japanese economy, the council insisted, would require extending upper secondary education to most
adolescents, shaping the motivational and cognitive orientations of
adolescents toward a complex society through upper secondary education, and training talented human resources to compete economically in the international domain. The report maintained that "economic competition among nations is a technical competition, and technical competition has become an educational competition." Notice
that the term competition was often used to characterize Japan's
emerging position. This was an indication that business strategists
were taking a more aggressive stance vis-à-vis other nations in the
economic domain and that they viewed education as a powerful instru-

ment for competition. They were concerned with training adolescents and youth not only in the secondary schools and colleges but also in the various vocational schools that operated outside that system.

The council emphasized the following four conditions to achieve the income plan: first, there would be a complete liberalization of international trade; second, Japan's ability to compete internationally would be strengthened; third, Japan would achieve full employment; and fourth, Japan would not lag behind international technological development. Those conditions would demand a new industrial structure requiring by 1970 an increase of 70,000 college-trained engineers and 440,000 technicians, to be provided by vocational high schools, and a vocational retraining of 1,600,000 employees for particular skills. Simultaneously, the council urged an expansion of teacher training, particularly in science and engineering, to meet such demands.

Subsequently, the major features of the council's report were incorporated into the Ikeda cabinet's economic policy. [11] Because of the new economic policy, labor shortages had already become a common problem by the early 1960s; industries could hardly wait for high school and college students to graduate and take jobs. When the industries were facing such a problem, the council submitted at the government's request recommendations concerning a policy on "human competence," in which it presented a positive view of the extension of high school and college education to a greater number of youth.

> In prewar Japan, it was a national task to train only leadership resources in politics, economy, science, engineering and other fields in order to increase rapidly national strength comparable to the level of the advanced nations. Hence higher and middle education was characterized as elite education. . . . But the postwar educational reforms and complexity of social phenomena changed the meaning of educational credentials. As compared with 15 percent [of the eligible population] advancing to the prewar middle school, recently 60 percent have attended high school and more than 70 percent are expected to attent it by 1970. Secondary education is no longer for a small portion of people but for the masses. With respect to college, while there were only less than 50 institutions in 1939, its recent numbers reached 250 (excluding two-year colleges), and 10 percent [of the eligible youth] attend college. The overemphasis on [elitism] attained through schooling has virtually changed. [12]

The council saw this trend as most conducive to the government's plan and even suggested that the practice of lifetime employment was out of date in the face of labor shortages.

Those changing social conditions, the council pointed out, required a new system of criteria to evaluate and employ individuals; in short, "In both education and society, achievement [merit] must be thoroughly emphasized." Thereafter, such phrases as "achievement orientation" and "human competence" were frequently used in education, business, and politics in the 1960s; they became popular concepts to evaluate the effectiveness of education. Additionally, an emphasis on developing skilled "manpower" was introduced.

As a part of the thorough emphasis on achievement orientation in education, a problem has risen in relation to the training of highly talented manpower. Here highly talented manpower refers to human competence that can play a leading role in various fields concerned with the economy and promote economic development. Despite the fact that education is well developed, there is no sufficient readiness to train these talented human resources and to offer unique educational programs. But a dynamic age of technological innovation requires human resources of high competence such as scientists and engineers who can introduce technological advancement, innovative managers who can open a new market with new technology, and labor-management leaders who can effectively deal with complex labor relations. An awareness of the need for highly talented resources should be developed on the part of the schools and the society as a whole. [13]

Note here the strong bias of the Economic Council toward the private industries. The council defined human competence in purely economic terms; it also referred to technology and science also from a merely economic point of view. What is even more significant, however, is that the government, as well as the Ministry of Education, accepted the council's definitions and views, in terms of which they modified the orientations of schooling. For example, in 1968-70 the second comprehensive curricular revisions at the elementary and secondary levels reflected the council's views; and the Central Council of Education also supported this position.

Following the Economic Council's recommendations, the Central Council of Education submitted its own recommendations in 1965, in response to a request by the minister of education, regarding the expansion of upper secondary education. In essence, the Central Council's recommendations represented nothing more than those made by the Economic Council. The Central Council, however, defined the purpose of education a little more broadly.

>Needless to say, education aims to form complete per-
sonality, and personality itself is an essential value that
integrates human beings' various innate personal qualities
and learned ability. In other words, the purpose of education is not only to develop human competence required
for the state but also to foster human beings, the essential elements that constitute the state. [14]

Then, the Central Council turned to the major problems that Japanese
would face in the immediate future:

>(1) How can individuals relate [shutaisei] themselves to
a society where technological innovation is rapidly
evolving?
>(2) How can they as Japanese cope with international
tension, given a peculiar Japanese position?
>(3) What efforts are they required to make in view of
present Japanese democracy? [15]

Although these problems are worded rather vaguely, it is apparent
that the Central Council saw the technological and economic problems
as paramount. The second problem seems to suggest, at least in
part, the international competition often referred to by the Economic
Council and FEA. Finally, the Central Council mentioned, although
ambiguously, the problem of democracy. Moreover, an emphasis on
human competence and talented resources led to the need for differentiation in curricula, as stressed by the Central Council of Education
the Economic Council, and FEA. Later we will discuss the implications of their stress on curricular upgrading with regard to these three
aspects, that is, human competence, talented resources, and differentiation.

In the meantime, the Central Council of Education made yet other
recommendations in "The Ideal Japanese." Addressing directly the
problem of Japanese adaptation to the spheres of economic and political pressures, the recommendations contained a significant political
implication. [16] In the face of a breathtaking transformation in the pattern of social organizations, an acceleration of mobility, rapid urbanization, and periodic political instability on the domestic scene,
the government required that a stable pattern of cognitive and motivational orientations be internalized on the part of the preadult Japanese. The government's concern was explicit in the Central Council's recommendations.

The Central Council pointed out that the drastic changes imposed
on the political, economic, educational, and social aspects of life in
the postwar period repudiated the Japanese tradition in favor of ab-

stract, foreign ideals and that they ignored Japanese history and national character; Japanese defeat, the Central Council asserted, gave the Japanese a false impression that their institutions and ideologies were totally wrong. In a word, Japanese culture was repudiated. Admitting Japanese extremism in the past, the Central Council held that ethnicity and uniqueness would have to be appreciated fully; given such an appreciation, according to the Central Council, the notion of the ideal Japanese could become fully meaningful. It also maintained that the Japanese must keep abreast of the world and cope with international economic and political problems, although such an adaptation would require maintaining a special awareness of themselves as Japanese.

To be more concrete, the Japanese would have to appreciate their nation and be loyal to it; that is, patriotism is an urgent issue. In the words of the Central Council:

> Today there are no individuals and ethnic groups in the
> world that do not constitute or belong to nations. The
> state is most organic and the strongest collectivity in
> the world. Individual happiness and security largely
> depend upon the state. It is commonly the state that con-
> tributes to the development of world mankind. To love
> the state rightfully is to be loyal to the state. In other
> words, proper patriotism leads to the love of mankind. [17]

While the object of national loyalty is Japan, according to the Central Council, it is also the emperor, the symbol of national integration. Therefore, the council stated, "It is logically natural that to love Japan is to love the Japanese symbol."

Coupled with the internal sphere of adaptation is the external aspect of Japanese accommodation. The Central Council repeatedly emphasized the development of human competence in order to accommodate the dynamics of international economy. The significance of the report on the ideal Japanese lies in its implication that the conservative government should attempt to strengthen national integration and promote effective economic expansion and competition through traditional institutions and ideology. It goes without saying that this is a reflection of the traditional pattern of adaptation par excellence.

Subsequently, all these repeated recommendations for curricular improvement and the development of a national awareness resulted in the second postwar set of sweeping changes in the elementary and secondary school curriculum. The second revision had a twofold purpose. First, it attempted to upgrade the courses of study, with particular emphasis on mathematics, natural science, and Japanese, and it allowed for a greater degree of differentiation. As a result, the number of instructional hours for those subjects increased; for example, at the middle school level, two additional instructional hours were required per week. At the high school level, "talented" students interested in a mathematics/natural science track were given special attention, whereas an engineering track was created as a primary priority at the vocational high school level. Second, the revision emphasized the notion of the ideal Japanese. This was clearly reflected in social studies curricula at all levels, which particularly emphasized the responsibility of each Japanese to the state.[18] Therefore, many previous recommendations partially, if not entirely, culminated in the curricular revision and the reorientation of schooling at the elementary and secondary school levels.

Otherwise, the demand of the private industries for more educated human resources was met by an increased number of high school graduates. High school students increased by one-third between 1960 and 1970. The percentage of the eligible population attending high school rose from 57.7 percent in 1960 to 64.0 in 1962, 70.7 in 1965, 75.4 in 1967, and 82.1 in 1970. As the government's original target for 1970 was 70 percent, the growth of secondary schooling was far ahead of expectations. Of a total of 4,231,542 high school students, one-third were attending private schools in 1970. At the level of higher education, the percentage of the eligible population attending four- and two-year colleges also rose from 10.3 percent in 1960 to 17.1 in 1965, and to 24.0 in 1970. The number of students in institutions of higher education increased dramatically from 711,618 (142,491 women) in 1960 to 1,715,042 (472,074 women) in 1970—a rapid rise of student enrollment by 241 percent. Seventy-five percent of all college students were enrolled in private institutions in 1970.[19] The expansion of college enrollment had also exceeded the government's expectation.

Both the government and private industries were content with the extension of upper secondary and college education to a greater number of Japanese and the subsequent increase of human resources, but they still confronted a shortage of skilled resources in science and engineering, on the one hand, and widespread student unrest all over the nation, on the other.

Because skilled labor continued to be in short supply in the last half of the 1960s, Japanese private industry pleaded for liberalized attitudes toward college education and employment practices, the amelioration of the bias against educational credentials obtained at less prestigious colleges, and the uniformity of higher education in Japan. Their plea was pragmatic and even opportunistic because only such a liberalization would offer them a greater supply of human resources. They were deeply concerned with student activism, too, since needed resources could not be efficiently channeled into the industrial organizations while activism was rampant. Despite the conservative nature of private industries, they were highly critical of the traditional structure of university governance and the hierarchical structure of social relations at academic institutions, which were partially to blame for the widespread student protests. Representing the private industries, the CED published two important reports in 1968 and 1969.[20] They overlapped with each other to a degree, but the 1969 report was more comprehensive and included a number of recommendations.

In 1968 nationwide student protests against university authorities and government policies began to accelerate, stimulated by medical students at Tokyo University. The student protests at the university instantly spread all over the campus and led to the resignations of the university president, the board of trustees, and ten deans, as well as several medical professors, all in the same year. University buildings were occupied by the protesting students, and the university's normal academic and research operations were disrupted for months, including the suspension of the entrance examinations in 1969. Thus, the nation's most prestigious university became the center and the focal symbol of Japanese university students' disenchantment, frustrations, and demands for institutional reform. The protests continued through 1970, based upon students' opposition to the extension of the Treaty of Mutual Security and Cooperation with the United States; high school students also were involved in the protests.

In the meantime, the Japanese began to feel the effects of economic prosperity. Personal income had already doubled, and the consumption of goods became greater than ever. As Japan's GNP approached the level of West Germany, Japanese industries were expecting a further expansion of the domestic economy, as well as their international market.

It was against that social and economic background that the CED's reports were prepared; small wonder that they expressed the deep concern of private industries regarding the future of Japanese higher education. Simultaneously, the Economic Council issued related recommendations to the government in 1969, and the Japanese Association for Economic Development (Nippon Keizai Chōsa Kyōgikai), a private corporation, also published a report in 1972 that presented recommendations for improving education.

CED expressed its deep concern with campus unrest on the grounds that it could also disrupt private economic organizations. In its report, "A Higher Education System for an Advanced Welfare Society," it was more critical of the existing university structure as a primary cause of the campus unrest than of the protesting students in general. It characterized the Japanese university as a "closed system," in which the lifetime employment of professors, the "undemocratic" practice of promotion based on longevity, factionalism among professors, and an "arbitrary and self-serving faculty" perpetuated the system that has continually existed despite the transformation of higher education into mass education, the functions, purposes, and ideals of which are different from those of a traditional, closed university. (Note, incidentally, that the practice of employment and promotion referred to here is also the dominant pattern among large corporations!) In CED's view, such a system lacked vision and could not respond effectively to students' frustrations and demands for institutional change. The report stated that the understanding of students' frustrations and the ability to respond flexibly to their expectations were of the utmost importance. Above all, it gave special consideration to the importance of mobilizing youth's "energy and passion," not for a destruction of institutions but for active participation in the "advanced industrial system as its bearers." This, CED stated, is the reason why college students and their education require particular attention by private industries.

In the report, the CED presented its visions of future Japanese society and higher education. CED spoke of what it called an "advanced welfare society" that could be confused with a popular notion of a welfare state. In its definition, however, the term referred to the prosperity and welfare of an advanced industrial nation, a society not ruled by government bureaucrats, but open, with opportunities for freedom. Such a society, it declared, is more advanced than the monolithic, government-dominated state of the past and will evolve to fulfill human needs better. In essence, what CED advocated was an industrial social order in which initiatives for social and economic innovations will be taken by private industries, which will also control the mobilization of human resources. "The private corporations exposed to severe competition," it stressed, "are the source for [social] development, and a simple welfare society lacking such corporate power is the one that cannot test its own power and cannot challenge its future problems." The basis of CED's notion of the advanced welfare society lies in the assumption that Japan is the leading industrial nation in Asia, that it has earned the trust and confidence of the free world, and that it requires a more efficient mobilization of human resources in society. Although this notion refers to various social problems—such as poverty, medical care, and the welfare of each individual—it is undoubtedly misleading; but that is beside the point here.

Turning to the universities, CED urged them to come to grips with the reality of social and economic developments taking place in Japan, in order to redirect their activities to meet the challenges of the advanced industrial order. It reminded them of their need to reorient themselves within a cultural and historical framework indigenous to Japan. The reason for stressing cooperation between academic institutions and private industry, it continued, is that the former constitute a closed system that exists only for its academic sake and has failed to respond to contemporary problems.

CED's proposals to reform the universities are presented here selectively. First, in order that the universities might assume direct accountability to society, which has often been evaded—particularly by the national universities controlled by the Ministry of Education—all national universities should be reorganized as independent corporations, each having a board of governors. As corporations, each institution's accountability would be clearly defined so that its administration and faculty might be more responsive to social change. Second, CED proposed the establishment of a public trust to govern all universities and colleges in Japan, whereby distinctions among private, national, and other public institutions would be eliminated. Operating funds would be secured from both the public and private sectors. Under the trust, the enormous differential in academic qualities between the private and national institutions, and the existing hierarchy of universities, would be reduced. Third, to eliminate closed and self-serving faculties, lifetime employment would be replaced by contractual employment. Fourth, the CEE system would be changed promptly to reduce the problems resulting from it. CED proposed that, as an experiment, 50 percent of the applicants be evaluated for admission on the basis of high school reports, and the other half be selected by CEE. This would provide some data as to the feasibility of using high school reports for admissions in general.

Finally, CED proposed that the current 6-3-3-4 system be superseded by a 5-4-4-x system, x representing a period of years necessary for specialized training at the level of higher education. Schooling would start one year earlier than at present, and the proposed system would consist of five-year elementary school, four-year middle school, and four-year lower-level higher education, of which the last two years would be devoted to general education equivalent to the current general education at the college level. A major characteristic of the proposal is that, under the proposed system, there would be much more extensive and intensive specialized training at the upper level of higher education. Furthermore, every student would be promoted according to his or her level of achievement, unlike under the present system in which such promotion is impossible.

As noted earlier, private industries were critical of general education at the college level and failed to see its significance; CED's proposal assigned general education to the earlier years, leaving time in the college years to devote to vocational and specialized training. The proposal was a response to the persistent demand of private industries for increased specialized and practical studies immediately relevant to the roles to be allocated to prospective employees in economic organizations. Anticipating that higher education would soon become mass education, however, CED proposed a single-track system, unlike FEA, which had preferred a dual system.

CED's proposal for changing patterns of management and financing in higher education is noteworthy and meritorious from the viewpoints of both industries and the public. Its criticisms that the national universities notoriously lack accountability is worth giving attention to, and its proposal is constructive. Nevertheless, CED's central interest lies in efficient college education that can supply skilled human resources to industries.

In addition, one notable point in CED's 1968 report was its renewed demand for the training of more college students in the fields of science and engineering. Its demand was justifiable in view of the fact that only 24 percent of the total college student population were in these fields in 1970. This percentage, however, represented a slight improvement over the 18 percent that had been obtained in 1960.

Turning briefly to the Economic Council's recommendations of 1969, their central emphasis was again on collaboration between economic and academic institutions.[21] The council pointed to the continued absence of such collaboration as a critical problem for Japan's industries and proposed regularly held joint conferences between the two groups of institutions. It proposed the establishment of open universities to provide students with greater access to higher education and suggested that the qualifications of employees be upgraded through retraining at the undergraduate and graduate levels. The practice of upgrading qualifications at colleges and universities is still nonexistent in Japan because of rigid restrictions against it imposed by the academic institutions, one of which is the entrance examinations.

Finally, let us turn to one aspect of the report issued by the Japanese Association for Economic Development (JAED) in 1972.[22] The Japanese economy was still growing at a rapid pace in 1972, and this was reflected in JAED's rather liberal view toward employment practice and educational credentials. The Japanese public in general, and employers and academics in particular, are excessively biased regarding educational credentials from universities; it has been noted already that this is one of the bases on which the hierarchy of Japanese universities is established. Employers contribute to reinforcing the hierarchy by deliberately differentiating applicants according to graduating universities (see Chapter 4). In view of this fact, JAED suggested that employers' biases toward educational credentials be eliminated and that access to employment be opened. It should be noted, however, that JAED advocated such a liberal policy because private industries required more college-trained personnel. In fact, after the oil embargo in 1973, which caused an extensive economic recession in Japan as elsewhere, industries rarely paid attention to the JAED suggestion.

CONCLUSION

This chapter derives from the assumption that education is a function of economic and political institutions. Goals and curricula are not defined by schools; they are in large measure defined by the predominant forces and imperatives of the economic and political systems. Japanese education has adapted to respond to pressures generated by the Japanese industries and the government for economic expansion and political stability. Business strategists in particular have seen schooling as a powerful instrument of adaptation, as they have made challenges in international economic competition. It has been seen that conditions for change in formal education are first generated by economic and political developments and that education follows initiatives taken by economic and political strategists.

It was noted that Japanese business emphasized achievement orientation, human competence, and differentiation of curricula as educational essentials for the improvement and differentiation of economic adaptation. The manner in which these aspects of emphasis in schooling are implemented, however, is culturally determined. Hence, one needs to understand them in the Japanese cultural frame of reference. Whether or not they have been accomplished as originally intended, what is significant about them is a business ideology imposed upon schooling—that is, efficiency.

During the period of economic expansion, Japanese industries were particularly concerned with an efficient mobilization of youth. Their particular interest in the widespread campus unrest was motivated by that concern. Meanwhile, both the government and business sought political stability. As institutional complexity and differentiation of adaptation to the Japanese environment increased, the government sought a greater degree of uniformity in terms of Japanese motivational orientations toward the state. Its policy on the ideal Japanese is uniquely Japanese.

Finally, let us note that the industries criticized the lifetime employment and promotion based on longevity practiced by Japanese universities, calling it closed and undemocratic. The fact is that the universities' practice reflects the general pattern of Japanese adaptation and is not different in kind from that of the business institutions, although it is probably more rigid. It is relevant to point out again that the relative absence of requisite horizontal mobility and the development of Japanese social stratification are functions of the general practices of lifetime employment and longevity-based promotion that have been extensively adopted by economic organizations. There have been few indications that the economic organizations have been radically changing their traditional practices.

There are areas of conflict between educational institutions and economic organizations, and the present chapter demonstrates that the economic organizations are a dominant force in resolving such dissonance for their own benefit. In other words, education is pressured to accommodate to the needs of economic, as well as political, organizations.

NOTES

1. John Kenneth Galbraith, The New Industrial State (Boston: Houghton Mifflin, 1971), p. 298.

2. Federation of Employers Association, "Shinkyōiku Seidono Saikentōni Kansuru Yōbō" [A recommendation for reconsideration of the new educational system], Tokyo, October 1952. Offset.

3. Federation of Employers Association, "Tōmen Kyōiku Seido Kaizenni Kansuru Yōbō" [A recommendation for the improvement of the current educational system], Tokyo, December 1954. Offset.

4. Federation of Employers Association, "Shinjidaino Yōseini Taiōsuru Gijutsu Kyōikuni Kansuru Iken" [Our viewpoint concerning technical education to meet challenges of an emerging age], Tokyo, November 1956. Offset.

5. Ibid.

6. Central Council of Education, "Kagaku Gijutsu Kyōiku Shinkōni Kansuru Iken" [On policies to promote education in science and engineering], Tokyo, December 1957. Offset.

7. Federation of Employers Association, "Kagaku Gijutsu Kyōiku Shinkōni Kansuru Iken" [Our view concerning the improvement of science and technical education], Tokyo, December 1957. Offset.

8. Federation of Employers Association, "Senka Daigaku Seido Sōsetsuni Taisuru Yōbō Iken" [A recommendation for the establishment of a technical college system], Tokyo, December 1960. Offset.

9. Asahi Shinbun (Asahi daily newspaper), July 10, 1960.

10. Economic Council, "Shotoku Baizō Keikakuni Tomonau Chōki Kyōiku Kukaku Hokōkui" [Report on the long-range educational plan oriented toward the doubling of income], Tokyo, October 1960.

11. See the cabinet's report, "Kokumin Shotoku Baizō Keikaku" [The plan to double personal income], Tokyo, December 1960. Offset.

12. Economic Council, "Jinteki Nōryoku Seisakuni Kansuru Tōshin" [Recommendations concerning a policy for human competence], Tokyo, January 1963. Offset.

13. Ibid.

14. Central Council of Education, "Kōki Chūtō Kyōiku Kakujū Seibini Tsuiteno Tōshin" [Recommendations concerning an expansion of upper secondary education], Tokyo, October 1965. Offset.

15. Ibid.

16. Central Council of Education, "Kitai Sareru Ningenzō" [The ideal Japanese], Tokyo, October 1966. Offset.

17. Ibid.

18. See Teruhisa Horio, "Keizai Seichōto Kyōiku" [Economic growth and education], in Sengo Nippon Kyōikushi [History of postwar education], ed. Takashi Ota (Tokyo: Iwanami, 1978), pp. 288-312.

19. For further statistical details, see Ministry of Education, Wagakunino Kyōiku Suijun [The educational standard of our nation] (Toyko: Ōkurashō Insatsukyoku, 1976).

20. Committee for Economic Development, "Daigakuno Kihon Mondai" [Basic problems of the university], Tokyo, November 1968; and idem, "Kōji Fukushi Shakaino Tameno Kōtōkyōiku Seido" [A higher education system for an advanced welfare society], Tokyo, July, 1969. Offset.

21. Economic Council, "Sangaku Kankeini Kansuru Sangyōkaino Kihon Ninshinki Oyobi Teigen" [Private industries' recommendations for and fundamental recognition of the relationship between academic institutions and industries], Tokyo, December 1969. Offset.

22. Japanese Association for Economic Development, "Atarashii Sangyō Shakaini Okeru Ningen Keisei" [Personality development in a new industrial society], Tokyo, March 1972. Offset.

7

CULTURAL AND
SOCIAL PERSPECTIVES

Having discussed the development of Japanese education, contemporary schooling, and socialization, as well as the accommodation
of education to economic forces, this chapter presents a cultural and
social perspective of Japanese education. This will help provide a
theoretical integration of the earlier discussion. The focus is first
on the isomorphism between the Japanese cognitive orientation and
the institutional system.

JAPANESE COGNITIVE ORIENTATION
AND INSTITUTIONAL ARRANGEMENTS

A people seek to legitimate and rationalize their way of life as
part of their adaptation to their social environment. Their adaptation
is guided by both explicit and implicit cultural premises that are
defined as orientations. Above all, implicit cultural premises constitute a dominant force shaping a society's pattern of adaptation.
George M. Foster terms a set of such premises a "cognitive orientation. "

> The members of every society share a common cognitive
> orientation which is, in effect, an unverbalized, implicit
> expression of their understanding of the "rules of the
> game" of living imposed upon them by their social, nat-
> ural, and supernatural universes. A cognitive orienta-
> tion provides the members of the society it characterizes
> with basic premises and sets of assumptions normally
> neither recognized nor questioned which structure and
> guide behavior in much the same way grammatical rules
> unrecognized by most people structure and guide their
> linguistic forms. All normative behavior of the mem-
> bers of a group is a function of their particular way of

looking at their total environment, their unconscious acceptance of the "rules of the game" implicit in their cognitive orientation.

. . . As Kluckhohn has pointed out, cognitive orientations (he speaks of "configurations") are recognized by most members of a society only in the sense that they make choices "with the configurations as unconscious but determinative backgrounds."[1]

Here Foster speaks of a culturally conditioned cognitive orientation that is internalized in individuals through enculturation and secondary socialization. It is a social representation of integrating principles accounting for a regularity of observed behavior and covert attitude.

Within this frame of reference, we have discussed the Japanese pattern of adaptation. The Japanese cognitive orientation, in Foster's sense, guides individual behavior and attitude in centripetal and vertical directions. Such behavior and attitude give expression to political, economic, and educational modes of activity. Hence, regardless of ideologies, educators, corporate employees, and members of different political parties exhibit the same cultural pattern in the appropriate arenas. It does not appear proper to interpret Japanese social relations and behavior with exclusive reference to ideologies and institutional arrangements, such as feudalism, communism, and capitalism, since they are significant cultural expressions. Nevertheless, as it was argued earlier, the cultural system interacts with the maintenance and integrative systems, that is, economic and political institutions.

To offer another example, we may refer to the People's Republic of China (PRC). It is a communist system based on Marxism, and it has developed probably the most extensive grassroots-oriented industrial democracy in the entire world. (Industrial democracy should not be confused with political democracy, which is now only emerging.) Industrial democracy refers to a pattern of participation and decision making as related to social and economic policies. It has been reported by Western observers that in the PRC such policies are first discussed extensively at the communal level, involving a high degree of the people's participation. This serves as a basis for formulating policies at a higher level.[2] The Japanese ringi system somewhat resembles the Chinese participatory pattern. Perhaps the most important variable that differentiates the Chinese from the Soviet system is the Chinese use of the centripetal pattern of social relations, based on a traditional kinship system, as a basis for the development of communes. Therefore, Chinese feel unalienated and actively involved in a political arrangement that is different from the traditional. In short, the Chinese example offers clear evidence of interaction among cultural, economic, and political institutions.

Without the isomorphism that exists between the Japanese cognitive orientation and the institutional arrangements of Japanese society, social dysfunction would frequently occur; one fundamental reason
why the Meiji reform succeeded, despite turbulent events, was the very
existence of this cognitive and institutional congruence. Similarly,
the perpetuation of the entrance examinations can be attributed to such
isomorphism; in other words, the Japanese cognitive orientation
toward the group, and particularly to vertical social relations and
social stratification, is congruent with an emphasis on the entrance
examinations—what Johan Galtung calls "degreeocracy"[3]—stressing
a particular type of credentials, lifetime employment, and the current economic and political systems.

Galtung contends that degreeocracy is "a substitute for the old
caste structure" that existed during the Tokugawa era.[4] Whether his
contention is correct or not, degreeocracy limits individual mobility
and leads to the creation of secondary, ascriptive conditions of life,
based not on birth but on academic credentials. Japanese often speak
of gakureki henchō, which refers to an excessive emphasis on academic credentials, but what is covertly meant (in terms of honne) is
not clearly conveyed by this phrase. It refers at the honne (implicit)
level to a bias or prejudice toward or against certain academic credentials. Degreeocracy, therefore, is an institutional practice in
which academic credentials received at different institutions are vertically structured according to the order of differential recognition
conferred on them by economic and political institutions. It involves
ascriptive and particularistic elements, since it tends to determine
one's future once and for all, reducing his or her alternatives to a
minimum.

> It is essentially an ascriptive system in the sense that
> once one is allocated to a group it is very difficult to
> change one's class. It is like being born into a class,
> only that in a degreeocracy social birth takes place later
> than biological birth. More precisely it takes place at
> the time of the various entrance examinations, and like
> all births it has its pains. There is the pregnancy pe-
> riod with some element of social isolation (preparation
> for the exam); the labour (the exam itself); and there are
> miscarriages and infant mortality (the high suicide rates
> for that particular age group, 20-24, in that particular
> period of the year, April). It is traumatic and dramatic;
> and it should be because it is the entrance to real life.
> Biological birth is dramatic and the social birth of fully
> conscious individuals even more so. As mentioned so
> often in speeches: the entrance examination is to be

born again, and once it has happened one's future life is
as predetermined as in [a feudal society]—only more effectively so because the society is more rational, more
technically adequate. [5]

Education takes place in a social context. Its system corresponds to the social, political, and economic institutions of a society,
It serves the functions defined by these institutions for reproducing
the institutional patterns as reflected by prevailing ideologies. Ac-
cordingly, as long as the patterns of such institutions are perpetuated,
the functions of schooling are likely to be the same.

In short, Japanese society is vertically structured, and its political and economic institutions are designed to perpetuate a vertical
structure through degreeocracy. Let us illustrate briefly how degreeocracy is reinforced by the government's policy. In 1974, for example, the government budgeted allocations to national universities and
colleges—using Tokyo University's allocation as a base line—as follows: 100 percent to Tokyo University, 70 percent to Kyoto, 51 per-
cent to Tohoku, 46 percent to Osaka, 43 percent to Hokkaido, 42 per-
cent to Kyushu, 34 percent to Nagoya, 13 percent to Yokohama, 10
percent to Akita, and 8 percent to Yamagata. [6] The first seven universities are former imperial universities and are currently the most
prestigious in Japan. The order of listing according to budget allocation corresponds to the order of degreeocracy. Yokohama, Akita,
and Yamagata represent typical, postwar institutions in terms of
budget allocation and student enrollment. Meanwhile, Tokyo University's budget equaled the combined budgets allocated to the 29 universities and colleges at the bottom of the degreeocratic structure of
the national institutions. It goes without saying that degreeocracy
and politics readily go hand in hand; sharp inequity among universities is deliberately created to perpetuate degreeocracy. Furthermore, it is reinforced by economic institutions that extend differential access to the institutions of higher education according to the
order of institutional prestige.

The evolution of the degreeocratic structure began with the establishment of Tokyo University in 1877. The primary purpose for
founding Tokyo University, early in the Meiji era, was to train high
level bureaucrats to fill strategic government positions. The historical eminence of this university derives partly from its complete
monopoly of that training for 20 years—until the establishment of
Kyoto University in 1897—and to its dominance thereafter. Shortly
after the establishment of Kyoto University, the 1903 education ordinance promoted some private technical schools (senmongakkō) to
"semiuniversities," but it was not until 1918 that they became full-
fledged universities. Five other imperial universities (Tōhoku,

Kyushu, Osaka, Hokkaido, and Nagoya) had been established between 1907 and 1939. Given the intention of the government to establish the imperial universities and the long period in which Tokyo University monopolized the training of government bureaucrats, it is understandable that Tokyo University should enjoy the greatest prestige in the nation. That the government attempted to produce particular human resources largely at one exclusive institution clearly reflects the centripetality of Japanese culture, which, incidentally, is conducive to fostering a uniformity of cognitive orientations. The uniformity of orientations developed at a single institution has served as the basis for the evolution of the Tokyo University clique (gakubatsu) into the most powerful interpersonal network in politics, law, academia, and even business.

According to Takane's study, the percentage of Tokyo University graduates who became members of the Japanese political elite is as follows: 4 percent in 1890, 40 percent in 1920, 49 percent in 1936, and 50 percent in 1969. On the other hand, the percentage of the elite having college education (or its equivalent in 1890) received elsewhere was 16 percent in 1890, 20 percent in 1920, 17 percent in 1936, and 28 percent in 1969.[7] The remaining members of the elite received no college education. By political elite, Takane means a group of individuals in the political category listed in Jinji Kōshinroku (the authoritative and selective Japanese Who's Who). His study reveals the dominant influence and exclusive privilege that Tokyo graduates have enjoyed in the political sphere. It also suggests that their cognitive orientations (in both Foster's and the narrow psychological senses) have dominated this particular sphere.

The contention was made earlier that the more Japanese society was modernized, the higher the degree of institutional complexity and differentiation it attained, and that achievement gradually replaced ascription as a criterion for social mobility. In the twentieth century, education became a major criterion for such mobility. In 1920, for example, while 64 percent of the exsamurai class in the political elite either had full college education or postcollege training (including study abroad), which had been received in the nineteenth century, only 52 percent of the commoners in the elite group were recipients of such education. But the 1969 data show that 86 percent of the exsamurai class and 81 percent of the commoner class had received college degrees or postbaccalaureate training.[8] Meanwhile, as education has become a more influential factor in determining one's membership in the elite, family background has lost its influence. In 1860, 75 percent of the elite members came from elite families, while in 1969 only 7 percent did.[9] What this suggests is that achievement has replaced ascription considerably, and education has become a major factor influencing one's elite membership in the political domain. Besides, the universities where individuals receive training exert a differential effect on access to the political elite. This historical and sociological background is a prototype of Japanese degreeocracy.

A similar pattern is reflected in what Mannari calls the Japanese business elite (limited to chairmen and presidents of corporations having ¥ 1 billion capital in 1960 and top officials of other economic organizations). As of 1960 the business elite had the following educational backgrounds: college graduates (prewar) constituted 66 percent, while graduates from technical schools (prewar), 23 percent; those with graduate training constituted only 2 percent, and the remaining 9 percent had middle school (prewar) education or less.[10] The predominance of college training as an attribute of the elite is again clearly evident. Furthermore, in 1960, 46 percent of the elite possessed credentials from Tokyo University; 9 percent from Kyoto University; 13 percent from Shitotsubashi University; 6 percent from Keiō University; and 26 percent from other universities.[11] Shitotsubashi was originally established as a national, commercial, and technical school in 1884 and later became one of the prestigious national universities. Keiō, however, was originally founded by Yukichi Fukuzawa in 1858 and became a private university of high reputation in 1918, along with Waseda and other private universities. What we have seen is the domination of Tokyo University graduates in the business sphere, too, and additional evidence supports the observation that educational credentials constitute an essential aspect of the qualifications for the elite.

The degreeocratic structure of Japanese society corresponds to its larger structure, which social anthropologist Nakane characterizes as a "monolithic society" (tanitsu shakai).[12] In other words, Japanese society is characterized by the relative absence of an institutional pluralism that could offer competing alternatives, and this is evident in the Japanese universities. Tokyo University is the model for all the others, which attempt to emulate it even though most of them are not able to replicate it in any viable sense. This is one reason why most Japanese universities do not exhibit individual characteristics; rather, uniformity is the underlying criterion of university policies. It is understandable why adolescents compete fiercely to seek admission to the most reputable university in the nation, in view of such a high degree of institutional uniformity and the relative lack of viable alternatives.

The lack of effective institutional complementarity is a function of the group-orientation of Japanese society, which emphasizes centripetality and uniformity. It is also a politically expedient phenomenon since it helps generate a homogeneous outlook for a majority of college youth, on the one hand, and homogeneous structural conditions of educational practice, on the other. Moreover, this observation applies equally to the secondary and primary levels of schooling.

SOCIAL EVOLUTION AND EDUCATION

Social evolution is characterized by a process of institutional differentiation and complexity facilitated by the development of technology and by a process that centralizes political and economic power. Schooling fulfills a special function relative to the centralization of power in political and economic institutions. Morton Fried has developed a useful taxonomy of societies that can be applied to the present discussion. He categorizes societies in evolutionary order: (1) egalitarian society, (2) rank society, (3) stratified society, and (4) state society. [13]

The minimal level of differentiation and complexity is found in simple, egalitarian societies. While egalitarian society is characterized by an absence of institutions and their related features, it provides all individuals with relatively equal social recognition and positions of valued status as long as they are capable of filling such positions. This type of society usually depends upon a hunting-and-gathering technology, which does not allow for the development of large political units and food surpluses; nor does it make possible the differentiation of roles, except in terms of sex and age. Egalitarian society is generally based on the social structure of a small collectivity composed of a small number of families. Its foundation is a network based on kinship, and its social order is characterized by the equal distribution of prestige and a system of economic reciprocity.

Rank societies represent the next stage in the development of social differentiation and complexity. Technology is not yet developed enough to introduce a complex division of labor; a rank society does not require an extensive development of social stratification. The division of labor is still inarticulate and is primarily based on the criteria of age and sex, as in an egalitarian society. Nevertheless, a rank society exhibits a social structure that establishes positions of valued status to which a limited number of persons have access, although it does not limit the access of individuals to the basic natural and social resources. The introduction of this elementary hierarchy of prestige becomes necessary as kinship systems and the size of the society grow larger. A rank society is most often based on horticultural and even rudimentary agricultural technology; relatively large villages and permanent settlements come into existence as a consequence of this new technology. Another emerging feature of a rank society is its economic system. Although the form of economic circulation is the reciprocal exchange, as seen in an egalitarian society, the exchange is more systematized in a rank society to achieve an integration of the economic system. There is a center of exchange to and from which goods flow. Individuals who administer the distribution of goods at the center receive high prestige.

An important aspect of social complexity in a rank society is the social relations articulated by the kinship system, which is paramount to the life of the people. In regulating people's interpersonal relations and activities, the kinship system is far more important in rank society than in egalitarian society. Though the web of kinship of an egalitarian society is determined by ecologically favored residential rules, the rank society focuses upon the ideology of kinship, that is, the functional and social significance of kin relationships that affect the framework of kinship. The development of the ideology of kinship is in part a consequence of the growth of sedentary settlement, which, in turn, contributes to the greater stabilization of social structure.

Another significant feature of differentiation and complexity lies in the formative stages of political authority, which rank society introduces. In rank society a regular form of authority emerges, which is consistently reinforced and extends to various aspects of social life. Authority is the religious and ritual expression of leadership stemming from the great influence that a person of high rank exercises upon the productivity of society through directing and scheduling productive activities.

Further development of differentiation and complexity leads to the formation of stratified society. Technology requires a more functional social structure not regulated by the kinship system, inarticulate political authority, or the rudimentary division of labor, but by an entirely new system of control and a complex division of labor. Stratified society creates specialized groups. This means the attenuation, and even the destruction, of the kin relationships that dominate rank society. Thus, kinship is no longer the means of social control and adjudication in a stratified society. Individuals of the same sex and equivalent age do not have equal access to the basic resources of society.

Stratified society is based upon a structure of differential access to the natural and social resources leading to the establishment of stratification as a mechanism of social control. The economic pattern of stratified society is represented by a new mode of production and distribution; it is based on a new division of labor incorporating differential types of power, control, and prestige. Economic transactions are conducted in terms of the objects to be distributed without special reference to interpersonal relations, which are highly important in the exchange of goods in a rank society. A system emerges here in which property relations constitute the basis of social relations.

A high level of political integration is attained in stratified society in terms of two kinds of social processes. The first is a great increase in the size of the political unit. The other is a growth of social stratification and the differentiation of people and occupational groups in terms of the differential rights and access to social and political positions of high prestige and power and to the natural and social resources. This process has to do with the emergence of complex socioeconomic classes associated with differential levels of living, security, and property. The growth of social differentiation and complexity is simultaneously accompanied by a rapid increase of population, a crucial condition for the establishment of a state.

We now arrive at the highest form of differentiation and complexity: the state. State society is a system of integrated political units in which complex institutions, both formal and informal, are developed to maintain an order of stratification. Its main concern is the perpetuation of its boundary system, which is made possible by the reinforcement of organizational principles associated with hierarchy, differential degrees of access to the natural and social resources, and compliance with the state's imperatives related to defense, territoriality, and official policies. It has specialized institutions of coercion employing physical force in the forms of an army and a police force. As Ferdinand Tönnies writes in Community and Society:

> The state, especially by legal definition, is nothing but
> force, the holder and representative of all natural rights
> of coercion. The state makes the natural law an instru-
> ment and part of its own will; it interprets that law. But
> the state can also alter what is thus under its control.
> It must be able to do so not only de facto but also de lege.
> For it can make the regulations of its interpretation of
> law legally binding for its subjects. Interpreting what
> in law amounts, for them, to announcing what shall be
> law, with all the ensuing legal consequences. [14]

At the level of the state, the kinship system has little to do with social control, and the complex institutions built on the functional need to defend the central order of social stratification replace those mechanisms of exercising power and control seen in the earlier types of society.

It is this last stage in which education became a particularly effective political and economic instrument in Japanese society. Remember that the Meiji leaders conceived of schooling as an institution of the formative nation-state for political integration and economic development. Otherwise, education has evolved as a sorting mechanism, as in other societies, the function of which is to allocate members of the society to roles and positions of differential status and power. In other words, in the Meiji era, education began to fulfill an important allocative function by providing individuals with differential access to social instititions; achievement was gradually replacing ascription. Thereafter, the ascriptive basis of role allocation had to give way to a new set of criteria defined by educational credentials. Hence, the state created a dual system of schooling; education for individuals, who were trained for strategic roles in the political and economic systems; and education for the masses, who were trained to increase the general labor force and, particularly, to develop motivational and cognitive orientations essential to the integration and continuity of the state. Therefore, teacher education received special attention and was defined by the state, for the teachers were primarily responsible for socializing and indoctrinating the young generation of the masses. Japanese degreeocracy commenced in that period.

While the allocative functions of schooling have remained the same, they have been further articulated and differentiated as more complex social and economic forces have hinged upon schooling. Upper secondary education has virtually become a social requirement for nearly all young citizens, although it is not compulsory. College education, on the other hand, is commonly required for white-collar jobs in secondary and tertiary industries. Furthermore, access to large firms also necessitates admission to those particular universities they patronize for the purpose of recruiting job applicants. Besides, in order to insure access to political, business, and academic elites, individuals must receive credentials at Tokyo, Kyoto, and only a few other universities.

In short, education is a fundamental instrument of the stratification system of society. Japanese degreeocracy, in particular, functions to articulate the system and, above all, to limit access to the most valued positions. Its functions are especially effective because horizontal mobility is inherently limited in Japanese social structure. Therefore, schooling in general and degreeocracy in particular are an essential basis of social stratification. It is, thus, defensible to argue that the most vital purpose of education in Japan is to stratify its citizens so as to establish differential access to social and natural resources. This argument is sufficiently supported by the discussion of the socialization for the college entrance examinations. The development of schooling in Japan is a process that has responded to the organizational principles governing social stratification, as well as to the political and economic imperatives of the state.

JAPANESE VIEW OF DEGREEOCRACY

To examine how Japanese view degreeocracy and its associated phenomena, we will draw on the findings provided by the Citizen's

Department of the Tokyo Municipal Government. [15] It conducted its
survey in 1975, using a randomly selected sample of 1,500 parents
in Tokyo who had children between the ages of three and eighteen.
Data were gathered by interview.

An overwhelming majority of the sample recognized Japanese
degreeocracy: 63 percent felt that it was currently pervasive. Five
parents out of ten thought that it would continue at least for some
time, but 40 percent were optimistic that it would be replaced by an
"achievement-oriented system." Seventy percent expressed the view
that the individual should not be evaluated by and rewarded for, his
or her academic credentials, and only 10 percent disagreed with that
view, and the remaining two parents did not have a clear opinion.
Nearly one-half of the sample (46.2 percent) insisted that the Japanese
social structure based on degreeocracy should be superseded by another structure. As a first step in that direction, they advocated the
elimination of discriminatory employment practices by private firms
based on degreeocratic criteria (69.2 percent). As another step,
they sought to eliminate income differentials based on academic credentials (65.7 percent). This indicates that they are well aware of
shiteikōsei and related practices.

The pattern exhibited in the Tokyo survey was reinforced by the
findings of a nationwide survey conducted in 1977 by Asahi Shinbun, [16]
according to which 83 percent of Japanese believe that Japanese society overemphasizes degreeocracy. Of those, 29 percent felt that
degreeocracy would develop further, and 26 percent agreed that it
would remain the same.

Most parents in the Tokyo survey expressed a sense of inevita-
bility regarding competition for the entrance examinations. They felt
that their children were forced to participate in them even though they
were unwilling to; only 8 percent of the parents refuted this inevitabil-
ity, and the remaining parents were unsure. The fact is that in most
cases parents are one of the sources of pressure for such competition.

A majority of the parents acquiesce in the current entrance examination system and, in turn, contribute to the perpetuation of the
system. Yet 81.7 percent of the parents supported education aimed
at developing individual growth, in spite of the pressures for the CEE.
This presents an obvious contradiction because such education is impossible under these pressures. Here is a conflict between tatemae
and honne. In other words, at the honne level they acquiesce in the
current pattern of examination-oriented schooling, while at the tatemae level they deny its usefulness. Furthermore, 51.4 percent of
the sample expressed the view that they would "nauseate" if students
whose education was completely devoted to preparing for the entrance
examinations became leaders of society. In stark contrast to this
view, most families in Tokyo are devoted to their children's prepara-

tory drilling for the CEE and ruthlessly compete with each other; again, we detect two different levels of attitude hinging on the CEE.

A similar pattern of contradiction is seen in the Asahi survey. Five Japanese out of ten are dissatisfied with schooling at the elementary and middle school levels, which is influenced by pressures for the entrance examinations. More than 40 percent held the view that juku is not useful, while fewer than 40 percent agreed that it is. Despite such views, the number of students attending juku grows every year. In the urban areas, 50 percent of the student population attend juku. Furthermore, even when nearly a majority of the Japanese are disenchanted with present education, the current pattern and its orientation do not change. One fundamental reason for these phenomena is that Japanese support the current educational practices and their ideology simply by acquiescing in the contradiction between the honne and tatemae levels.

In fact, there is a tendency on the part of parents, as well as children, to keep it secret when children attend juku or receive private tutoring at home so that they may unavowedly prepare for examination competition. This observation was repeatedly shared by my informants, including teachers, parents, and children. That is, in the uchi (private and inner) world they not only support the examination-centered institutional practices of schooling but also intensify them, but in the yoso (public and outer) world they express frustrations with these practices. Such an attitude is often characterized by Japanese as "a psychology of island people," which refers to the notion that people are shrewd, narrow minded, concerned with the immediate, and insecure, since their natural and social resources are perceived as limited in their small islands. Foster speaks of this psychological pattern in terms of "the image of limited good":

> Broad areas of [people's] behavior are patterned in such fashion as to suggest that [people] view their social, economic, and natural universes—their total environment— as one in which all of the desired things in life, such as land, wealth, health, friendship and love, manliness and honor, respect and status, power and influence, security and safety, exist in finite quality and are always in short supply. . . . There is no way directly within [their] power to increase the available quantities. [17]

Foster derived this notion from a peasant society, but it can be applied to the Japanese as well, as far as their orientation and behavior in education are concerned. Consequences of the image of the limited good are a lack of cooperation, fierce competition, excessive drilling, personal and familial sacrifices, and incomplete personality growth.

THE INDIVIDUAL AND SOCIETY

In a centripetal society such as Japan, the individual is subjected to group pressures and expectations. Group-centered Japanese society imposes pressure upon individuals to conform to group norms that take precedence over the individuals, permitting them only a limited scope of alternatives. This is one of the basic reasons why degreeocracy is rigid in Japan and why individuals compete for the same goals. It has led to the development of the cognitive orientation characterized by the image of limited good. Such an orientation is a part of the ideology underlying the Japanese pattern of adaptation.

The Japanese pattern of adaptation is taxing to the individual. Since individuality, or the development of all individual potentials, is generally not encouraged in Japanese society, social conditions militate against the development of the average Japanese into an individual who has an articulate self-consciousness and distinctness in behavior and attitudes. Most Japanese do not adequately comprehend what individuality is and, hence, they often confuse it with selfishness and the lack of personal maturity. In this regard, Ronald Dore astutely observed that "in a typically Japanese way, the necessary revolution in individual attitudes—a revolution which is only possible through the self-awareness and effort of each individual—is being omitted."[18] The revolution in individual attitudes has long been resisted because of Japanese cultural emphasis on the group, in which the individual becomes an indistinct, though highly valued, person, while Japanese "revolution" in the economic and industrial spheres is phenomenal and drastic.

The lack of critical self-awareness on the part of the Japanese makes an individual susceptible to cultural and social pressures for attitudinal and behavioral duality. Consequently, Japanese entertain two conflicting levels of behavior—such as tatemae/honne and yoso/uchi—without a deep sense of dichotomy. Such a behavioral dichotomy is more or less taken for granted in Japanese life. This dual tendency makes an individual's view less convincing and defensible. Generally, Japanese individuals find it difficult to defend themselves against social pressures and to resist general trends of various events and institutional practices. This is evident in terms of their attitudes toward Japanese degreeocracy and examination-centered education. Therefore, it becomes the burden of the individual to bear and repress conflicts caused by dual behavior. The Japanese have developed the capacity to tolerate and acquiesce in conflicts and contradictions in education, politics, business, and social life in general. But this is toilsome, just as it is to undergo the socialization for the CEE on the part of adolescents and their mothers and fathers.

The Japanese pattern of adaptation also limits alternatives available to individuals, since it does not allow for a sufficient degree of horizontal mobility. Group-centered social organizations in Japan do not operate on the assumption that the horizontal mobility of individuals is a requisite means to secure human resources. Lacking alternatives, Japanese tend to be enculturated in given organizations for their lifetimes, and they live with constant pressures for behavioral and cognitive conformity. Such pressures for conformity are not peculiar to work organizations; they constitute a basic condition of social life in general. Apparently, this causes a psychological malaise for many Japanese.

While the Japanese pattern of adaptation is taxing to the individual in various respects, its group-centered orientation is highly conducive to the protection of individual group members. Unlike a highly centrifugal society, such as in the United States or Britain, where individuals must be constantly concerned with their self-protection and the defense of their own interests, Japanese society has developed social organizations that offer individuals security and personal anchorage. There is a high degree of isomorphism between individual concerns and organizational goals. This is a basis of employees' loyalty to their firms. Japanese industrial efficiency is a function of such isomorphism and the symbiotic relations between individuals and their work organizations.

It should also be noted that this pattern of adaptation has enabled Japanese society to achieve relatively smooth transitions during the critical periods of historical events in the past one and a half centuries. It has been the stabilizing mechanism with which Japanese social transformation has been carried out. At the same time it has contributed to the development of unique education, business, and politics and to political integration and industrial development. Japanese society, with its emphasis on centripetality, is much less class-structured and more egalitarian than some other highly industrialized societies, such as the United States, since inclusiveness is a basic principle.

YOUTH AND SOCIETY

We discussed earlier the education and socialization imposed by the CEE, the social structure characterized by centripetal social relations, and the high degree of isomorphism between Japanese cognitive orientation and social structure. Given such a pressured enculturation and tightly knit society, one might assume that young Japanese men and women have sufficiently internalized societal expectations and limitations as functional dimensions of their lives. This assumption is by and large correct in the long run, but the durability of what is enculturated and the conditioning forces of society are often subject to modification.

In fact, it is interesting to note that young Japanese are resentful and critical toward their society. An international Gallup Study
of youth attitudes was conducted in 1972 under the partial sponsorship
of the Japanese government to measure youth satisfaction with society
in 11 countries: Japan, the United States, Britain, West Germany,
France, Switzerland, Sweden, Yugoslavia, India, the Philippines,
and Brazil. Each sample (randomly selected) consisted of 2,000
young men and women between the ages of 18 and 24.[19] The survey
does not address education in Japan, but it offers a useful and relevant perspective for understanding the psychology and culturally conditioned attitudes of young Japanese who have been brought up in the
social conditions that have been given extensive attention here.

It was noted earlier that Japanese youth experience a period of
"self-process" characterized by uncertainty and instability after the
rigorous, one-dimensional socialization for the CEE. Eventually,
this period is superseded by submergence in the centripetal social
relations of permanent groups, which become a source of contentment
and acquiescence. The survey also reveals other cultural expressions
of Japanese youth, which are closely related to our exploration of the
Japanese cultural orientations.

The survey data indicate that, among the 11 groups of youth,
the Japanese reacted most negatively toward their society. This puz-
zled sociologists and social psychologists in Japan and became a lively
topic for debate. First, let us look briefly at the findings: 73.5 percent of the Japanese youth expressed dissatisfaction with their society,
whereas the next highest percentage of dissatisfaction, exhibited by
U.S. youth, was 35.7 percent. This was followed by the Swedish and
West German groups, 35 and 34 percent of whom expressed dissatisfaction toward their societies. Brazilians exhibited the least degree
of dissatisfaction, although theirs is a politically dictatorial society.
It is interesting to note that the negative reaction of the Japanese was
twice as strong as the American, despite the prosperity and the political and social stability that prevailed in Japan in 1972, in contrast
with the controversial involvement in the Vietnam War and the widespread political dissension that characterized the United States at that
time.

It is also noteworthy that when asked, "Does your country sufficiently protect your rights and welfare?" 88.5 percent of the Japanese responded negatively against 54.4 and 48.1 percent for the British and Americans, respectively. Despite their living in a dictator-
ship, only 22.7 percent of the Filipinos answered negatively. The
same pattern emerged when the participants were asked whether industrial development took precedence over individual life and happiness. Once again, the negative attitude of the Japanese, 90.4 percent, outstripped all the others: 76.2 percent for the Swedes; 69.3

percent for the Americans; and 64.7 percent for the British. At that time, precisely because of the extensive industrial development, the Japanese were suffering from probably the severest ecological problems of all the industrial nations. And in that connection, the survey was revealing as to why individuals do not take positive action to improve a society with which they are dissatisfied. More than 70 percent of the Japanese surveyed, again the highest of all groups, felt that individuals are powerless; 50 percent of the West Germans and 30 percent of the Americans agreed with this view.

When asked whether human nature is good or evil, 33 percent of the Japanese called it evil, whereas fewer than 20 percent of those in France, the United States, Britain, Switzerland, and West Germany—where the Christian notion of fundamentally evil human nature has a special significance in life—concurred. Although the religious concept of an evil human nature is generally weak in the fabric of Japanese life, the Japanese sample exhibited the highest degree of agreement with that view. Even more remarkable, in view of that belief, 68.8 percent of the Japanese sample favored close association among friends, whereas 44.5 percent of the American sample, 36 percent of the British, and only 12.1 percent of the French favored it. According to Jirō Matsubara, a noted Japanese sociologist, Japanese youth probably equate an evil human nature with a lack of confidence in individuals. From these findings it appears that the Japanese distrust each other more than the other groups, yet they prefer close social relations much more than any other group.

There is small wonder that these findings perplexed Japanese scholars, as well as some social scientists in other countries. Understandably, they believed that the Japanese pattern of preadult socialization and the internalization of the Japanese cognitive orientation in adolescents would lead youth to conform to general social expectations in significant measure, particularly because the Japanese are generally resilient conformists who maintain their centripetal orientation regardless of generational differences.

In order to resolve this contradiction, let us examine the social and cultural variables that likely affected the Japanese responses in the survey. It appears that one of the variables is related to the pattern of preadult socialization, a part of which was discussed extensively earlier as it bore on preparatory instruction for college entrance examinations. Socialization coerces adolescents to cultivate uniformity, self-denial, perseverance, and achievement for the sake of the entrance examinations. Also, because the predominant character of secondary schooling is similarly shaped by pressures to do well in high school entrance examinations, education is not intended to develop personal and social maturity, and this produces a notable negative effect on adolescents. Those who will attend college are certainly willing to accept psychological multilation and other aspects of the rite of passage imposed on them, but those who are not bound for college suffer alienation from the dominant orientation of schooling and are compelled to assume the ignominious status of second-class adolescents. In both cases, Japanese society continuously imposes rigid socialization on adolescents when they are in the most formative stage of personality development. The Gallup survey reveals that, to an appreciable extent, Japanese youth who have undergone such socialization are resentful toward their society and distrustful of each other.

The second variable relates to the Protean pattern of youth personality in Japan (see Chapter 3). Two major psychocultural conditions of our time have created the Protean individual: psychohistorical dislocation and the flooding of imagery produced and propagated by the mass communication networks. While the former implies a breakdown in the traditional system of symbols, as a result of rapid social transformation, the latter refers to a phenomenon in which the individual's self is split and diffused by the overwhelming influx of superficial messages, trivial and spurious headlines, and unpromising alternatives. It appears that many Japanese youth undergo variable degrees of psychohistorical dislocation, given the postwar transformation of Japan, and experiences influenced by the flooding of imagery. The life of Arinori Mori was discussed earlier in terms of the Protean personality, but it is relevant to consider a more contemporary example:

A young Japanese (aged 25 in 1962), who is now a sarariiman, "salaried man," in a big firm. Born into an intellectually oriented family, he grew up as a middle-class boy in the prewar traditional social structure, a fiery patriot whose hatred for Americans was extreme. After Japan's surrender, he became extremely confused in his beliefs. However, he developed his curiosity about America, aroused by contacts with American soldiers and postwar education, and became an exponent of democratic life in contrast with the traditional Japanese way of life, while at the same time maintaining appreciation of the Japanese arts. During his high-school days, he became an outspoken Marxist in his circle of acquaintances. Yet, being fairly fluent in English, he spent a year as an exchange student in an American high school, where he was converted to Christianity. On his return to Japan, finding himself not well accepted by his group since he had become Americanized, he decided to immerse himself again in Japanese culture. At Tokyo University he became a fanatic

Zengakuren (the National Federation of Students) member, advocating "pure Communism: but he declined an offer of a top position in the organization and then, convinced that he was not suited for revolutionary life, became a drifter and heavy drinker, engaging in affairs with bar girls. Eventually, he graduated from the university and became a sarariiman. Now he apparently does his job satisfactorily; he is no longer a Marxist, but rather a seeker of sophisticated pleasure. . . . This case illustrates the reorienting and reconditioning of the individual in both the preadult and the adult stages. [20]

In addition, the Japanese Protean personality is characterized by another attribute. Since the group takes precedence over the individual and the individual tends toward immersion in the group, individuals are generally inclined to develop their own critical and articulate views on a variety of pertinent matters or to confront controversial issues directly. Such a personality is likely to be vulnerable to the flooding of imagery. This tendency should not be overgeneralized, however, since there are situations in which the opposite tendency is strong.

The third variable concerns a tatemae (spurious) and honne (genuine) conflict. According to Matsubaba, Japanese scholars emphasized that a quantitative survey, such as the Gallup, tends to elicit spurious responses at the tatemae level, at least in Japanese society. [21] Therefore, the Japanese responses may not have sufficiently indicated their honne attitudes. Given Japanese culture, where honne and tatemae are clearly differentiated in attitudes and behavior, the Japanese scholars' view is plausible.

At any rate, most Japanese youth generally submerge themselves, sooner or later, in large groups and become devoted members of their groups and acquiescent citizens of their society. In other words, the Japanese cultural orientations endure to serve as the framework for group life and social integration, and the Japanese pattern of adaptation is effectively at work.

CONCLUSION

This chapter has presented a cultural and social perspective, emphasizing Japanese cognitive orientation, the evolution of education, and the relationship between the individual and society. We have noted that Japanese cultural orientations are a persistent force guiding individual behavior and the development of institutional activities, including education. The cultural and social perspectives presented here further clarify the interaction between cultural orientations and institutional practices, particularly educational activities.

NOTES

1. George M. Foster, "Peasant Society and the Image of Limited Good," American Anthropologist 67 (1965): 293-94.

2. This discussion is based on my extensive dialogue with Myles Horton, director of the Highlander Research and Education Center (Tennessee), who has made three trips to China to study Chinese industrial democracy.

3. Johan Galtung, "Social Structure, Education Structure and Life Long Education: The Case of Japan," Reviews of National Policies for Education: Japan (Paris: OECD, 1971), p. 139.

4. Ibid., p. 140.

5. Ibid., p. 139.

6. Yomiuri Shinbun, ed., Taishū Daigaku [Colleges for the masses] (Osaka: Yomiuri Shinbun, 1976), p. 99.

7. Masaaki Takane, Nipponno Seiji Eriito [The political elite of Japan] (Tokyo: Chūōkōronsha, 1976), p. 135.

8. Ibid., p. 138.

9. Ibid., p. 79.

10. Hiroshi Mannari, Businesu Eriito [Business elite] (Tokyo: Chūōkōronsha, 1977), p. 23.

11. Ibid., p. 125.

12. See Chie Nakane, Tate Shakaino Ningen Kankei [Human relations of a vertical society] (Tokyo: Kōdansha, 1976).

13. See Morton H. Fried, The Evolution of Political Society (New York: Random House, 1967).

14. Ferdinand Tönnies, Community and Society, trans. and ed. Charles Loomis (New York: Harper Torchbooks, 1963), p. 216.

15. Citizens' Department of Tokyo Municipal Government, Kyōiku Mondaini Kansuru Yoron Chōsa [Opinion survey concerning educational problems] (Tokyo: Citizens' Department of Tokyo Municipal Government, 1975).

16. Asahi Shinbun (Asahi daily newspaper), March 1, 1977.

17. Foster, "Peasant Society and the Image of Limited Good," p. 296.

18. Ronald Dore, City Life in Japan (Berkeley: University of California Press, 1958), p. 393.

19. Sōrifu, Sekaino Seinen Nipponno Seinen [Youth of the world and Japan] (Tokyo: Sōrifu, 1972).

20. Nobuo Shimahara, "Enculturation—A Reconsideration," Current Anthropology 11 (1970): 145-46.

21. Jiro Matsubara, Nippon Seinenno Ishiki Kōzō [Japanese youth and the structure of self-awareness] (Tokyo: Kōbundō, 1976), p. 2.

8
CONCLUSION

CENTRIPETAL SOCIETY

The two concepts, centripetality and centrifugality, introduced in Chapter 2, serve as conceptual tools for the formulation of a continuum of orientation toward social relations in various societies; one pole of the continuum emphasizes the centripetality of social relations and human interaction, while the other pole marks their centrifugality. Japanese society reflects the former emphasis, and societies, such as those of the United States and Britain, the latter; other societies, meanwhile, can be placed between the two poles. Of the variety of ways of comparing societies, the centripetal-centrifugal continuum is one of the better explanatory tools with which to appreciate that of Japan.

Centripetality is probably the most significant variable that distinguishes Japan and Euro-American societies. It characterizes modes of Japanese institutional activities in the educational, political, and economic spheres and differentiates them from those of other societies.

Contemporary Japanese group orientation is the expression of centripetality that has been accentuated throughout Japanese history. Its antecedent forms were found in ie (household), dōzoku (corporate group of households), and iemoto (kin-tract based on the ie and dōzoku models), and it results from the historically vital economic, ecological, political, and social conditions of Japan. The development of Japanese group orientation is a cultural consequence of social strategies adopted to cope with social and natural conditions of the environment. Once it was developed as a prominent mode of responding to environmental pressures, it constituted a vital basis of the Japanese pattern of adaptation. Today, it continues to be a dominant mode of orientation guiding Japanese behavior and attitudes.

Although Japan is highly modernized and one of the most productive industrialized societies, its traditional group orientation still persists. Centripetality constitutes the mainstay of social relations in Japanese industry, where it accounts for generating high productivity and also coping with the economic crises that occur from time to time.

Thus, in Japanese society, the group, rather than the individual, is the primary basis of life and activity and claims precedence over the individual; the group mediates all relationships between individuals and their society. So pervasive is Japanese group orientation that it has produced a system of social stratification that, being built upon institutions rather than individuals, is quite unlike the stratification common to Euro-American industrial societies. The Japanese group is characterized by its stress on motivational and cognitive conformity, inclusiveness, hierarchy, and exclusiveness vis-à-vis other groups, traits that effectively require individuals to secure permanent membership in work organizations as soon as they are eligible. In general, transferring one's group membership is culturally and socially frowned upon and difficult to do. Consequently, individuals become locked into certain groups for their lifetimes. Individuals derive their social status from the status of their groups, and they are expected to carry that distinction with them into society. A relative lack of horizontal mobility by individuals among different organizations is a function of Japanese group orientation and social stratification. Hence, although Japanese social structure is organized to protect its members, it sharply constrains their individual mobility.

SOCIAL AND CULTURAL FUNCTIONS OF EDUCATION

The educational reforms of the Meiji era make it apparent that education in Japan has been developed primarily to respond to the political and economic needs of the state. They also suggest that education functions as an adaptive activity of society only when it is patterned after, and guided by, the general cultural framework governing the Japanese pattern of adaptation. As evidence to support this observation, the failure of the two reforms in 1872 and 1879 that did not adequately consider Japanese cultural orientations was noted. Just as Itō rejected the American, British, and French political systems for incompatibility with Japan, Mori, minister of Education in the first Itō cabinet, judged their educational systems incompatible with Japanese cultural tradition and the emerging needs of the new state.

Subsequently, in 1886 Mori issued a series of education ordinances to develop a unifrom structure of elementary and higher education. His reform was perfected with the promulgation of the Imperial Rescript on Education. Incorporating elements of Confucian ethics,

Shinto statism, and a modern orientation toward learning into the imperial frame of the state, the Rescript defined the purpose of education and the responsibilities of the citizen of the new state. It continued to be the ideological mainstay of Japanese education until 1945.

With Japan's defeat in 1945 came postwar education, intended to eradicate the foundations of prewar education in the imperial state and to transplant the educational system and orientation developed by the United States Education Mission to Japanese society. Subsequently, new legislative measures were enacted to implement that reform. Yet no matter how ideal the reform, from the educational viewpoint of the mission, it was bound to face Japanese resistance and require a great deal of modification to become educationally useful to the Japanese. The inevitable resistance was caused, at first, by the lack of isomorphism between the reforms and the Japanese pattern of adaptation and, subsequently, by the inconsistency between the ideological and pedagogical purposes of the reform and the political and economic goals of Japan, which by the 1950s had become an independent state. The Japanese government's modification of the reform—in order to make education a more effective political and economic instrument of the state—became increasingly evident with the centralization of control over educational administration, content, and underlying ideology; comprehensive curricular changes also occurred in response to the emerging political goals of the state. In brief, education was promptly accommodated to the political climate of the 1950s.

The focus in the late 1950s and 1960s, however, shifted toward the training of the human resources required by the expanding economy and the emerging structure of industry; both state and industry looked to education as a way to meet new challenges. As the Japanese economy was evolving from recovery to expansion around 1955 and to further international expansion in the late 1950s and the 1960s, it was apparent that the state and the industrial system were inseparable aspects of an "organic" entity. The state was an instrument of the industrial system, and the industrial system was an arm of the state. Thus, the political and economic systems fused to permit the state to undertake policies that enhanced the development of corporate institutions and their profits.

Private industry assumed an active role in issuing a series of recommended educational policies aimed at increasing the supply of "human resources" and promoting industrial development. The recommendations reflected the views and common interests of such highly influential and effective industrial associations as the Federation of Employers Association and the Committee for Economic Development. These groups had their counterparts in government—the Central Council of Education and the Economic Council—which enjoyed advisory capacities and infused the strategies of the industrialists into the government's policies.

The fusion of the political and industrial systems became most obvious in 1960, when the Ikeda cabinet launched a major economic policy to double personal income. Private industry enthusiastically welcomed the policy for two reasons: first, it would enhance the economic expansionism stated earlier and, second, it would encourage the public to shift its attention from the internal, political issues of the late 1950s to economic matters. It goes without saying that both government and industry thought the economic policy highly successful because they accomplished their goals much sooner than expected.

Meanwhile, the schools were increasingly being called on to meet the needs for labor, science, and engineering. In response to industry's pressure to upgrade schooling for the masses and to make it more responsive to the changing industrial structure, the government undertook comprehensive curricular changes and developed policies to expand secondary and higher education. Consequently, the percentage of the eligible population attending high school and college, respectively, rose from 57.7 and 10.3 percent in 1960 to 82.1 and 24.0 percent in 1970.

THE COLLEGE ENTRANCE EXAMINATIONS
AS A FUNCTION OF JAPANESE ADAPTATION

Japanese education was presented as a rite of passage to the adult world. It is a uniquely intensive and unusually forced preparation for the passage. Pressures for personal achievement peak around the age of 18, when preadults take the CEE. Covert pressures for the examinations start around the age of 12, however, via high school entrance examinations, success in which can eventually provide superior preparation for the CEE. The expectation of individual achievement to pass the entrance examinations intensifies throughout the years of adolescence.

The CEE, with its attendant pressures, epitomizes Japanese education. Secondary schooling has become, in large measure, a preparatory process for the high school and college entrance examinations. Hence, priorities in education are established to meet the demands of the entrance examinations. This contradicts the formal purposes of education, but the contradiction is resolved in the interest in honne (intended and genuine), as opposed to tatemae (formal and spurious) goals.

Exploiting students' critical needs for intensive preparation for the examinations, private industries that specifically cater to those needs have developed. They include publishing industries, preparatory schools, tutoring services, testing agencies, bookstores, and the like. Such industries have increased rampantly, even though their sole contribution is to intensify competition among adolescents. Ironically, however, the more anxious and competitive the mood they generate, the more they thrive.

Adolescents are subject to variable patterns of socialization for the CEE, depending on such socializing agents as schools, parents, tutors, preparatory schools, and other examination-centered industries. However variable such patterns may be, a singular concern of adolescents is to secure access to particular universities through the CEE.

The well-defined hierarchy of universities and colleges in Japan corresponds to the differential degrees of access their graduates can secure to employment in large private firms and governmental bureaus. When assessing the qualifications of job applicants, the foremost employers consider the prestige of their respective universities a major criterion. Dozens of universities are usually patronized by major firms for the purpose of recruiting university graduates; hence, Japanese degreeocracy motivates adolescents to strive for admission to competitive and prestigious institutions, no matter how difficult it is to enter them. It is this degreeocracy that produces numerous rōnin students (see Chapter 4), who now constitute nearly 40 percent of the total college applicants.

The most significant factor underlying the competitive CEE and degreeocracy is the Japanese pattern of adaptation, the core of which is group orientation. As mentioned earlier, each individual's initial membership in a given organization tends to determine his or her career and social status because of the relative lack of individual horizontal mobility among different organizations. Therefore, the university entrance examination is the primary sorting device for careers in Japanese society.

The CEE shows how the Japanese pattern of adaptation typically functions in modern Japan. It is not an accidentally devised mechanism but a culturally and socially functional system that promotes traditional Japanese adaptation. It is a politically instrumental device that contributes to the development of adolescents' cognitive and motivational conformity. Likewise, it is an instrument of the state that serves to stratify individuals according to cultural dictates. It is no wonder that the CEE is perpetuated despite the prolonged anxiety and tension it creates for adolescents and their families; after all, it is expected that individuals in Japanese society can be temporarily sacrificed to maintain the organizational principles of the group.

COGNITIVE ORIENTATION AND
INSTITUTIONAL ARRANGEMENTS

Finally, turning our attention back to the larger social and cultural context of education, the existence of isomorphism between institutional arrangements and Japanese cognitive orientation should be pointed out. The latter guides individual behavior and attitudes in directions compatible with the traditional pattern of adaptation, in the educational, economic, political, and other spheres. Institutional arrangements in Japanese society, on the other hand, have developed in such a way that they do not contradict the dominant pattern of cognitive orientation. Institutional arrangements and cognitive orientation reinforce each other in their major features, and this reinforcement also is manifested in Japanese social stratification and degreeocracy, where dominant cultural orientations have influenced the shaping of their structures.

Japanese are, however, not entirely content with their social structure, where horizontal mobility—a form of expression of individuality—is rather severely limited and degreeocracy is imposed a priori upon them. They are not always enchanted with the tightly knit, group-oriented society; as individuals, they are unhappy with the CEE system. Yet, their disenchantment with these dimensions of life does not lead to significant change, for most Japanese are socialized to endure hardship, repress frustration, and accept group norms with great resilience. Acceptance into the group and the social and psychological security accorded by it take precedence over individuality and the risky divergence into a centrifugal world. Japanese are protected by their groups and enjoy inclusive protection at the price of individuality and individual freedom; the discussion of the CEE illuminates this dilemma.

A final word: The evolution of education in Japan clearly indicates that formal education is a function of political and economic institutions—the thesis stated at the outset of this volume. While it may enhance personal interest in one way or another, its primary goals are to mold individuals so as to promote organizational imperatives. For this purpose, Japanese are trained to be diligent, resilient, and convergent and to endure organizational pressures. They are remarkably disciplined people.

APPENDIX

TABLE A.1

Percentage of Eligible Population Attending Schools

	High Schools			Colleges			Graduate Schools			Other Institutions of Higher Education		
	Total	Male	Female	Total	Male	Female	Total	Male	Female	Total	Male	Female
1955	51.5	55.5	47.4	10.1	15.0	5.0	n.a.	n.a.	n.a.	10.1	15.0	5.0
1956	51.3	55.0	47.6	9.8	14.7	4.9	n.a.	n.a.	n.a.	9.8	14.7	4.9
1957	51.4	54.3	48.4	11.2	16.8	5.4	n.a.	n.a.	n.a.	11.2	16.8	5.4
1958	53.7	56.2	51.1	10.7	16.0	5.2	n.a.	n.a.	n.a.	10.7	16.0	5.2
1959	55.4	57.5	53.2	10.1	15.0	5.1	n.a.	n.a.	n.a.	10.1	15.0	5.1
1960	57.7	59.6	55.9	10.3	14.9	5.5	n.a.	n.a.	n.a.	10.3	14.9	5.5
1961	62.3	63.8	60.7	11.8	16.9	6.5	n.a.	n.a.	n.a.	11.8	17.0	6.5
1962	4.0	65.5	62.5	2.3	18.1	7.4	n.a.	n.a.	n.a.	12.9	18.2	7.4
1963	66.8	68.4	65.1	15.4	21.7	9.0	n.a.	n.a.	n.a.	15.5	21.8	9.0
1964	69.3	70.6	67.9	19.9	27.9	11.6	n.a.	n.a.	n.a.	20.0	28.0	11.6
1965	70.7	71.7	9.6	17.0	22.4	11.3	4.2	4.7	1.9	17.1	22.7	11.4
1966	72.3	73.5	71.2	16.1	20.2	11.8	5.2	5.7	2.3	16.3	20.6	11.8
1967	74.5	75.3	73.7	17.9	22.2	13.4	5.0	5.5	2.4	18.1	22.7	13.4
1968	76.8	77.0	76.5	19.2	23.8	14.4	4.8	5.3	2.4	19.5	24.3	14.5
1969	79.4	79.2	79.5	21.4	26.6	16.1	4.9	5.5	2.3	21.8	27.2	16.1
1970	82.1	81.6	82.7	23.6	29.2	17.7	4.4	5.1	1.5	24.0	30.0	17.8
1971	85.0	84.1	85.9	26.8	32.5	20.8	3.8	4.4	1.5	27.2	33.4	20.8
1972	87.2	86.2	88.2	29.8	35.7	23.7	4.0	4.6	1.7	30.3	36.7	23.7
1973	89.4	88.3	90.6	32.2	37.5	26.6	4.2	4.7	1.7	32.7	38.5	26.7
1974	90.8	89.7	91.9	34.7	39.9	29.3	4.0	4.6	1.6	35.3	41.0	29.4
1975	91.9	91.0	93.0	37.8	43.0	32.4	4.3	5.1	1.7	38.4	44.1	32.4
1976	92.6	91.7	93.5	38.6	43.3	33.6	4.4	5.2	1.6	39.2	44.4	33.7

n.a.: data not available

Source: Ministry of Education, Monbu Tōkei Yōran [Educational statistical abstract] (Tokyo: Ōkurashō Insatsukyoku, 1977).

173

TABLE A.2

Number of Postwar Schools

	Elementary Schools	Middle Schools	High Schools	Higher Technical Schools	Two-Year Colleges	Colleges and Universities
1955	26,880	13,767	4,607	n.a.	264	228
1956	26,957	13,724	4,575	n.a.	268	228
1957	26,988	13,622	4,577	n.a.	269	231
1958	26,964	13,392	4,586	n.a.	269	234
1959	26,916	13,135	4,615	n.a.	272	239
1960	26,858	12,986	4,598	n.a.	280	245
1961	26,741	12,849	4,602	n.a.	290	250
1962	26,615	12,647	4,637	19	305	260
1963	26,423	12,502	4,811	34	321	270
1964	26,210	12,310	4,847	46	339	291
1965	25,977	12,079	4,849	54	369	317
1966	25,687	11,851	4,845	54	413	346
1967	25,487	11,684	4,827	54	451	369
1968	25,262	11,463	4,817	60	468	377
1969	25,031	11,278	4,817	60	473	379
1970	24,790	11,040	4,789	60	479	382
1971	24,540	10,839	4,791	63	486	389
1972	24,325	10,686	4,810	63	491	398
1973	24,592	10,836	4,862	63	500	405
1974	24,606	10,802	4,916	63	505	410
1975	24,650	10,751	4,946	65	513	420
1976	24,716	10,719	4,978	65	511	423

n.a.: data not available

Source: Ministry of Education, Monbu Tōkei Yōran [Educational statistical abstract] (Tokyo: Ōkurasho Insatsukyoku, 1977).

174

RECOMMENDED READINGS

CHAPTER 2

de Vos, George. Socialization for Achievement. Berkeley: University of California Press, 1973.

Doi, Takeo. The Anatomy of Dependence. Tokyo: Kōdansha, 1977.

Fukutake, Tadashi. Japanese Society Today. Tokyo: Tokyo University Press, 1974.

Hall, John Whitney, and Richard K. Beardsley. Twelve Doors to Japan. New York: McGraw-Hill, 1965.

Hsu, Francis. Iemoto: The Heart of Japan. Cambridge, Mass.: Schenkman, 1975.

Nakane, Chie. The Japanese Society. Berkeley: University of California Press, 1972.

_____. Kinship and Economic Organization in Rural Japan. London: London School of Economics, 1967.

Reischauer, Edwin O. The Japanese. Cambridge, Mass.: Harvard University Press, 1977.

CHAPTER 3

Readings Available in English

Dore, Ronald. The Diploma Disease. Berkeley: University of California Press, 1975, chap. 3.

_____. Education in Tokugawa Japan. Berkeley: University of California Press, 1965.

Hall, John W., and Richard Beardsley. Twelve Doors to Japan. New York: McGraw-Hill, 1965, chap. 9.

Passin, Herbert. Society and Education in Japan. New York: Teachers College Press, 1965.

Shiveley, Donald H. , ed. Tradition and Modernization in Japanese Culture. Princeton, N.J.: Princeton University Press, 1971, chap. 2.

Readings Available in Japanese

Kaigo, Tokiomi. Kyōiku Chokugo Seiritsushino Kenkyu [A study of the development of the imperial rescript on education]. Tokyo: Tokyo University Press, 1965.

Kaigo, Tokiomi, ed. Kyōiku Kaikaku [Educational reform: postwar Japanese educational reform I]. Tokyo: Tokyo University Press, 1975.

Kaigo, Tokiomi, and Masao Terasaki, eds. Daigaku Kyōiku [University education: postwar Japanese educational reform IX]. Tokyo: Tokyo University Press, 1969.

Nagai, Michio. Kindaikato Kyōiku [Modernization and education]. Tokyo: Tokyo University Press, 1969.

Tsuchiya, Tadao. Meiji Zenki Kyōiku Seisakushino Kenkyū [A study of the development of educational policies in the first half of the Meiji era]. Tokyo: Azekura Shobō, 1963.

Yamauchi, Taro, ed. Gakkō Seido [School system: postwar Japanese educational reform V]. Tokyo: Tokyo University Press, 1972.

CHAPTERS 4 AND 5

Readings Available in English

Organization for Economic Cooperation and Development. Reviews of National Policies for Education: Japan. Paris: OECD, 1971.

Passin, Herbert. Society and Education in Japan. New York: Teachers College Press, 1965.

Vogel, Ezra. Japan's New Middle Class. Berkeley: University of California Press, 1965.

Readings Available in Japanese

Asahi Shinbun. Ima Gakkōde [Schooling at present]. 6 vols. Tokyo: Asahi Shinbunsha, 1973-77.

Asō, Makoto, and Morikazu Ushiogi, eds. Gakureki Kōyōron [The utility of academic credentials]. Tokyo: Ūhikaku, 1977.

Hashizume, Sadao, ed. Gakureki Henchōto Sono Kōzai [Bias toward academic credentials: merit and demerit]. Tokyo: Daiichi Hōki, 1976.

Mainichi Shinbun. Kyōikuno Mori [Educational forest]. 11 vols. Osaka: Mainichi Shinbunsha, 1965-68.

_____. Ranjuku Jidai [Rampant juku]. Tokyo: Mimul, 1977.

Masuda, Koichi, et al. Nyūgaku Shiken Seidoshi Kenkyū [Study of the history of entrance examinations]. Tokyo: Tōyōkan, 1961.

Nippon Kyōiku Shinri Gakkai, ed. Daigaku Nyūshio Kangaeru [A reconsideration of college entrance examinations]. Tokyo: Kaneko Shobō, 1974.

Shinbori, Michiya. Gakubatsu [Academic clique]. Tokyo: Fukumura Shuppan, 1969.

Yomiuri Shinbun. Taishū Daigaku [Colleges for the masses]. Tokyo: Yomiuri Shinbunsha, 1976.

CHAPTER 6

Asō, Makoto. Daigakuto Jinzai Yōsei [Universities and the training of human resources]. Tokyo: Chūōkōronsha, 1970.

Nagai, Michio. Kindaikato Kyōiku [Modernization and education]. Tokyo: Tokyo University Press, 1969.

_____. Nipponno Daigaku [Japanese university]. Tokyo: Chūōkōronsha, 1965.

Ogawa, Toshio, and Satoki Ikezaki. Sengo Minshushugi Kyōikuno Shisōto Undō [The thought and movement of postwar democratic education]. Tokyo: Aoki Shoten, 1971.

Ota, Takashi, ed. Sengo Nippon Kyōikushi [History of postwar education]. Tokyo: Iwanami, 1978.

Shimizu, Yoshihiro. Kyōikuto Shakaino Aida [Between education and society]. Tokyo: Tokyo University Press, 1973.

CHAPTER 7

Readings Available in English

Cohen, Yehudi, ed. Man in Adaptation: The Institutional Framework. Chicago: Aldine, 1971.

Dore, Ronald. City Life in Japan. Berkeley: University of California Press, 1958.

Fried, Morton H. The Evolution of Political Society. New York: Random House, 1967.

Readings Available in Japanese

Mannari, Hiroshi. Bizinesu Eriito [Business elite]. Tokyo: Chūōkōronsha, 1977.

Matsubara, Jiro. Nippon Seinenno Ishiki Kōzō [Japanese youth and the structure of self-awareness]. Tokyo: Kōbundō, 1976.

Nakane, Chie. Tate Shakanino Ningen Kankei [Human relations of a vertical society]. Tokyo: Kōdansha, 1976.

Takane, Masaaki. Nipponno Seiji Eriito [The political elite of Japan]. Tokyo: Chūōkōronsha, 1976.

Yomiuri Shinbun. Taishū Daigaku [Colleges for the masses]. Osaka: Yomiuri Shinbunsha, 1976.

BIBLIOGRAPHY

The following selected bibliography includes books in both English and Japanese relevant to the problems dealt with in this volume.

Abegglen, James C. Management and Worker: The Japanese Solution. Tokyo: Kōdansha, 1973.

Amano, Ikuo. Kyūsei Senmon Gakkō [The technical institute]. Tokyo: Nikkei Shinsho, 1978.

Anderson, Arnold, ed. Education and Economic Development. Chicago: Aldine, 1965.

Ariga, Kizaemon. Ariga Kizaemon Chosakushū VII: Shakaishino Shomondai [The collection of Ariga Kizaemon's works VII: problems in social history]. Tokyo: Miraisha, 1969.

Asahi Shinbun. Ima Gakkōdewa [Schooling at present]. Tokyo: Asahi Shinbunsha, 1976.

Asō, Makoto, and Morikazu Ushiogi, eds. Gakureki Kōyōron [The utility of academic credentials]. Tokyo: Ūhikaku, 1977.

Azumi, Kōya. The Recruitment of University Graduates by Big Firms in Japan. New York: Columbia University Press, 1968.

Bellah, Robert. Tokugawa Religion. Glencoe, Ill.: Free Press, 1957.

Benedict, Ruth. The Chrysanthemum and the Sword. Tokyo: Charles Tuttle, 1976.

Bennett, John W., Herbert Passin, Robert K. McKnight. In Search of Identity. Minneapolis: University of Minnesota Press, 1958.

Borton, Hugh. Japan's Modern Century. New York: Ronald, 1970.

Brzezinski, Zbigniew. The Fragile Blossom: Crisis and Change in Japan. New York: Ronald, 1970.

Campbell, Alexander. The Heart of Japan. New York: Alfred Knopf, 1961.

Citizens' Department of Tokyo Municipal Government. Kyōiku Mondaini Kansuru Yoron Chōsa [Opinion survey concerning educational problems]. Tokyo: Citizens' Department of Tokyo Municipal Government, 1975.

Cohen, Yehudi. The Transition from Childhood to Adolescence. Chicago: Aldine, 1974.

Coleman, James, ed. Education and Political Development. Princeton, N.J.: Princeton University Press, 1965.

de Vos, George. Socialization for Achievement. Berkeley: University of California Press, 1973.

Doi, Takeo. Amae Zakkō [Collected essays on Amae]. Tokyo: Kōbundō, 1976.

_____. The Anatomy of Dependence. Tokyo: Kōdansha, 1977.

Dore, Ronald. British Factory-Japanese Factory: The Origins of National Diversity in Employment Relations. Berkeley: University of California Press, 1973.

_____. City Life in Japan. Berkeley: University of California Press, 1958.

_____. Education in Tokugawa Japan. Berkeley: University of California Press, 1965.

Dore, Ronald, ed. Aspects of Social Change in Modern Japan. Princeton, N.J.: Princeton University Press, 1967.

Eisenstadt, S. N. From Generation to Generation. New York: Macmillan, 1971.

_____. Tradition, Change and Modernization. New York: John Wiley, 1973.

Erikson, Erik H. Identity, Youth, and Crisis. New York: W. W. Norton, 1969.

Frank, Isaiah. The Japanese Economy in International Perspective. Baltimore: Johns Hopkins University Press, 1975.

Fried, Morton H. The Evolution of Political Society. New York: Random House, 1967.

Fukutake, Tadashi. Japanese Society Today. Tokyo: Tokyo University Press, 1974.

Funayama, Kenji. Sengo Nippon Kyōiku Ronsōshi [Controversial history of postwar education]. Tokyo: Tōyōkan, 1963.

Galbraith, John Kenneth. The New Industrial State. Boston: Houghton Mifflin, 1971.

Hall, John W., and Richard Beardsley. Twelve Doors to Japan. New York: McGraw-Hill, 1965.

Hashizume, Sadao, ed. Gakureki Henchōto Sono Kōzai [Bias toward academic credentials: merit and demerit]. Tokyo: Daiichi Hōki, 1976.

Horimatsu, Buichi. Nippon Kindai Kyōikushi [Modern educational history of Japan]. Tokyo: Risōsha, 1959.

Hsu, Francis. Clan, Caste and Club. New York: Van Nostrand, 1963.

_____. Iemoto: The Heart of Japan. Cambridge, Mass.: Schenkman, 1975.

Ishida, Takeshi. Japanese Society. New York: Random House, 1971.

Japan Teachers Union. How to Reform Japan's Education. Tokyo: Japan Teachers Union, 1975.

Kahl, Joseph A., ed. Comparative Perspectives on Stratification— Mexico, Great Britain, Japan. Boston: Little, Brown, 1968.

Kaigo, Tokiomi. Kyōiku Chokugo Seiritsushino Kenkyū [A study of the development of the imperial rescript on education]. Tokyo: Tokyo University Press, 1965.

Kaigo, Tokiomi, ed. Kyōiku Kaikaku [Educational reform]. Tokyo: Tokyo University Press, 1975.

Kaigo, Tokiomi, and Toshiaki Murakami, eds. Kindai Kyōikushi [Modern history of education]. Tokyo: Seishin Shobō, 1959.

Kawashima, Takeyoshi. Ideologī Toshiteno Kazokuseido [The familial institution as an ideology]. Tokyo: Iwanami, 1957.

Kazamias, Andreas M., and Bryon G. Massialas. Tradition and Change in Education: A Comparative Study. Englewood Cliffs, N.J.: Prentice-Hall, 1965.

King, Edmond J. Other Schools and Ours. New York: Holt, Rinehart and Winston, 1967.

Kitano, Seiichi. Ieto Dōzokuno Kisoriron [The fundamental theory of ie and dōzoku]. Tokyo: Miraisha, 1976.

Kobayashi, Kazuo, Noboru Toyosawa, and Shiro Hoda. Kindai Nippon Kyōikuno Ayumi [Development of modern Japanese education]. Tokyo: Rissōsha, 1960.

Kobayashi, Masaaki, et al., eds. Nippon Keieishio Manabu I [A study of the history of Japanese management I]. Tokyo: Yūhikaku, 1976.

Lipset, Seymour Martin, and Leo Lowenthal, eds. Culture and Social Character. New York: Free Press, 1961.

McClelland, David. The Achieving Society. New York: Van Nostrand, 1961.

Mainichi Shinbun. Kyōikuno Mori [Educational forest]. 11 vols. Osaka: Mainichi Shinbunsha, 1965-68.

Mannari, Hiroshi. Bizinesu Eriito [Business elite]. Tokyo: Chūōkōronsha, 1977.

Masuda, Koichi, et al. Nyūgaku Shiken Seidoshi Kenkyū [Study of the history of entrance examinations]. Tokyo: Tōyōkan, 1961.

Matsubara, Jiro. Nippon Seinenno Ishiki Kōzō [Japanese youth and the structure of self-awareness. Tokyo: Kōbundō, 1976.

Ministry of Education. Japan's Growth and Education. Tokyo: Ministry of Education, 1965.

_____. Wagakunino Kyōiku Suijun [The educational standard of our nation]. Tokyo: Ōkurashō Insatsukyoku, 1976.

Ministry of Labor. Keizai Hakusho [Economic white paper]. Tokyo: Ōkurasho Insatsukyoku, 1976.

Miyazawa, Seiichi, ed. Kyōikushi [History of education]. Tokyo: Tokyo Keizai Shinpōsha, 1965.

Mori, Akira. Keikenshugino Kyōiku Genri [Educational principles of experimentalism]. Tokyo: Kanko Shobō, 1952.

Nagai, Michio. Kindaikato Kyōiku [Modernization and education]. Tokyo: Tokyo University Press, 1969.

Nakane, Chie. Japanese Society. London: Penguin Books, 1973.

_____. Kinship and Economic Organization in Rural Japan. London: London School of Economics, 1967.

_____. Tate Shakaino Ningen Kankei [Human relations of a vertical society]. Tokyo: Kōdansha, 1976.

Nippon Kyōiku Shinri Gakkai, ed. Daigaku Nyūshio Kangaeru [A reconsideration of college entrance examinations]. Tokyo: Kaneko Shobō, 1974.

Okita, Saburo. Japan in the World Economy. Tokyo: Japan Foundation, 1975.

Organization for Economic Cooperation and Development. Reviews of National Policies for Education: Japan. Paris: OECD, 1971.

Ōta, Takashi, ed. Sengo Nippon Kyōikushi [History of postwar education]. Tokyo: Iwanami, 1968.

Parsons, Talcott. The Social System. Glencoe, Ill.: Free Press, 1959.

Parsons, Talcott, and Gerald M. Platt. The American University. Cambridge, Mass.: Harvard University Press, 1973.

Parsons, Talcott, and Edward Shils, eds. Toward a General Theory of Action. Cambridge, Mass.: Harvard University Press, 1951.

Passin, Herbert. Japanese Education: A Bibliography of Materials in the English Language. New York: Teachers College Press, 1970.

_____. Society and Education in Japan. New York: Teachers College Press, 1967.

Riesman, David. The Lonely Crowd. New Haven, Conn.: Yale University Press, 1961.

Sahlins, Marshall, and Elman Service, eds. Evolution and Culture. Ann Arbor: University of Michigan Press, 1970.

Sansom, George. History of Japan. 3 vols. Stanford, Calif.: Stanford University Press, 1958-63.

Shimahara, Nobuo K. "A Study of the Enculturative Roles of Education." Ph.D. dissertation, Boston University, 1967.

Shimahara, Nobuo K., ed. Educational Reconstruction. Columbus, Ohio: Charles Merrill, 1973.

Shimahara, Nobuo K., and Adam Scrupski. Social Forces and Schooling. New York: David McKay, 1975.

Shinbori, Michiya. Gakubatsu [Academic clique]. Tokyo: Fukumura Shuppan, 1969.

Shively, Donald H., ed. Tradition and Modernization in Japanese Culture. Princeton, N.J.: Princeton University Press, 1971.

Slater, Philip. The Pursuit of Loneliness. Boston: Beacon Press, 1970.

Smelser, Neil J., and Seymour M. Lipset, eds. Social Structure and Mobility in Economic Development. Chicago: Aldine, 1966.

Sōrifu. Sekaino Seinen Nipponno Seinen [Youth of the world and Japan]. Tokyo: Sōrifu, 1972.

Spaulding, Robert M. Imperial Japan's Higher Civil Service Examinations. Princeton, N.J.: Princeton University Press, 1967.

Steward, Julian. The Theory of Culture Change. Urbana: University of Illinois Press, 1972.

Takane, Masaaki. Nipponno Seiji Eriito [The political elite of Japan]. Tokyo: Chūōkōronsha, 1976.

Tonnies, Ferdinand. Community and Society. Translated and edited by Charles P. Loomis. New York: Harper Torchbooks, 1963.

Tsuchiya, Tadao. Meiji Zenki Kyōiku Seisakushino Kenkyū [A study of the development of educational policies in the first half of the Meiji era]. Tokyo: Azekura Shobō, 1963.

van Gennep, Arnold. The Rites of Passage. Chicago: University of Chicago Press, 1969.

Vogel, Ezra. Japan's New Middle Class. Berkeley: University of California Press, 1965.

Ward, Robert E., and Dankwart A. Rustow, eds. The Political Modernization of Japan and Turkey. Princeton, N.J.: Princeton University Press, 1964.

Yanai, Hisao, and Akira Kawai. Gendai Nipponno Kyōiku Shisō [Educational thought of modern Japan]. Tokyo: Reimei Shobō, 1963.

Yomiuri Shinbun. Taishū Daigaku [Colleges for the masses]. Osaka: Yomiuri Shinbunsha, 1976.

INDEX

achievement orientation, 10, 40, 78–79, 122, 127, 134–35, 143, 150–51, 155

adaptation, definition of, 8–9; Japanese pattern of, 1, 47, 59–60, 62–63, 67–68, 74, 93, 125–26, 127, 129, 137, 143, 147, 158–59, 167–68

Ainu, 19

Allied powers, 63, 68, 74

allocation of jobs, 92

amae, psychology of, 24–26, 38–39, 60

Amano, Teiyū, 68–69

archetype of Japanese group, 26–27

Asanuma, Inejirō, 132

ascription, 10, 122, 150–51, 154–55

Australian tribes, 78

Barnard, Henry, 48–49

basic personality, 37

batsu, 35

behavioristic conditioning, 67, 74

Benedict, Ruth, 37–38

bunke, 28–29

bureaucratic batsu, 36

business ideology, 143

Central Council of Education (Chūkyōshin), 64, 124–25, 128–29, 130–31, 167; recommendations of, 130–31, 135–37

centralized political structure, 16

centrifugal society, 81

centrifugality, 19, 21, 109, 166

centripetal orientation, 19, 21, 71, 90, 105, 150, 158, 159–60, 161, 166

China, People's Republic of, 147

Chūtō test, 107–8, 110

Civil Information and Education (CIE) Service, 64, 66

cognitive orientation, 44, 47, 67, 81–82, 85, 97, 121, 122, 125, 133, 136, 146, 148, 155, 169–70; definition of, 146–47

Cohen, Yehudi, 45

college entrance examination as cultural focus, 4

College Entrance Examination Center, 123–24

Committee for Economic Development (CED) (Keizai Dōyūkai), 128, 167; recommendations of, 132, 139–42

Confucian education, 51–52, 53–54; ethic, 32, 46, 50, 55, 97, 166; lecturer, 53; literature, 46

conscription, 16

control of education, 71

cooperation between educational institutions and industry, 132, 142

cultural archetypes of Japan, 26–27

cultural evolution, 9–10

cultural ideology, 131

cultural orientation, definition of, 2; of Japan, 8, 9–10, 26–27, 73, 84, 90, 91–92, 93–94, 105, 126, 143, 157, 163, 166

cultural revitalism, 53–54

culture and personality studies, 37

culture core, 59

curricular revisions, 67, 72, 74, 82, 127, 131, 137–38, 166–67

daigakkusei, 105

de Vos, George, 38

ABOUT THE AUTHOR

NOBUO K. SHIMAHARA is   Professor in anthropology of education and Chairperson of the Department of Social and Philosophical Foundations of Education at the Graduate School of Education, Rutgers University, New Brunswick, New Jersey.

He has published Burakumin: A Japanese Minority and Education (The Hague, 1971); Educational Reconstruction: Promise and Challenge (as editor, 1973); Social Forces and Schooling: An Anthropological and Sociological Perspective (with Adam Scrupski, 1975). Educational Reconstruction was translated into Japanese and published in three volumes in Japan (1977-78). His articles have appeared in the Encyclopaedia Britannica and a number of journals, including: Current Anthropology, Human Organization, Teachers College Record, Comparative Education, Phi Delta Kappan, School and Society, Cutting Edge, and others.

Dr. Shimahara received a bachelor's degree from Shimane University, Japan, and an Ed.M. and Ed.D. in anthropology of education from Boston University.